Reverberations across Small-Scale British Theatre

Reverberations across Small-Scale British Theatre
Politics, Aesthetics and Forms

Edited by Patrick Duggan and Victor Ukaegbu

intellect Bristol, UK / Chicago, USA

First published in the UK in 2013 by
Intellect, The Mill, Parnall Road, Fishponds, Bristol, BS16 3JG, UK

First published in the USA in 2013 by
Intellect, The University of Chicago Press, 1427 E. 60th Street,
Chicago, IL 60637, USA

A catalogue record for this book is available from the
British Library.

Cover designer: Holly Rose
Copy-editor: MPS Technologies
Cover image: © Geoffrey Fielding
Production managers: Jessica Mitchell and Tim Elameer
Typesetting: Contentra Technologies

Print ISBN: 978-1-78320-297-3
ePDF ISBN: 978-1-78320-216-4
ePub ISBN: 978-1-78320-217-1

Printed and bound by Hobbs the Printers Ltd, UK

Contents

Acknowledgements

This project has been supported by many people over the years of its gestation, in many different ways. Particular thanks are due to our colleagues Jane Bacon and Vida Midgelow, whose input and support in the very early stages of the work was fundamental in developing the book out of an initial project to curate a series of live conversations between artists and academics. We'd like also to thank the University of Northampton for the seed-funding that enabled us to begin work on the book and Jessica Mitchell at Intellect for her support in getting it finished. Above all, however, we would like to thank the artists and academics who have so generously contributed their time and energy to the production of this volume: thank you.

Setting the Scene: Introducing *Reverberations*

Patrick Duggan and Victor Ukaegbu

What are the conceptual consequences of thinking about culture as a *verb* instead of a *noun*, process instead of product?

(Conquergood 1991: 190. Emphasis original)

Reverberation, n.: Something repeated or transmitted further; a continued or knock-on effect, likened to that of reverberating waves of sound; a repercussion.

(Oxford English Dictionary: online)

Context

In 2004 the then Culture Secretary, Tessa Jowell argued that:

Culture has an important part to play in defining and preserving cultural identity – of the individual, of communities, and of the nation as a whole … today we have the new melding of cultural traditions that is the result of population transfer and globalization… So we are inventing new forms of dance, of music, of drama that transcend traditional boundaries, and help give us a national identity which is uniquely ours. Culture defines who we are, it defines us as a nation. And *only* culture can do this.

(Jowell 2004: 17–18)

The cultural landscape of Great Britain has radically shifted since Jowell's report was written, not least because the ongoing global economic downturn (arguably beginning in September 2008 with the collapse of Lehman Brothers and still ongoing as we go to press in 2013) has ensured that funding for the arts is being radically and universally slashed. Nevertheless, theatre maintains an important place within the cultural landscape and economy: 'touring companies … are the lifeblood of the UK's theatre ecosystem. It is vital they are able to flourish, now more than ever' (Smith 2010: online).

Smith's article was a response to the perceived (in 2010) threat to touring theatres that impending changes to Arts Council's funding strategies, as a result of central government fiscal planning, might herald. Undoubtedly, the funding landscape in Britain has changed since the beginning of the global financial crisis and the implementation of massive cuts to arts (and higher education) funding since May 2010 when the Tory-led coalition government came to power. This is not intended as a statement of politicisation for the volume, but to highlight that while the shifts in funding have made life difficult for many theatre companies, one of the binding features of the companies within the volume is their resilience and so a more positive narrative emerges around a chameleon-like ability of small-scale theatres to adapt to survive the political and economic landscapes they inhabit [1].

Current social, political and news discourse on the place of the arts in the United Kingdom is wide ranging and in many cases inflammatory. Whether a cause *du jour* (such as the absence of creative and cultural subjects from the newly proposed English Baccalaureate under scrutiny in November 2012), the implicit denigration of arts subjects within higher education, or debates around the broader 'productivity' of the arts *per se*, the centrality of debates connected to the funding and function of arts is rarely far from some aspect of social consciousness via news or popular media representation. It is, perhaps unsurprisingly, also a present part of academic consideration.

The 2008 worldwide financial crisis and subsequent economic squeeze on all sectors of the economy brought the arts world to a new historical juncture. For the first time in more than three decades the performance industry and theatre companies both large and small, marginal and mainstream have faced similar resource challenges and concerns about the future of the arts in general. At the same time, academics worry about the fates of drama and theatre as subjects and as academic disciplines in schools, colleges and universities. The full, long-term impact of these changes remains to be seen but there have been and will continue to be effects on financial sustainability, organisational structures, artistic policy and practices of small-scale theatre companies like the ones represented herein. These shifts are directly linked to the dwindling resources available to and thus granted by the Arts Council for England (ACE), Heritage Funds, and by private donor organisations. The usually financially robust Arts and Humanities Research Council (AHRC) has not been spared either. While it is not the focus of this volume to engage with this area of current discourse it is a concern undoubtedly inflected in all of the chapters below. There have been studies that have analysed such challenges, including: 'Eclipse Report' (2001) collaboratively published by ACE, the East Midlands Arts-Theatrical Management Association and Nottingham Playhouse; Dominic Shellard's 'Economic Impact Study of UK Theatre' (2004) for ACE; the ACE, Baring Foundation and Paul Hamlyn Foundation's hybrid study of 2008 on arts, refugees and asylum seekers in UK society; the Equity Manifesto for Theatre (2011) was a report on 'the way forward' and was conducted after ACE cut the grants it made to 185 companies in 2007. Dorney and Merkin's excellent book-length study, *The Glory of the Garden: English Regional Theatre and the Arts Council 1984–2009* (2010), examines the ambiguous links between ACE's financial and policy interventions and their impact on the practices and products of regional theatres. In different ways, these studies highlight the undeniable benefits and cultural capital that regional and small-scale theatre companies provide for society and the economic, cultural and social 'dangers' inherent within their demise. The chapters in this volume do not necessarily re-visit these sentiments but in bringing to light the historical challenges, conflicts and tensions that small-scale theatre companies have faced in Britain, they provide important lessons for new and emergent companies.

In July 2012, the University of Reading and the V&A Museum, London, hosted a conference entitled 'Subsidy, Patronage and Sponsorship: Theatre and Performance Culture in Uncertain Times' as part of the AHRC funded project 'Giving Voice to the Nation: The Arts Council of Great Britain and the Development of theatre and performance in Britain 1945–1995'. Even before the presentations were accepted, the conveners raised some of the many issues that confront theatre and performance scholars and practitioners today with the titles of two of the 11 sub-themes of the conference: 'Subsidy, Patronage and Policy in the Regions' and 'Embracing the Economic Crisis – Opportunities for Innovation'. We currently occupy a moment in history when the Arts Council of England has had to defend itself against charges that its actual and planned funding cuts (in response to current global economic down-turn and to government spending and cutting directives) are detrimental to ambitious theatre-making and to the arts in general. As such, the timing of the conference seems, if nothing else, an acknowledgement that the need for British theatre to meet its current challenges is as crucial as the need to understand where it has been, what it has done and how far it has changed.

For us, this fundamentally suggests a need for theatre academics and practitioners to take stock of developments in the discipline over a period, such as 1970 to present (2013), when British theatre could be said to have arguably experienced some of it most stimulating and challenging times in the modern era, aesthetically and financially. The period covered is one of great expansion in the number of theatre companies and venues, types of work on offer, aesthetic and logistical strategies and methodologies, and significant increases in the numbers of people engaged in and attending performances.

The current moment of flux, change and 'austerity measures' – socially, politically and artistically – is precisely the moment, it seems to us, in which to look back at the history of small-scale British theatre for valuable lessons about 'survival' in moments of economic crisis and political resistance to arts practices as a formal part of social processes. Moreover, such a retrospective could, and in this volume does, illuminate the importance of the contributions of small-scale theatres to 'the bigger picture' of British social, political and cultural life. Most importantly, however, in combining practitioner and academic voices this volume presents new primary source material alongside analyses of these contributions to theatre and cultural histories in a form that is accessible to theatre and performance practitioners, academics and critics, students and the wider public.

Frames

At almost the same moment that Smith was typing his report on the importance of British touring theatres (cited above), we were in a meeting discussing and planning this volume. It started with a desire to bring academic voices together with practitioners in a sustained and productive dialogue that might, as no other volume has, open up the multivalent territory of 'contemporary' British small-scale, touring theatre through a focus on company history, ideological outlook and aesthetic practices [2]. In so doing, we sought to engage with questions of multi- or interculturalism, national identity or (what we have self-consciously problematically termed) 'Britishness', and politics [3]. Ultimately, the chapters fuse historiographical and 'cultural materialist' analyses to explore the work of each company within its immediate historical context(s) and more broadly to look at the productive reverberations their work has caused in the British theatrical landscape.

Nadine Holdsworth proposes that at a basic level, theatre is

'something intrinsically connected to [understandings of] nation because it enhances "national" life by providing a space for shared civil discourse… Theatre, as a material, social and cultural practice, offers the chance to explore histories, behaviours, events and preoccupations in a creative, communal realm that opens up potential for reflection and debate' (Holdsworth 2010: 6).

As such, theatre is part of any cultural discourse on understandings of national identity or 'Britishness'. Theatre is a fundamental part of imaginatively constructing ideas about and understandings of 'the nation', thus it provides a site where 'the nation can be put under the microscope' (Holdsworth 2010: 6). As such, it often self-consciously uses its content, innovative dramaturgies and its function as entertainment to creatively enter into dialogue with problems and tensions within the national psyche or sociopolitical discourse. It is precisely these concerns and practices that are 'under the microscope' in the work of the companies represented in this volume and which each of the chapters contained herein seeks to elucidate.

Britain has a long and rich history of small-scale theatre companies attending to questions of politics and nation – explicitly and more obliquely – in content and form, aesthetically and ideologically; a concern to be sociopolitically engaged is perhaps one of the defining features of the companies collected in this book and while questions of national identity are not essential to that engagement (for the companies), it is certainly a recurrent element of each chapter's analysis of the work. This is more than at the level of holding a mirror up to nature, so to speak. Rather, each of the companies included here grapple with the complexities of their social and cultural contexts through nuanced and innovative dramaturgical practices and praxis models in order to attempt to find modes of productively moving forward. This is not to suggest that these companies are attempting to define Britain or British culture, rather they and their work are *part of* a wider cultural discourse that is multifarious, nebulous, fluid and always already *in process*. While cultural products are fundamental to any understanding of nation and national identity, any such understandings are going to be 'performative' because, as Homi Bhabha has argued, they are always partial and '*in medias res;* and history may be half-made because it is in the process of being made; and the image of cultural authority may be ambivalent because it is caught, uncertainly, in the act of "composing" its powerful image' (1990: 3). The companies interrogated in this volume represent a cluster of related companies that share some identifiable aesthetic and/ or ideo-political features, such as the links between Talawa and Tiata Fahodzi theatres, or between Tara Arts, Red Ladder and The Paper Birds. By charting specific sociopolitical and cultural terrains each cluster, no matter its distinguishing characteristics, is a significant part of how small-scale theatres play a big role in shaping developments and movements inside British theatre landscape.

Anthony Gormley's *One and Other* [4] was a 'performance' that attempted to stage a snapshot of Britain in 2009 that was at once representative and incomplete. As Holdsworth argues of the piece:

> Rather than presenting a homogeneous picture of the nation, Gormley invited a rampant polyvocality... In the sum of the 2,400 parts, Gormley created a unique composite, a snapshot of the nation – but one underlined by the fact that given another 2,400 participants the picture would have been completely different (2010: 77–78).

What Gormley's project highlights is that the notion of Britishness and of what defines the nation of Britain, its inhabitants and its cultural and political discourses is invariably complex and as such, any single definition is likely to be incomplete at best and fatuous at worst. The ultimate goal of this volume is not one of definition but rather of representation and dialogue. In its selection of companies and in the focus of the chapters, the book tries to represent different views, questions and voices from within the small-scale theatre ecology of the United Kingdom. We are not trying to suggest that the companies included are entirely representative of the whole, but that their work seems to us to key into and explore important sociopolitical questions and dilemmas. And while each chapter is productively self-contained, the strength of the volume lies in the dialogic (*vide* Bakhtin) relationship between the contributions (which we will elucidate in more detail below) and how together the companies use their work, in the words of Gormley, to 'test their sense of self and how they might communicate this to a wider world' (Gormley: online).

So while this book will not (could but should not) attempt to *define* Britishness, we must – for framing sake, if nothing else – suggest some form of definitional work on this idea as one of the fundamental groundings of the volume. We do not suggest a definitive, overarching definition that neatly summarises what it means to 'be' British, for this would be to problematically homogenise a rich and multicultural body of people that might be grouped together as the populous of the landmass of Great Britain, geographically at least. Rather we offer some theoretical framing around the concepts of nation and national identity within which the theatre companies discussed in this book might be seen to be operating.

At a basic level, the British frame of the volume is defined merely by the borders of the United Kingdom and as such means we have looked at companies making work in the territorial community made up of England, Northern Ireland, Scotland and Wales. While this geographic taxonomy is broadly accurate, it does, however, suggest too narrow a conception of national identity as it (figuratively) cuts off the fluidity and diversity that comes with migration and immigration flows, globalisation (positively and negatively) and representations from the internet, entertainment and news media sources. Although there are multiple theoretical perspectives that can be brought to bear in thinking about nation and national identity, in the current context we find that philosophical approaches are more productive than geographic, governmental, modernist or ethnic ones [5]. Given that we are attending to art practices and forms of creativity and imagination, Benedict Anderson's widely circulated idea of the 'imagined community' is both useful and seductive in this regard.

Anderson's proposition is that, broadly speaking individuals imaginatively conceive the nation to be 'a deep, horizontal comradeship' and as such social and political inequalities within that imagined community are ignored (Anderson 2006: 6–7). Despite the limitations of this idea and its possible push towards depoliticisation (cf. Holdsworth 2010: 19–21), it does provide a dynamic and useful model with which to contemplate nationhood in so far as it sets the parameters of any nation both within an imaginative sphere and as flexibly composed rather than solidly defined. This is important in considering the possibility that the theatres in this volume might be engaged in reflecting and changing/creating understandings of Britishness through imaginative, creative processes. The place of aesthetic practices within such process is well documented; however, the fluidity of the process is perhaps less well established. Dana Arnold in *Cultural Identities and the Aesthetics of Britishness*, for example, has argued that a desire for a single, unified cultural identity is fundamental to understanding ones nation and that aesthetics might be part of that process: 'The aesthetics of architecture, landscape, painting, sculpture and literature [are] used … in the furtherance of particular social and political aims. In this way aesthetic culture reinforce[s] the culture of the dominant political and social ideologies' (2004: 1).

While the relationship between cultural aesthetic practices and national identity is usefully highlighted, the implied solidity and rigidity as well as the idea that aesthetic culture reinforces hegemonic structures are problematic for our concerns. While the theatres discussed throughout this volume are all in some way part of an analogous process to the one Arnold highlights – reflecting social concerns and structures back to the producing society – they are also, without exception, problematising and deconstructing those discourses in order to push understandings of national identity beyond the established norms. Not only do their concerns and composition match the cosmopolitan nature of contemporary Britain but they also fundamentally suggest that British national and cultural identities are intertwined, dynamically and productively in flux, and impossible to locate geographically, ideologically, racially or politically. A brief return to Bhabha's introduction to *Nation and Narration* highlights the importance of this and neatly points to a common concern, though differently expressed, of each company and chapter of the book:

The 'locality' of national culture is neither unified nor unitary in relation to itself, nor must it be seen simply as 'other' in relation to what is outside or beyond it. The boundary is Janus-faced and the problem of outside/inside must always itself be a process of hybridity, incorporating new 'people' in relation to the body politic, generating other sites of meaning and, inevitably, in the political process, producing unmanned sites of political antagonism and unpredictable forces for political representation.

(Bhabha 1990: 4)

Ultimately, the collected chapters in this volume seek to consider what Britishness might mean in relation to the small-scale theatre work of *circa* the last 35 years. The book thus contemplates how the work of these companies might come to constitute/reflect/problematise/develop notions of Britishness and how an ideological sense of Britishness might be reflected in the goals, 'manifestos' and aesthetics of the companies represented within these pages.

The companies

Understanding, let alone theorising a common aesthetic for the many small-scale theatre companies in Britain would be a daunting undertaking given the disparate, complex sociopolitical and cultural conditions under which such companies operate (locally, regionally and nationally) and which define their places and performance conventions within the broader British (multi-)cultural landscape. Moreover, any such undertaking would be problematic in and of itself because of artistic, philosophical, ideological, cultural, regional and logistic differentials that would influence the selection of a 'representative' sample of companies. Although we evaded the temptation to try to define 'small scale' and 'small-scale aesthetics' in any particular terms, making decisions about the composition of this volume raised several related questions; principal among them was, of course, which companies should we include and why? This overarching question pushed us towards others that impacted upon the content, structure and form of the volume. We grappled with the problem of selecting a handful of examples from more than 100 companies, each of which is defined by a thoroughly grounded aesthetic and praxis and how to arrange the chapters whilst avoiding chronological reading and unintended prioritisation of a company over others. In the background, meanwhile, were considerations regarding how best to arrange and organise the chapters and to ensure that each is suitably positioned to provide readers with a reading 'map' that reflects the numerous links the companies share in the field.

These overarching concerns led to others that are picked up throughout the volume as authors and companies articulate their understanding and definition of small scale and its associated aesthetic as analytical categories. For example, Grid Iron, Red Ladder, Talawa, Tiata Fahodzi, Tara Arts and Tinderbox might be seen to regard their aesthetic approaches, subject matters and company size as the defining constructs of their work and place on the theatre landscape. Meanwhile, Foco Novo, Lone Twin, The Paper Birds, salamanda tandem and Volcano steer beyond aesthetic and topographic constructs. The conversation between such positions facilitated by this book opens new vistas for interrogating the wider sociocultural and political terrains of small-scale theatre companies. Despite the Arts Council 'defining' them through the subsidy they receive and the inevitable external control they may be subject to thereof, questions will remain as to whether small-scale theatre is about the size of a company in terms of personnel, annual budget and turnover or the scale of work, if there is a small-scale performance aesthetic and, how this might be different from mainstream theatres. Similar questions surround the connection between scale, funding and quality of work produced. By interrogating how the artistic vision and policy, the philosophy and ideology underpinning the work of the companies represented here tie them to or distance them from others (included and absent), the volume throws light on whether the companies' production processes, organisational and management structures have remained faithful to their founding visions or radically changed, how, and for 'better' or 'worse'.

At first glance, the inclusion of salamanda tandem might seem to sit outside the focus of the volume given they do not conform to a 'theatre' label (Chapter 11). Their presence in this volume is not intended to define them as a small-scale theatre, but rather to suggest that the aesthetic, economic and political strategies of such companies find purchase and functionality within a connected but different type of small-scale touring arts company. At the very least, this is insofar as salamanda tandem confronts the same issues as the other companies in this volume. The working of these concerns – artistic, philosophical, aesthetic, financial and audience – is a signpost to the links between small-scale to mid-scale (a category to which Tara Arts and Talawa theatre now also belong by their own development and admissions) and mainstream commercial theatres. The aesthetic developments of companies such as salamanda tandem, Tara, Talawa, and to some extent Red Ladder, and their abilities to travel to and from the small scale to the mainstream spectrum when it suits them for ideological and artistic reasons, mirror how small-scale theatre companies contribute much to the entirety of the British theatre landscape. Without necessarily prioritising or using any of our questions or answers as yardsticks for the selection of companies and for the organisation of the volume, the companies presented herein share these concerns and arguably owe their success in part to how effectively they have grappled with and interrogated them.

Another compelling question for us has been why some companies endure and others disappear despite enormous efforts to sustain them. We do not necessarily think this volume provides definitive answers to this or to the other questions, how could it, but the discussions and interviews on each company provide telling clues and important arguments towards such answers. Each of the many theatres, old or new, defunct, moribund, in limbo, or still active and functional were inspired by specific sociocultural conditions and settings. Some of the conditions that gave birth to them have remained the same, such as with Tinderbox's interest in contemporary social themes and materials that subvert conventional readings of the here and now (of Belfast) 'despite the system' (Chapter 2) and Red Ladder's return to new writings, working with women and its socialist radical roots under Rod Dixon since 2006 (Chapter 6). Foco Novo (Chapter 1), though now defunct, was predicated on a socialist, anti-class, non-gendered, multicultural leaning that gave it birth and sustained it, while Volcano theatre, starting as part of a British physical theatre aesthetic that includes the likes of Brith Goff, Kneehigh and Frantic Assembly, evolved without losing its core principles, in Somers' words, from 'counter culture' 'punk anger' to 1990s 'cool' (Chapter 3). In this mix, Lone Twin has remained resolutely steadfast in its improvisational techniques, episodic storytelling, infectious humour and loose structure integrating music and dance (Chapter 8). The Paper Birds, the youngest of the lot, is steadily bedding its root whilst exploring new dimensions of the social and political (Chapter 9); whilst Tiata Fahodzi has become very comfortable in its Nigerian, West African British niche (Chapter 4).

Some of the small-scale theatre companies have given way to new ideas to the extent of changing aesthetically and/or ideologically in response to their own internal dynamics and external realities. Companies such as Red Ladder, salamanda tandem, Tara Arts (Chapter 7) and Talawa (Chapter 5) are arguably some of the latter category whose founding aesthetics and methods have grown in thematic and stylistic complexities. Originally small-scale, they have become what we might think of as medium scale and while they have evolved through different vicissitudes they retained their ideological/sociopolitical identities and artistic visions whilst adapting to changing cultural and social conditions. Grounded in understandings of their own histories and acknowledging the importance of them, these companies have developed a responsive malleability that has ensured they not only keep pace with societal changes and cultural trends but also stay relevant to their primarily audiences while developing new ones [6]. Meanwhile, companies like The Paper Birds, Volcano, Lone Twin Theatre and Grid Iron (Chapter 10) are engaged in very particular readings and re-readings of the particularities of the contemporary moment in which they are or were making work and which spawned their theatrical and aesthetic sensibilities.

It is no doubt due to the endurance of their aesthetic distinctiveness that the small-scale theatres discussed in this volume have become essential pieces of Britain's unique theatrical topography. In the case of Tara Arts, for example, its syncretic utilisation of materials from various cultures and canons has ultimately evolved a small-scale performance aesthetic with little of the *us-them, margin-centre* binaries that might be associated with particular vectors of postcolonial discourse that such works could be seen to be responding to. Tara's performances and production conventions transcend migrant-immigrant-migration marginalisation discourse as well as problematising the politics of British cross-cultural performance. Although taking more a 'traditional' text based (occasionally canonical) approach, the work of Talawa Theatre and Tiata Fahodzi speaks to similar concerns. While each has its roots in 'negotiating black-British experience on and off the stage', as Igweonu puts it in his chapter on Talawa, their works attend to broader questions of diaspora, marginality, community and race politics through precise, nuanced and dynamic theatre practices that revise established texts and new writing. Moreover, while both are black-led companies their work attracts significant and diverse audiences and in so doing they have become companies of fundamental importance within the British theatre ecology. As such, all three companies – Talawa, Tara and Tiata Fahodzi – are actively engaged in countering the silencing and othering associated with what Trinh Minh-ha terms 'a conversation of "us" with "us" about "them"' which results in '"[t]hem" always stand[ing] on the other side of the hill, naked and speechless, barely present in its absence' (1989: 67).

Meanwhile, Red Ladder, Tinderbox and The Paper Birds share a common interest in exploring and critiquing contemporary political 'problems' through engaging, theatrically ambitious performances that veer away from agitprop or heavy handed didacticism that is commonly associated with 'Political theatre' (cf. Kirby 1975 and Patterson 2006). With recent productions such as *Big Society! A Music Hall Comedy* (2012) and *Promised Land* (2011), Red Ladder has recaptured its socialist, collective, feminist base to make a return to the overt political agenda of its founding years. The much 'newer' company The Paper Birds (founded in 2003) foreground pressing political issues and questions about contemporary feminism through a physical theatre aesthetic influenced by The Wooster Group, Complicité, Robert Wilson and Pina Bausch. The Northern Irish theatre company, Tinderbox, takes a slightly more obliquely political route as they sought (and still seek) to make work that 'resonate[s] with audiences in Belfast, Northern Ireland *and beyond*' (Tinderbox: online; emphasis added). As Grant points out in Chapter 2, this was within the violent and troubled context of the 'notorious "Troubles" which … cast such a shadow over every aspect of life in Northern Ireland for more than three decades' while maintaining a 'resolute determination for "business as usual".

The Coda provides a 'rounding off' for the book as Franc Chamberlain provocatively reflects on his reading of the volume and as well as thinking 'beyond' it. Chamberlain reprieves some of the recurrent themes of the book – value, 'Britishness', culture, aesthetics and politics – to positively contemplate the inevitable omissions a volume such as this involves as well as highlight some of the questions it stimulates for him. In so doing, he remembers some of his own theatre experiences to highlight the diversity and dynamism of the residual, current and possible futures of British theatre ecologies.

Mapping

While a historical line is discernible across the companies discussed here, the fact that most of them are still making work and actively engaged in exploring the contemporary epoch led us away from a simple chronological ordering of the chapters, based on company age, for example. Similarly, grouping by genre was impossible because of the multifaceted and dynamic aesthetic processes each company embraces and because of a desire to avoid homogenising by 'type' of any kind (aesthetic, geographic, racial; an issue that is raised in many of the chapters). So, in moving towards the final structure of the book, we played with various ways of organising the contributions and using various sections to create groupings but ultimately these were rejected on the grounds that each would reduce the dialogic potential of the whole. Instead, we have been led by the title of the volume and organised the chapters to reverberate within and around their immediate neighbours, to in some way problematise, echo, develop or counterpoint them.

The dialogic underpinning of this structure is further facilitated by allowing each chapter to engage with a form that best suits its local objectives. While each contribution is roughly comprised of an even split of primary interview material and academic analysis/reading, we have resisted the temptation to adopt a common format for the chapters. The internal structure and organisation of each one reflects the respective authors' reading of the style and aesthetics of the selected companies and their engagement with practitioners. Thus, authors capture the essence of each company and the links between the interview and critical analysis sections of each chapter in different ways. A similar approach has been employed for the organisation of the volume. The aim is to steer readers towards a fluid, multivalent mode of engagement with the chapters; the interviews with practitioners, the analysis of aesthetic fundamentals and discussions of productions are not sections in themselves. Readers are advised to consider each section as integral to their understanding of the chapter if they are to encounter the diversity of forms and praxis in the small-scale theatre terrain that is arguably, distinctively British. Consequently, while some authors mediate the interviews and chapters actively, some set the scene and withdraw, giving the floor to practitioners and the company to speak in their own voices. In a third approach, authors voice their views without in any way attempting to steer readers one way or another; these authors simply set up dialogues for readers to mediate the work of companies themselves. Some authors combine some or all the approaches mentioned.

This publication is a contribution to ongoing debates about and an attempt to map, using carefully selected examples, the aesthetic trajectories of small-scale theatre companies in relation to mainstream theatres. It is also an attempt to record and analyse for posterity some of the important aesthetic changes and shifts that were either necessary or contingent on small-scale theatres as they journeyed through history to where they are today and as they prepare for challenges ahead. One of the features of the volume's organisation is that in the bid to speak about small-scale theatres, the volume also draws attention to sociocultural issues and politics across all sections of contemporary Britain. The result, we hope, is a vibrant and exciting reading-scape, a variegated theatre topology with polyphonic voices that speak across theatre and performance boundaries. In other words, a volume that truly and completely erodes any sense of stultifying homogeneity, monotony or the feeling of *déjà vu* that a volume such as this one may be prone to.

References

Anderson, B., 2006. *Imagined Communities*. London: Verso.

Arnold, D. (ed.), 2004. *Cultural Identities and the Aesthetics of Britishness*. Manchester: Manchester University Press.

Bhabha, H., 1990. *Nation and Narration*. London: Routledge.

Brown, S., et al., 2001. *Eclipse Report: Developing Strategies to Combat Racism in Theatre*. http://www.artscouncil.org.uk/publication_archive/eclipse-developing-strategies-to-combat-racism-in-theatre/ (accessed 7 March 2013).

Conquergood, D., 1991. 'Rethinking ethnography: Towards a critical cultural politics'. *Communication Monographs*, 58: 2, pp. 179–94.

Dorney, K. and Merkin, R. (eds), 2010. *The Glory of the Garden: English Regional Theatre and the Arts Council 1984–2009*. Cambridge: Cambridge Scholars.

Doustaly, C., 2012. 'Review of *the Glory of the Garden: English Regional Theatre and the Arts Council 1984–2009*'. *Cultural Trends*, 21: 4, pp. 339–41.

Equity, 2011. *The Manifesto for Theatre*. https://www.equity.org.uk/documents/manifesto-for-theatre (accessed 4 March 2013).

Holdsworth, N., 2010. *Theatre and Nation*. Basingstoke & New York: Palgrave Macmillan.

Gormley, A., 2009. *Anthony Gormley's One and Other*. http://skyarts.sky.com/antony-gormleys-one-other (accessed 5 November 2012).

Jowell, T., 2004. *Government and the Value of Culture*. http://www.shiftyparadigms.org/images/Cultural_Policy/Tessa_Jowell.pdf (accessed 1 November 2012).

Kidd, B., et al., 2008. *Arts and Refugees: History, Impact and Future*. http://www.phf.org.uk/downloaddoc.asp?id=392 (accessed 5 March 2013).

Kirby, M., 1975. 'On political theatre'. *The Drama Review: TDR*, 19: 2, pp. 129–35.

Minh-ha, T., 1989. *Woman, Native, Other: Writing Postcoloniality and Feminism*. Bloomington: Indiana University Press.

Patterson, M., 2006. *Strategies of Political Theatre: Post-War British Playwrights*. Cambridge: Cambridge University Press.

Shellard, D., 2004. *Economic Impact Study of UK Theatre*. http://www.artscouncil.org.uk/publication_archive/economic-impact-study-of-uk-theatre (accessed 8 March 2013).

Smith, A., 2010. 'Touring Theatre Has Never Been More Important'. *The Guardian*. https://www.guardian.co.uk/stage/theatreblog/2010/nov/10/touring-theatre-never-more-important (accessed 8 March 2013).

Tinderbox Theatre Company. http://www.tinderbox.org.uk/ (accessed 8 November 2012).

Notes

1   Even though now disbanded, Foco Novo demonstrated phenomenal 'staying power' in the difficult funding landscape of the 1970s and 1980s.

2   We use 'contemporary' loosely; the companies represented in this volume have long histories and while most are still making work some are not. What makes them all contemporary, in our view, is that their histories, past productions, aesthetic interventions and engagement in wider political discourse are still being 'felt' today – in the work of other companies and the history of small-scale touring theatre in Britain. 'Contemporary' is then a reference to their ongoing influence and importance.

3   We are using 'Britishness' in an analogous way to Homi Bhabha's use of 'nationness' in *Nation and Narration* (1990).

4   *One and Other* was a 100 day 'performance' instillation by the artist Anthony Gormley in which members of the public applied for a one hour slot on the empty forth plinth in

London's Trafalgar Square. In this hour the participants were able to use the time and the space in any way they wished; there was an even gender split and regional representation across the 2400 participants.

5   Holdsworth covers these areas well in *Theatre & Nation*, 2010.

6   Talawa's recent collaboration with the Almeida Theatre (London) on David Waton's *The Serpent's Tooth* (7–17 November 2012) is an excellent example of such development and malleability.

Chapter 1

Foco Novo: The Icarus of British Small-Scale Touring Theatre

Graham Saunders

In histories of British Fringe touring companies specialising in new writing, two names dominate: Portable and Joint Stock. Long after disbandment both have acquired almost mythic status. Portable were the buccaneering young idealists in a van, taking vivid and anarchic shows such as Howard Brenton's *Christie in Love* (1968) and Snoo Wilson's *Pig Night* (1971) to new audiences, often in non-theatre venues, while Philip Roberts considers William Gaskill and Max Stafford-Clark's Joint Stock 'the most important Fringe group of the seventies' (Roberts and Stafford-Clark 2007: xvi). Yet Foco Novo, which was in existence for almost the same time as Joint Stock, also staged the work of new writers as well as specially commissioned versions of modern European dramatists including Brecht, Büchner and Genet. Its history is defined by radical shifts in artistic policy – from overtly socialist theatre including *Nine Days and Saltley Gates* (1976) to promoting black drama – and interspersed throughout with large-scale productions of European classics. Foco Novo represented both the opportunities and later the increasing tensions of small-scale touring theatre in Britain during the 1970s and 1980s.

Foco Novo was the vision of its co-founder Roland Rees. Howard Brenton has called him the 'unsung hero of contemporary theatre' (Brenton 1995: 34), and Rees remained Foco Novo's artistic director throughout its lifetime. The company was established by Rees and David Aukin in 1972. Its first two productions *Foco Novo* (1972), by the American playwright Bernard Pomerance (and the title from which the company subsequently took its name), and Bertolt Brecht's *Drums in the Night* (1973) established its subsequent artistic policy: new writing and specially commissioned adaptations of modern European classics.

However, Foco Novo's inauguration as a dedicated touring company did not come about until 1975 with another production of Brecht – this time Bernard Pomerance's adaptation of *A Man's a Man*. In the interim had been Jamaican born playwright Alfred Fagon's *Death of a Black Man* (1975), and Rainer Werner Fassbinder's *Cock Artist* (1974). However, these London productions did not tour. Its identity as a small-scale British touring company specialising in mounting large-scale productions of Brecht also underwent a distinctive change of direction that same year. After *A Man's a Man*, Foco Novo produced *The Arthur Horner Show* by Phil Woods. The eponymous title referred to the miner and political activist from the 1930s and 1940s, and its tour departed from an established fringe theatre circuit to play at miner's clubs and welfare halls. Foco Novo had now mercurially switched to a style of British socialist drama practised by contemporaries such as 7.84, Red Ladder and North West Spanner.

Foco Novo's new found identity coincided with their move from the Arts Council's designation of Project Grant status, which funded one-off shows for the relative stability of annual revenue. With additional financial support from the unions who also helped publicise the shows, one can see the attractions for entering this new artistic phase. The first outcome of this phase was Jon Chadwick and John Hoyland's *Nine Days and Saltley Gates* (1976), two linked documentary-style plays that explored key moments in British socialist history. *Nine Days* was written to mark the 50th anniversary of the 1926 General Strike, and while seen as defeat for the Labour Movement, its companion piece *Saltley Gates* recalled the action of pickets at the West Midlands Saltley coke depot during the 1972 miner's strike that was widely credited in bringing down the Heath government. *Nine Days and Saltley Gates* was followed in 1977 by *Tighten Your Belts*, a play based on Labour government spending cuts to public services.

During this phase Foco Novo had a certain credibility as a socialist theatre group and even achieved the notoriety that companies such as 7.84 and North West Spanner periodically attracted when Scottish Tory MP Nicholas Fairburn questioned in the press Foco Novo receiving Arts Council funding for political propaganda (Rees 1992: 90). However, their direct involvement in the politics of the Labour movement also led to a split on Foco Novo's Board over its artistic direction. Members such as Bernard Pomerance wanted to see a more pluralistic approach whereby other forms of work could be produced, while others such as John Chadwick rejected this policy (Rees 1992: 90).

The question of touring to a single constituency also became an issue. Chadwick and Hoyland argued that "'art' shows' would not be well received in miner's clubs and that 'Labour Movement audiences required Labour Movement shows' (Rees 1992: 90). Conversely, others on the Board thought it unlikely that theatre audiences would enthusiastically embrace plays such as *Tighten Your Belts*. Notes from meetings taken by Clive Tempest, Foco Novo's Arts Council drama officer, reveal what he calls 'the fundamental clash within the artistic direction' (ACGB 1977c), with one faction wanting to become a socialist collective while another wished to pursue a broader artistic direction. In a memo Tempest concluded:

> Foco Novo is a curious hybrid. All of its problems stem from the unholy alliance between its two parts… Hire and fire your actors/Have a permanent company. The 'artistic director'/The 'collective'. High standard metropolitan work/Work aimed at club or Trade Union Council audiences.
>
> (ACGB 1977b)

The playwright Nigel Gearing, whose play *Snap!* was later produced by Foco Novo in 1981, summarised this predicament best when he commented that while the company 'had a strong political bent … it was never interested in agit-prop, or on the other hand, social realism' (Rees 1992: 95). Rees had also come to the conclusion that Foco Novo's identity as a socialist company had resulted in an 'insularity [that] was circumscribing the work I wished to do' (Rees 1992: 94). Rees won the day, and plans for a documentary-style project about the ongoing Grunwick dispute in North London were abandoned.

The change in artistic policy came after *Tighten Your Belts* in Foco Novo's next production for its 1978 season. Originally entitled *Deformed* (changed during its tour to *The Elephant Man*), Bernard Pomerance's play based on the life of John Merrick, a one-time freak-show exhibit in the nineteenth century, remains Foco Novo's best-known work. Yet its success paradoxically served to exacerbate frustrations over constraints imposed by the small-scale touring circuit. The playwright Howard Brenton has commented that institutions such as the National Theatre enable 'big formal plays of Shakespearian size' whereas in Fringe touring 'You just can't write a play that describes social action with under ten actors. With fifteen you can describe whole countries, whole classes, centuries' (Itzin 1980: 187). Foco Novo, which regularly employed casts of ten, shared this outlook, and by the late 1970s increasingly began to resent what they saw as confinement by the Arts Council to its small-scale touring circuit. Although it played to small audiences on its national tour, *The Elephant Man* played to capacity houses on its final London dates at the Hampstead Theatre (with most critics noting the extraordinary central performance by David Schofield). Subsequently the play enjoyed a long run on Broadway and later a new revival at the National Theatre, directed by Rees in 1980.

The change in direction can be seen in the programme notes to *The Elephant Man*. Under its statement of artistic policy, while a commitment remains to finding new audiences and taking performances to 'Trades Halls, Community Halls, and Theatres', gone are the earlier rallying calls about Foco Novo being 'one of the theatre groups best known and most experienced within the Labour movement' (Foco Novo c. 1976). In its place was a more aesthetics-led approach that spoke of wanting to 'highlight issues in a graphic and theatrical form about Britain in the '70s' (Foco Novo 1977). Following the success of *The Elephant Man* policy also moved towards approaching dramatists 'to write particularly for the company's requirements and on subjects and themes mutually interesting' (Foco Novo 1978). The full extent of this change of direction can be discerned in the choice of plays for the following 1978 season. These included C. P. Taylor's *Withdrawal Symptoms*, which explored physical and emotional dependency as well as class through its central character of a middle-class drug addict, and two plays by unknown writers – Colin Mortimer's *The Free Fall* (which used documentary sources in a story about the activities of a religious cult operating in Britain) and Tunde Ikoli's *On the Out*. Ikoli's play also marked the beginning of another significant strand to Foco Novo's artistic policy that would continue throughout the 1980s – namely championing black British drama.

The international success of *The Elephant Man* emboldened Foco Novo. Ever since the early productions of Brecht its identity as a small-scale touring company hid wider ambitions. *The Elephant Man* now gave Foco Novo the opportunity to pressure the Arts Council into funding their move from small-scale to middle-scale touring. Early on with *Drums in the Night* the Arts Council had considered Foco Novo for inclusion into their middle-scale touring circuit based on venues of between 300 and 800 seats (ACGB 1973).

However, the company's radical shift of identity after 1975, from large-scale productions of Brecht to tours of miners' community centres and trades union halls, crucially seems to have persuaded the Arts Council that Foco Novo had deliberately opted to remain a small-scale touring company. From this point onwards the Arts Council's mindset would prove very difficult to change.

Perceptions of inflexibility by the Arts Council towards its clients had been a long-standing source of grievance by touring companies who, having established themselves on the Fringe circuit and built up a loyal following, wanted to expand. Howard Brenton, who produced work for both Portable and later Foco Novo, argues that by the 1980s the whole policy of small-scale touring on the Arts Council's circuit (or 'grid') was looking increasingly outdated. This loose network of colleges, universities, arts centres and studio theatres inside repertory theatres convinced Brenton that the Arts Council was 'living off a version of alternative theatre that we knew was long dead' (Rees 1992: 219). In a somewhat ironic reversal, Brenton was to return to small-scale touring when he collaborated with Foco Novo on several projects during the 1980s after his play *The Romans in Britain* (1980) – a venture that had promised to be the culmination of his journey from the Fringe to the National Theatre's Oliver stage – collapsed after an attempted prosecution for obscenity.

Foco Novo's resentment can be seen clearly in publicity materials for its 1977–78 season in which they openly state that 'many of the plays the Company would like to present are being taken out of their reach' and has resulted in the necessity of developing two strands of artistic policy – 'small scale productions relying on documented research by writers on specific issues' – alongside 'a continuation of the original policy of the Company to present plays requiring a cast which can capture a real social cross-section' (Foco Novo c. 1978). The declaration is clear: small-scale touring is seen as a necessity imposed by the Arts Council whereas the company's main interests are in large-scale productions.

However, by June 1979 with the first royalties appearing from the Broadway and American tour of *The Elephant Man*, Foco Novo was now, temporarily at least, able to ignore the Arts Council. By mounting a large-scale production of their own, a compelling case could be made that would persuade the Arts Council to fund the company at a level commensurate with a middle-scale touring company.

It had been a long-held ambition of Rees to produce an early play by Bernard Pomerance called *Quantrill in Lawrence* (ACGB 1973). Set in the American Civil War about a gang of criminals (including Jesse James and his brother) known as the Quantrill Raiders, its Shakespearian-sized cast and historical setting had long put it beyond the company's resources. Now, thanks to *The Elephant Man*, *Quantrill in Lawrence* was presented in 1980 as an additional show to Foco Novo's work that season. The play employed a cast of 14 and the considerable sum for the time of £2000 was spent on design. However, while *Quantrill in Lawrence* demonstrated that Foco Novo could successfully mount large-scale productions, significantly it did not tour. Although approaches were made to Nottingham Playhouse and Birmingham Repertory Theatre to mount a co-production, the £8500 required from the partner theatre would prove too costly (ACGB 1979).

A great deal was staked on the success of *Quantrill in Lawrence*. Foco Novo's administrator Valerie Mainz took the unusual step of writing directly to the Arts Council's drama director requesting that all members of the drama panel attend performances as the company 'are under no illusions about being able to present a production on the scale of *Quantrill* again', but hope to show 'the potential and scope of our company given adequate funding' (Foco Novo 1980a). As well as being presented as incontrovertible evidence for their suitability to move into middle-scale touring, the premiere that year also coincided with a major funding review of all the Arts Council's theatre clients.

In truth the Arts Council had been unable to summon much enthusiasm for *Quantrill in Lawrence* even before it premiered. Jonathan Lamede, Foco Novo's drama officer at the time had commented in an internal memo, 'this play has been an obsession with Roland [Rees] for a couple of years now, I think we must let them get on with it and get it out of their systems' (ACGB 1980a). Dubbed 'a Jacobean western' (ACGB 1980g) in one Arts Council Show Report, reviews were largely negative and audiences poor. While all seven members of the drama panel echoed these criticisms, many also agreed that *Quantrill in Lawrence* had been 'a failure, but an interesting failure' (ACGB 1980c), and persuaded the Arts Council in its review of the company that a compromise should be reached. While rejecting funding at a level that would allow transition from small- to middle-scale touring, permission was granted for existing annual funds to pilot one middle-scale tour for its next season (ACGB 1980h).

Foco Novo's choice in their tenth anniversary year saw a return to their origins with Brecht's *Edward II*. Despite remonstrations from the Arts Council's Touring Officer Ruth Marks and their own drama officer 'about the scant interest in Brecht in the middle-scale' (ACGB 1982a), Rees was determined to go ahead. However, *Quantrill in Lawrence*'s four-week residency at London's Institute for Contemporary Art (ICA) had sent out worrying messages to the Arts Council over Foco Novo's commitment to touring. Two weeks before the production previewed, its Financial Director Anthony Field had written expressing concern that this 'expensive production will be seen only in London and will not tour at all, despite your Company's policy to operate as a touring company' (ACGB 1980d). A question over whether London had been prioritised over the regions was also raised at Foco Novo's Review Panel in October (ACGB 1980i).

The tour of *Edward II* to Theatr Clwyd, Basildon, Croydon and London received mixed reviews. While there was praise for aspects of the production, with Michael Billington declaring 'it is heartening to see Foco Novo entering the big league', Billington, and others, also felt that an early play by Brecht was a poor choice (Billington et al. 1982). Attendance was also disappointing despite letters to Rees from Theatr Clwyd and the Towngate Theatre praising the production and wanting to see the company return. As one manager pointed out, 'Brecht is not easy to market even to Theatr Clwyd audiences' (Foco Novo 1982a).

The Arts Council saw *Edward II* as further proof that Foco Novo was unable to sustain itself as a middle-scale touring company. In a letter its Drama Director John Faulkner points out that based on returns for the tour, audience figures averaged 185 a performance, far short of the 300 minimum that would justify promotion to middle scale. Concerns were also raised over Foco Novo's commitment to touring in its 1982–83 season over a proposal to split half of its touring between London and the region, while its forthcoming tour of Brecht's *Puntilla and His Man Mati* to Edinburgh, Mold and Croydon meant that only one other English venue outside of its London run would be undertaken (ACGB 1982c). Although the Arts Council reluctantly allowed a further middle-scale production during the one-year trial period, this arrangement was abruptly discontinued when Foco Novo's co-production with Leicester Haymarket on Howard Brenton's *Bloody Poetry* (1984) consisted of a 'tour' that included only Leicester and the Hampstead Theatre in London.

However, it would be wrong to assume that Foco Novo had abandoned small-scale touring; in its 1980 Panel Review it could confidentially state that tours were still being undertaken at venues appropriate to this kind of work (Foco Novo 1980b). In fact, the inroads made here in the development of black drama through its work in the South London district of Peckham remains one of the most innovative features of Foco Novo's work.

This interest had been a continual, if intermittent strand of Foco Novo's work since Alfred Fagon's *Death of a Black Man* (1975). However, it was Rees's championing of British-born Tunde Ikoli that saw Foco Novo moving away from plays set outside Britain such as Mustapha Matura's *Independence* (1979). Ikoli's work for Foco Novo including *On the Out* (1978), *Sink or Swim* (1982), *Sleeping Policeman* (1983, a collaboration with Howard Brenton), *Week in Week Out* (1985) and *Banged Up* (1986) directly addressed the experiences of second generation British-born Afro-Caribbeans.

Foco Novo's application for an Arts Council Special Initiatives Grant in 1982 to produce a show on the effects of youth unemployment in South London began this new direction. Known originally as The Peckham Project, the grant, together with funding from Greater London Arts (GLA) and Southwark Council, saw the development of shows such as *Sink or Swim* and *Sleeping Policeman* derived from devised workshops with the local community.

This strand of work also saw Foco Novo for the first time since the Chadwick/Hoyland Labour plays touring to a variety of non-theatre venues and playing to audiences with little or no previous experience of theatre. For instance, Ikoli's *On the Out* during its national tour played at venues including the Normington Junior School Hall, Derby, Highfields Youth and Community Centre in Leicester and the Valley Road Family Centre in Coventry.

Yet Rees's predilection for operating on a grand scale was also pioneering in that it resisted the assumption that black writing somehow belonged to small-scale community projects. A case in point was Ikoli's adaptation of Maxim Gorki's novel *The Lower Depths* (1986), transposed to contemporary London. This ambitious co-production between Foco Novo and Birmingham Rep included a cast of ten, while in 1988, just before the company folded, Ikoli had been commissioned to produce a rewriting of Shakespeare's *The Tempest*.

However, Foco Novo's move into community projects, its choice of material and the decision to tour the plays outside London were questioned in some quarters. For example, while the Ikoli/Brenton collaboration *Sleeping Policeman*, which was about life in Peckham, was generally well reviewed in London, Philip Hedley, then Artistic Director of Joan Littlewood's Stratford East Theatre, questioned the policy of touring of plays that were so geographically and culturally specific. After seeing *Sleeping Policeman* at the University Theatre Colchester, Hedley wrote in his Arts Council Show Report,

> [w]hat on earth was this play about six random characters in Peckham doing playing to about 200 [in total for the nights played at this venue] ... on an Essex campus? How heavily subsidised were each of those audience members for what tuned out to be an act of non-communication?
>
> (ACGB 1983)

Although Rees never saw the work produced in Peckham as 'Community Theatre' (Foco Novo 1982c), others did when it came to touring shows to 'theatre' audiences. As far back as Tunde Ikoli's debut *On the Out*, in his Arts Council show report, despite commenting 'it will go down like a bomb in youth clubs', Jonathan Lamede notes at the Bush Theatre, on the night he attended with less than 30 people, the show 'does not seem to have appealed to London audiences' (ACGB 1978).

Doubts were also raised about Foco Novo's commitment to the community it proposed to work amongst. Fellow director Mike Alfreds, one of the members of the Arts Council's Special Initiatives Panel, commented 'I'm very suspicious of "community based projects" – a fashionable OK thing. Is the company *committed* to community work? What will happen (to the community) when the project is over?' (ACGB 1982b). Jonathan Lamede reporting on Ikoli's *Sink or Swim* at the Peckham Settlement returned to his misgivings about *On the Out* four years previously, stating that while its audience of 'fifty youngsters, mostly black ... most of whom wouldn't go near a theatre ... to save their lives' enjoyed the show, Lamede concludes that for regular theatregoers 'it would have come across as a rather feeble documentary, simplistic and rosy-viewed, if not patronising' and rather than representing a development in Foco Novo's work the Peckham project 'could even be seen as a regression' (ACGB 1982c).

Nevertheless, with the Arts Council's move towards actively encouraging companies to develop work with ethnic minorities after the inner city riots of 1981, Foco Novo could demonstrate a genuine commitment going back as far as 1972. This makes their cut in revenue funding and relegation to single project status in 1988 seem inexplicable. Even during the previous year when the company was in deficit by £55,000, in a memo to the Drama Director Ian Brown, Foco Novo's new Drama Officer Michael Haynes stressed their long pedigree of working with black writers and mentioned that 'there is still a great deal of potential in the company and if it is allowed to marshal its resources, in 1988/89, there may well be much fine work coming from Foco Novo' (ACGB, 1987).

Howard Brenton has commented that Foco Novo had a reputation for being difficult (Rees 1992: 219), and consultation of Arts Council's files makes it clear that the company had stored up a considerable amount of ill will since the late 1970s over the issue of touring: namely the impression of wanting to shed commitments to small-scale touring and concentrate on major regional theatres and London venues. On the Arts Council's part their argument had always been that middle-scale touring was unsustainable for a company who, on average, attracted audiences of less than 100 per night. These factors, combined with a tendency to run into deficit due to the scale of its productions gave Foco Novo a reputation, rightly or wrongly, for being a touring company who did not want to tour.

Moreover, due to Foco Novo's mercurial artistic identity, switching between socialist theatre, modern European classics and black British writing, the Arts Council, with its need for firm categories, never quite knew where to place the company. With hindsight, if Rees had concentrated on developing a sustained policy towards black theatre, Foco Novo would still likely be in operation today. However, his insistence that British theatre traditions could be merged with others from Europe and elsewhere never sat easily with audiences or the Arts Council. In many respects, Foco Novo provides a salutary lesson for touring companies today.

With its restless ambition and almost wilful refusal to avoid artistic or ideological categorisation, Foco Novo ended up failing to secure influential allies. Its final project in rehearsal at the time was a typically ambitious play entitled *Consequences,* written collaboratively by a group of eight writers [1]. The title is ironic in that it was the desire to transcend limiting assumptions about small-scale touring that eventually had consequences of its own for Foco Novo.

Interview with Roland Rees and Trevor R. Griffiths

(Roland Rees was the co-founder of Foco Novo from 1972 until 1988. Professor Trevor R. Griffiths is a theatre historian and was Chair of the Foco Board during the 1980s.)

Wednesday 28 September 2011, Peckham London

Saunders: *How far did you feel at the time that Foco Novo and other small-scale touring companies during the 1970s and 1980s were producing an identifiable political, social and political aesthetic?*

Rees: *Firstly, politically speaking, during the mid-1970s Foco Novo toured all the major coalfields in West and South Wales, Kent, Midlands and Scotland with* Nine Days and Saltley Gates. *These tours were made possible through the auspices of the secretary of the National Union of Miners in South Wales, Dai Francis. In 1973 I was working with the Welsh Theatre Company at the Sherman Theatre, Cardiff, producing a play by Phil Woods based on the pantomime* Aladdin, *complete with Abanazar the owner of a coalmine, Ping and Pong oil sheiks and the hero Aladdin, the miner. After the Sherman Theatre,* Aladdin *played Maerdy and other Miner's Halls and Social Clubs. Dai Francis liked it and the company Foco Novo met him in 1975. What interested him was a play portraying the history of the miners' struggle, which ultimately led to the Saltley Gates picket line. So* Nine Days and Saltley Gates *was born. The two writers were Jon Chadwick and John Hoyland. There were other political theatre groups such as Red Ladder and Belt and Braces but we believed we were the first company to compose a tour exclusively of a play written for a mining audience, which was staged in local halls and was a part of their community. We toured to Miners' and Labour Clubs, sports centres for one night, doing five or six performances per week for five or six weeks, with an audience of 300–400 sitting around drinking beer and enjoying the show. This was truly 'Sponsorship', at a time when the Labour Movement, and in particular, the NUM, had the desire and wherewithal to promote cultural activities. Sponsorship took on an entirely different meaning from that which was handed down by the Arts Council.* Nine Days and Saltley Gates *and* Tighten Your Belts *all followed a pattern of touring, which avoided arts centres and theatres except for the London bookings at the Oval House and the ICA, but that heyday of trade union support was soon past.*

Secondly, Foco Novo contributed socially and politically with our policy of promoting black theatre. We commissioned plays by black writers, thus providing leading parts for black actors instead of leaving them on the sidelines. We also followed the policy of 'integrated casting', placing black actors in parts that would normally have been cast with white actors. We must remember this was a period – the 1970s and 1980s – when this rarely happened. Foco Novo was ahead of its time in this respect. A case in point was the London-born Nigerian Tunde Ikoli who wrote six plays for the company. I believe this broke new ground for other companies, particularly black companies.

Griffiths: *One thing we did do that we didn't get enough credit for was our championing of black actors and black writers. Roland had been instrumental in getting more opportunities for black writers and actors before he founded the company and it was always a key element of the company's work to try to continue to nurture them. But I also remember that we were very concerned that we weren't doing enough to champion women writers, hence our last production, Marguerite Duras's* Savannah Bay *(1988). But of course doing that also challenged the pigeonholing of the company: we weren't a 'woman's company' so that simply added to the confusion about what we were. If you could have telescoped all our shows into a five-year period we would have looked something like a national theatre in terms of the range and scope of what we did. But spread over time it looked like we didn't have a niche and weren't focused; we lacked a 'unique selling point' and our shelf-life was limited.*

Rees: *In terms of its aesthetic contribution the company was named Foco Novo after the title of its first produced play by Bernard Pomerance. In 1972 the presentation of this production drew on many of the forms employed by me in past work – particularly the influence of Brecht. He purposefully walked a line between agit-prop and social realism and it became a hallmark of my own work: clarity rather than ornamentation; the juxtaposition of image against image; the singular use of objects; the emphasis*

11

Brecht placed on the inter-disciplinary and collaborative nature of theatre continues to be a covert influence on much of the most contemporary theatre, even though Brecht is dismissed as an irrelevance. That is why the company presented five plays from amongst the earliest of his canon [2] and the ones least often presented from his work. The dip into Brecht was for us a learning process, both for the company, for the audience, and for other companies for whom Brecht was foreign territory. We chose other European playwrights as well, because their plays, like those of Brecht, lent a different voice to the productions such as Genet's Deathwatch *(1985), Fassbinder's* Cockartist *(1974) and Büchner's* Woyzeck *(1980) for instance.*

It was the policy of Foco Novo to learn from the European play, but at the same time to produce brand new plays that reflected the ideas and aims of the company. A considerable amount of the company's work was commissioned from playwrights who took on the mantle of sharing Foco Novo's interests. This was evidenced most clearly by A Seventh Man *(1976), John Berger's documentary book. We commissioned the poet Adrian Mitchell to produce a play based on the book. He transformed the text into songs, poetic stories in their own right. Each character was making a journey from the Mediterranean littoral, first by donkey from their Turkish village, then by bus to Istanbul, then by train towards southern Germany. A migrant was born. The whole was accompanied first by Turkish instruments, Oud and Balalaika, then by increasingly electronic music. The set was designed by Ralph Steadman. Backdrops of a village, and a long road of telegraph poles, whilst rectangular blocks of wood were manhandled by the cast to form shapes of a village, finally they reached the big city where they moved industrial packing cases in time with the music. It was hard work.*

Foco Novo always had a high standard of set and costume design and lighting, making great use of live music, largely jazz. Most of the designers were well established in their own right as freelancers, having trained at the Slade – Adrian Vaux, Ariane Gastambide, Bernard Culshaw, Sheelagh Killeen, Iona Mcleish and Tanya McCallin from Central-St. Martins. The same approach was adopted whether the design was for small-scale touring or middle scale. For example, the jazz musician Mike Westbrook required a concert grand whatever the size of the acting area.

Griffiths: *I think as well, during that period for me as a theatregoer, there was a shared aesthetic, or a shared philosophy more probably in the sense of being interested in the margins in terms of what was being done in more established areas. It was marginal in the sense that it was new writing; it was marginal in the sense that it was new subject matter. It was probably marginal in terms of the design aesthetics and it was also literally marginal in terms of touring to places that weren't getting much in the way of theatre. There was also particularly a coming together of various elements – such as the building of the new universities and the new repertory theatres, which had their own little studio theatres. The transport system had also changed – one of the things you get in the Arts Council papers is the interest in the* transit van and the Gulbenkian Foundation's part in funding those transit vans. That van in itself also influenced the type of scenery that could be toured and that made a big difference to the much older kinds of touring companies with their trains full of scenery. So although you were going to see very different shows, one or more of those elements united many of the companies.

Saunders: What was the company's relationship like with the Arts Council?

Griffiths: I wasn't very surprised by what you found in the Arts Council archives. I suppose it is a little unfair that we now have access to internal memos that were never designed for publication but my impression was always that we kept falling foul of different people's agendas and that we were also too awkward to be neatly pigeonholed. The paradox of our situation was that what you call the restlessness in artistic policy made us very vulnerable, because we could be seen as marginal to a whole number of agendas and not central to a single one. Clearly touring was always a major bone of contention in the time I was associated with the company, and the decision to stage Quantrill in Lawrence out of The Elephant Man royalties was, in retrospect, a major financial disaster because it gave the Arts Council a weapon to use against us in future years: both because they could say we had managed to do three shows once so why couldn't we do it again, and secondly because it didn't tour, which fuelled their belief that we were a company that didn't want to tour. They never acknowledged that the money for the production was a one off that made it possible for us to do something for which they hadn't funded us.

Rees: The Arts Council dearly loved to box you into categories of small-, medium- or large-scale touring, and did not like it when their boxes could not be ticked – in Foco Novo's case we did medium-scale touring sometimes, whilst also doing small-scale touring, which meant the Arts Council could not pin us down; the boxes could not be neatly ticked. Our intention was not to aggravate, only to do the work we wanted to do, which meant we were more than likely chose, out of financial reasons, to produce 'small-scale' touring shows but sometimes chose to produce what was termed 'middle-scale' touring. In fact over the many years we toured there was an ever-changing variety of job descriptions for different venues. Again there was a long and disputatious period when there was uncertainty whether Croydon was London, or Croydon! Was a show with a cast of 14 to be labelled as London and middle scale, or was the show with ten actors playing in a converted building literally just down the road, 'small' scale and out of London? There was a period of time when you could ratchet up your work rate, by touring to Scotland, but could not be considered in the same breath if you drove over the line that divides Wales from England. It must be remembered that this was a period of time when what was now called Arts Council England was the Arts Council of Great Britain.

Saunders: How did the situation with touring change between the 1970s and the 1980s?

Griffiths: Of course the new writing companies would always find it difficult to get bookings of any length because most venues by the 1980s were very concerned about survival *as the economic situation and government policies both worked against challenging work. It became increasingly difficult for venues to justify taking say Paine's Plough, Joint Stock and Foco Novo in the same year. I was working at Strathclyde University until 1981 and we were able, in one year alone, to have all of those companies and Gay Sweatshop and Actors Touring Company at our venue but that simply stopped for a variety of complex reasons. I think also that one of the attractions of companies like Complicite, Shared Experience and Cheek by Jowl was that their product may have been aesthetically challenging but it was still recognisable as somehow 'classical' and politically less threatening: it didn't overtly suggest the need for political action to change the status quo, so there was a kind of sleight of hand in which the Arts Council could say we're supporting new approaches to theatre-making while minimising support for work that might get antagonistic newspaper coverage. A lot of the more obviously political product found itself a home in stand up, and companies like Foco Novo and 7.84 came to seem anachronistic.*

Saunders: *What do you think were the factors that led to the demise of the company?*

Griffiths: *In many ways what happened to us was an almost glacial process of destruction as a whole spectrum of forces combined against us, not in the sense of a conspiracy but as a gradual shifting of forces to the point where it became impossible to continue. Obviously the economic climate had changed and the political climate had changed and the institutional climate had changed. Big organisations like the Arts Council will always operate with an (often unconscious) imperative towards their own survival, and when there is pressure on them from above (governmental) and a contradiction between their need to support artistic endeavour and the funding available there's likely to be great pressure to find solutions that square the circle. Hence, in part, the proliferation of appraisals and hoops for companies to jump through.*

There's also a personal communication element here: we weren't very good at cultivating friendships and contacts within the Arts Council and, perhaps ironically for a 'political' company, we didn't play the personal politics particularly well. My view is that when I was on the board in the 1980s our drama officers weren't fully convinced by our approach and that we didn't see that well enough or try to convince them of why they should support us. Also we had been going for a decade or so, which meant that to some extent we weren't the cherished project of any one drama officer and we were in a trap where we couldn't move 'onward and upward' because we didn't have support to do that (and there probably wasn't actually anywhere to go) and the alternatives were stagnation or collapse. So, my feeling is that for some in the Arts Council we became a kind of roadblock in respect of their ambitions for new companies and projects. The whole funding model was built on assumptions about expansion, and the process of dealing with contraction was bound to bring casualties.

I think it's true to say that there was a restlessness and ambition of the company, that we wanted to do so much but that we didn't fit into categories or tick enough boxes to make our case for survival. There's also a crude Darwinian argument to be made that sees subsidy as only pump-priming: if the oil doesn't flow in enough quantities, you cut your losses and move on to more promising territory. In a 1986 document we said, 'If we remain dogpaddling where we are, we will fall away' and the erosion of funding made it increasingly difficult to stay afloat, until it reached a point where we simply couldn't keep our heads above water.

Looking through the Arts Council archives, I was struck by how a number of other companies made a very good job of cultivating interest in their work by, say, personal letters to Arts Council officers. There's a very good account of the trials and tribulations and excitements of a highland and islands tour by another company that functions brilliantly to draw the reader into the whole experience. We didn't do that kind of thing and I think we suffered because we didn't.

Saunders: *In Roland's book* Fringe First *I thought Howard Brenton made a very interesting comment about the Arts Council's small-scale touring 'grid' becoming, by the 1980s, more like a prison for companies who had established themselves and wanted to move into middle-scale touring, but there was no mechanism in place to facilitate this move.*

Griffiths: *You had to stay in your box – and one of the reasons for this was because the economic climate was changing. A lot of Arts Council funding was based on an expansionist idea about money supply. It would've been great if a situation had arisen where the Arts Council could've said that a gap had now arisen into which we could move Foco Novo, or someone like Joint Stock who were also having the same ideas about moving into middle-scale touring; or a mechanism where Foco Novo could take over a venue like the Palace Theatre in Watford. But because people were staying on in the really big theatres, because of the economic climate, this wasn't possible. By the time the companies had established themselves and done the good work you were getting into the 1980s and a change of government that was crucial. So with a lack of money the audiences also didn't grow, so there wasn't the opportunity to move companies onto the next level of touring. Some people like Max Stafford-Clark, with Joint Stock, managed to move sideways and then upwards and other companies managed to carry on, perhaps because they had a brand image. So, 'yes' says the Arts Council 'do new work, but oh you're only getting 14% audiences', but Foco Novo's shows were playing in theatres that were only in any case getting 20% with Noel Coward. I think the two things – touring and doing new work – are both very difficult. Yes, you can tour new work to Edinburgh and Glasgow to a certain extent and probably Birmingham and Manchester and a couple of places in Wales, but in somewhere like Hemel Hempstead it was a very different matter.*

Rees: *When we toured* The Elephant Man *to Welwyn Garden City the venue was only able to house an audience of 100.*

Griffiths: *And it's always something that can be used to beat people with. When you compare it with a company like the Actors Touring Company who did things like* The Beaux

Stratagem, *which is slightly off-centre but it's a classic, and you'll get audiences of 50–60 a night, whereas for some of the things we did you'd be lucky to get 20–30 a night.*

Rees: *Also, the people who ran venues like arts centres and all the different places we played thought that the incoming company would promote itself and we couldn't do that.*

Saunders: *What lessons do you think the experiences of Foco Novo provided, for touring companies that came after them?*

Rees: *We are talking about the 1970s and 1980s, and it was a very different world to what came after. Before, it was about staying together on tour, week in week out, touring in the transit van. Now, the touring world has been subsumed into mainstream theatre. There is not much alternative. What at first was a separate world, comprised of a variety of people with different disciplines, is now actors hoping they will have left drama school, with a degree, ready to be in a play with excellent actors, paid an equity minimum, and the next step is looking for a part in a film. It is not what they can learn from a company like Foco Novo, but which agent they need to get the work they want. I don't think the type of touring we did in the transit bus really exists anymore – perhaps with TIE groups, but even most of those have disappeared. Work isn't toured now and tends to play in just one venue.*

Those plays are now done once off in a theatre and usually in London, or the other major cities. We would do a tour and we'd end up in London. It was the carrot of London that allowed me to get the best actors.

Griffiths: *I know that people still set up their loss share companies and head out after they've graduated.*

Saunders: *What do you feel Foco Novo contributed to notions of Britishness in its touring work? Here I'm thinking about that period of working with John Hoyland and John Chadwick in producing the industrial workplace plays and also your work with the black community in Peckham during the 1980s.*

Griffiths: *I think a lot of the new companies during the 1970s and 1980s wanted new audiences, but where those new audiences were going to be found was an interesting question. It probably relates to the way that David Edgar developed that idea of communities in that you're not necessarily going to a 'Birmingham community' but you might be going to a gay community – or in our case trying to address a multicultural audience, long before people were talking about that kind of thing. And it could be that your multicultural audience would much more likely to be found in Peckham rather than somewhere like Hemel Hempstead. So yes, the Arts Council wants new work. Yes, the Arts Council believes in the right to fail – but not too much – and the Arts Council believes in attracting new audiences, but it's defining new audiences in a geographical rather than a non-geographical way. If you took a show to Peckham, the chances are that a significant percentage of that audience wouldn't be a traditional theatregoing audience – so in that way have you fulfilled your mission? Strictly speaking, no you haven't.*

Saunders: *Was the new writing by black British playwrights such as Tunde Ikoli difficult to tour outside of places like London during the late 1970s and early 1980s?*

Rees: *We did* Sleeping Policeman *at some of the venues outside London and the audiences seemed totally frightened, and even when it went to the Royal Court with Howard's imprimatur on the play it didn't do well. However, when we took it to the Albany [in Deptford, South London] it did fantastically.*

Saunders: *It struck me that as a company you refused to accept the term 'small-scale touring'. For example from the outset you paid your actors equity minimum rates. You also employed large casts and musicians in your productions.*

Rees: *We were the first company to do so. It was also a selfish thing too because I realised that I'd get better actors. We always had a production manager and two stage managers and that was more than anyone else had in that area at the time, when the actors were also the stage managers.*

Griffiths: *Our actors weren't unloading the van!*

Very often touring is associated with the 'B' tour. Although the 1970s aesthetic was fairly spartan – it had to be for touring – at the same time it was going to use proper sets and proper lighting. In the 1970s the companies I saw up in Glasgow were evangelical in one sense in terms of their 'political' messages, but they were all conscious of trying to not give us a second-class aesthetic experience.

References

Arts Council of Great Britain Archives, 1973. '"Foco Novo" Productions', 5 February, ACGB 43/43/6.

——, 1977a. Letter from Anthony Kearey to Dave Weeks, ACGB 34/43/2.

——, 1977b. Internal Memo, Memo from Clive Tempest, 'Foco Novo Meeting', 10 May, ACGB 34/43/2.

——, 1978. Jonathan Lamede, Show Report for Foco Novo's *On the Out,* 10 May, ACGB 34/43/3.

——, 1979. Internal Memo, Jonathan Lamede, 'Foco Novo Board Meeting', 9 November, ACGB 34/43/2.

——, 1980a. Jonathan Lamede, 'Report on Foco Novo Board Meeting Held on 18 January 1980', 21 January, ACGB 34/43/2.

——, 1980b. Jonathan Lamede, 'Foco Novo Board Meeting', 26 March, ACGB 34/43/4.

——, 1980c. Marghanita Laski, 'Drama Department Show Report', *Quantrill in Lawrence,* 23 May, ACGB 34/43/4.

——, 1980d. Letter from Anthony Field to Valerie Mainz, 12 May, ACGB 34/43/4.

——, 1980e. Jonathan Lamede, 'Drama Officer's Report', 3 June, ACGB 34/43/4.

——, 1980f. Memo from Chris Cooper, 'Foco Novo at the ICA: *Quantrill in Lawrence',* 12 June, ACGB 34/43/4.

——, 1980g. Nicholas Barter, 'Show Report on *Quantrill in Lawrence',* 14 June, ACGB 34/43/4.

——, 1980h. Jonathan Lamede, 'Foco Novo Review: Recommendations', 14 November, ACGB 34/43/4.

——, 1980i. 'Foco Novo Review Meeting: Summary', 18 November, ACGB 34/43/3.

——, 1981. Jill Davis, 'Show Report for *Snap!*', 5 February, ACGB 34/43/3.

——, 1982a. Jonathan Lamede, 'Foco Novo Board Meeting', 9 March, ACGB 34/43/5.

——, 1982b. Memo from Jonathan Lamede, 'Special Initiatives', 16 April, ACGB 34/43/6.

——, 1982c. Letter from John Faulkner to Anne Louise Wigman, 4 May, ACGB 34/43/6.

——, 1982c. Jonathan Lamede, 'Show report for *Sink or Swim*', 11 August, ACGB 34/43/6.

——, 1983. Philip Hedley, 'Show report for *Sleeping Policeman*', 28 October, ACGB 34/43/7.

——, 1987. Memo from Michael Haynes to the Drama Director, 7 May, ACGB 34/43/9.

Billington, M. et al., 1982. Reviews of *Edward II*. *London Theatre Record*, 11–24 February, pp. 98–101.

Brenton, H., 1995. *Hot Irons: Diaries, Essays, Journalism*, London: Nick Hern Books.

Foco Novo, undated c. 1976. 'The Grunwick Dispute', ACGB 34/43/1.

——, 1977. *The Elephant Man*, programme notes, ACGB 34/43/1.

——, undated c. 1978. Policy and Future Productions, ACGB 34/43/2.

——, 1979. Roland Rees, 'Letter to Anthony Field', 7 February, ACGB 34/43/3.

——, 1980a. Letter from Valerie Mainz to John Faulkner, 29 April, ACGB 34/43/4.

——, 1980b. Submission to Arts Council Review Panel 1980, 30 April, ACGB 34/43/4.

——, 1982a. Letter from Roger Tomlinson to Anne Louise Wigman, 8 February, ACGB 34/43/5.

——, 1982b. Letter from Roger Tomlinson to Anne Louise Wigman, 8 February, ACGB 34/43/5.

——, 1982c. Letter from Roland Rees to John Faulkner, 14 April, ACGB 34/43/6.

——, 1987a. Letter from Carolyn Lewis to Alan Rivett, 23 January, ACGB 34/43/9.

——, 1987b. Memo from Michael Haynes to Drama Director, 'Request from Foco Novo to do only one Production on its present Subsidy in 1987/88', 7 May, ACGB 34/43/7.

Itzin, C., 1980. *Stages in the Revolution: Political Theatre in Britain*. London: Eyre Methuen.

Rees, R., 1992. *Fringe First: The Pioneers of Fringe Theatre on Record*. London: Oberon Books.

Roberts, P. and Stafford-Clark, M., 2007. *Taking Stock: The Theatre of Max Stafford-Clark*. London: Nick Hern.

Notes

1   The writers included Howard Brenton, Nell Dunn, Trevor Griffiths, Tunde Ikoli, Joshua Sobol, Nigel Williams, Snoo Wilson and Olwyn Wymark.

2   *Drums in the Night, A Man's a Man* (1975), *Conversations in Exile* (1982), *Puntila and His Servant Matti* (1983) and *Edward II* (1982).

Chapter 2

Insider Knowledge: The Evolution of Belfast's Tinderbox
Theatre Company

David Grant

It may seem strange to readers from outside Northern Ireland that in an interview about a Belfast theatre company in a book about small-scale British theatre, the question of scale should loom larger than the concept of Britishness. After all, haven't issues of national identity dominated the region's political and historical discourses for more than a century? The cultural agenda, however, has been much less single-minded. In fact, throughout most of the notorious 'Troubles', which, from their onset in the early 1970s, cast a shadow over every aspect of life in Northern Ireland for more than three decades, the attitude of many local artists has been governed by a resolute determination for 'business as usual'. Whereas in December 1971 a reference to 'an acceptable level of violence' [1] by British Home Secretary Reginald Maudling was widely seen as a gaffe, by 1988, when this story begins, its key protagonists, in common with most of those around them, had, to a large extent, come to internalise the pervasive influence of the Troubles – the routine searches, the almost daily news reports of violence, the ordinariness of it all. It was only with the first IRA ceasefire in 1994 that it became possible realistically to imagine a different dispensation. Even then, it was to be another four years before the signing of the Good Friday Agreement began the protracted Peace Process, which is still underway. As for the theatre, after an initial reticence to engage with the violence around it, issues of local politics had been so well rehearsed by 1988 (both directly in a series of 'Troubles-Plays' in the late 1970s and early 1980s and more indirectly in historical allegories like *Translations* (Friel 1980) and *Observe the Sons of Ulster Marching Towards the Somme* (McGuinness 1986)) that a new generation of theatre artists were hungry to relocate their work within a less parochial context.

It was in this climate that Tinderbox Theatre Company was established in Belfast in November 1988 by Tim Loane and Lalor Roddy, two individuals who, as Loane says in this interview, were motivated by the desire to make the idea of a new theatre company work 'despite the system'. There were very few models in Northern Ireland at the time for small-scale theatre. As Ophelia Byrne has observed, 'the decline of the region's theatre tradition in the 1970s was only partly due to the outbreak of the "Troubles". The loyal audiences that had helped sustain commercially viable live drama at the city's Group Theatre for most of the twentieth century had already fallen away and other venues such as the Grand Opera House and the Arts Theatre quickly closed or struggled to remain open. As Byrne concludes: 'It was not, then, that the violence … caused the collapse of theatre in Ulster [2]. It simply finished it off' (2001a: 6). The Lyric Theatre alone managed to continue operating throughout this turbulent period and a once vibrant theatre community began to wither away. By the early

1980s, however, the background of violence had become normalised to an extraordinary extent. The Grand Opera House was meticulously refurbished and reopened in 1980; restaurants and cinemas followed suit, and by the mid-1980s the green shoots of a resurgent cultural life were emerging across the city centre. But the pre-existing theatre infrastructure had all but disappeared.

Frustrated by the general lack of acting work, which was compounded by an even greater dearth of roles for women, in 1983 the five founder members of Charabanc Theatre Company secured funding from the Department of Economic Development to research and perform a play about the Belfast Linen industry (Grant 1993: 61). They conducted extensive interviews with women who had worked in the mills and created a devised play called *Lay Up Your Ends,* which brought capacity audiences back to the Arts Theatre for the first time in many years. Despite the success of this and subsequent productions, Charabanc's funding base was very insecure. The principal funder, the Arts Council of Northern Ireland, had limited resources based on the expectation of there being only one major client in each discipline (the Lyric Theatre, the Ulster Orchestra etc.), while the Belfast City Council, preoccupied with factional in-fighting, took a very restrictive approach to arts funding. Indeed, individual councillors, when lobbied, showed concern only for activities that they believed would directly win votes in their own electoral ward. Despite Charabanc's energetic example as Belfast's first independent theatre company for more than a decade, in 1988 the outlook for new initiatives was poor. The Field Day Theatre Company, established in Derry by Brian Friel and Stephen Rea in 1980, had blazed something of a trail for independent theatre with the international success of the premier of Friel's *Translations*, but even they had to come cap-in-hand to the Arts Council on an annual basis (Byrne 1997: 66). Thus, the prospects in 1988 for an unproved theatre company consisting of unknown actors were not encouraging.

And yet, there was an energy and a sense of cultural expectation in the air. As Loane makes clear, the absence of formal theatre training (or indeed specialist undergraduate drama programmes) throughout Ireland was compensated for by a lively university drama scene. Queen's University's own drama society (Dramsoc) boasted many illustrious alumni, including Stephen Rea and Simon Callow, and in March 1988 hosted the annual festival organised by Irish Student Drama Association (ISDA), which Loane, as festival director, helped to organise. There, the Queen's students and graduates who would shortly form the core membership of Tinderbox were able to share their work with peers from Galway, Cork and Dublin, and heard talk of the companies that inspired their visitors. The Druid Theatre Company had been founded by Garry Hynes and other recent University College, Galway graduates in 1975. Younger, but no less illustrious, Dublin's Rough Magic Theatre Company had been founded in 1984 by a group of graduates from Trinity College, including artistic directors Lynne Parker and Declan Hughes. Nearer home, two recent graduates from the University of Kent, Zoe Seaton and Jill Holmes, were in the process of setting up Big Telly Theatre Company, basing themselves in Flowerfield Arts Centre in Portstewart, a seaside town on Northern Ireland's north coast. In Belfast too, a newly emerging arts centre was in the early stages of its development at the city's then semi-derelict Old Museum.

The Old Museum was a fortuitous choice of base for the nascent Tinderbox Theatre Company. It had been built in the 1830s through the enthusiasm of a group of young men who came together as the Belfast Natural History and Philosophical Society (Nesbitt 1979: 9). Like many of the founder members of Tinderbox, they were recent graduates (in their case of the nearby and newly opened Royal Belfast Academical Institution) and were driven by a zeal for the ideas of the Enlightenment that had not been entirely extinguished by the bloody suppression of the United Irishmen's rebellion in 1798. This was a radical heritage that would later inform Tinderbox's decision to produce Stewart Parker's *Northern Star* to mark the rebellion's bicentenary, but at this early stage of the company's development, no political motivation can be discerned. The building fell into disuse in the early stages of the Troubles until it was discovered by a number of community arts organisations including Neighbourhood Open Workshops (Grant 1993: 17) and the Belfast Community Circus (Grant 1993: 27) in the mid-1980s who secured permission from its owners to use it as a temporary rehearsal and performance space. By 1988, a development campaign had been launched, and the building was finally reopened as the Old Museum Arts Centre in 1989. It was at this cardinal stage in the building's development that its connection with Tinderbox began. The company set up a makeshift office in a dilapidated back room, where they were soon to become neighbours of Replay Productions, now Belfast's longest established Theatre-in-Education company (Byrne 1997: 75).

Despite their zeal, it is clear from Loane's account that the decision to produce two short plays by Harold Pinter (*The Dumb Waiter* and *One for the Road*) in June 1988 was informed by no better developed an artistic policy than the desire to work on plays the actors knew and liked. But from this initial impetus, a firm commitment to try and make the idea of a theatre company work for at least 12 months rapidly followed. The company name was formally adopted in preparation for a lunchtime production of Edward Bond's *Stone*, which was accepted for that November's Belfast Festival at Queen's. Auspiciously, the venue was the Group Theatre, the long established former home of Ulster Theatre. Jules Maxwell and Stephen Wright, recent Queen's graduates, joined the company to work on music and lights, respectively [3]. Despite some bold if naive experiments in stagecraft, the radical nature of Bond's play, which had originally been written for Gay Sweatshop, seemed less important to the company than the fact of being included in the Belfast Festival, with the status and recognition that this implied.

While development of the company in its early stages was characterised by certain spontaneity, it is significant for the purposes of this volume that all the early plays were by established British dramatists. As Loane makes clear in his interview, notwithstanding the obvious geographic connection with the rest of Ireland and a diversity of political views within the company, there was a pragmatic cultural connection with the English theatre. These were the plays that the company was most aware of and that felt most readily available to them. But a more complex network of influences becomes clear as the interview progresses. Loane's own experience of working with Druid in Galway and with artists from Dublin such as Lynne Parker clearly had some impact on the way the company's work developed.

But so had Stephen Wright's sojourn at the London's Bush Theatre. A Scottish connection also becomes clear through the influence of the late John McGrath, one of whose plays (*The Last of the MacEachans*) Tinderbox toured throughout Northern Ireland in 1997; and more recently through the return from Dundee Repertory Theatre of Mick Duke (now Artistic Director of Tinderbox) with his play, *Revenge*, directed by Anna Newell, who had also worked extensively in Scotland.

These diverse influences recall the critic Edna Longley's description of Northern Ireland as a 'cultural corridor, a zone where Ireland and Britain permeate each other' (1990: 24). In part, this suggests the open-endedness of the Northern Ireland cultural experience. But it also vividly evokes the sense in which for outsiders it can seem something of a 'non-place'. As Loane's interview demonstrates, artists from Northern Ireland often experience a sense of indifference (or perhaps Troubles-fatigue!) from their audiences when they take their work elsewhere. This is particularly the case in Dublin where the expression 'the North' often seems to Northerners to convey the sense of a direction rather than a place – as if in implicit denial of the existence of their politically volatile neighbour.

Northern Ireland's inherent liminality has profound implications for any construction of Britishness there. In *Staging the UK*, in which Tinderbox's production of *Convictions* is used as a major case study, Jen Harvie contends 'that national identities are neither biologically nor territorially given; rather, they are creatively produced or staged' (2005: 2). One need not look far in Northern Ireland for stagings of Britishness. The Orange Order marching season, with its banners sporting patriotic slogans and images drawn from nineteenth-century imperial history, is a signal example. But Harvie's analysis implies that these identities are not immutable. They are susceptible to political, historical and demographic change, and Tinderbox's programme has responded accordingly over the years to the rapidly evolving dynamic of the Northern Ireland context. In more recent times, this has led Tinderbox to seek directly to engage with the political process as with *Vote, Vote, Vote* – a series of sketches performed to coincide with the 2003 assembly election campaign. The company has also been at the forefront of work with Belfast's mushrooming population of ethnic minorities, most notably through the work of outreach director from 2000 to 2008, John McCann as recorded in *Gathering Ground* (2007).

Tinderbox's status as a small-scale company has contributed to its adaptability. Unencumbered by the often overwhelming overheads of a building, the company has been better able to shape its programming around their shifting fortunes. As Tom Maguire records: 'The company members largely subsidised their work for much of the company's initial period of operation, working for other companies, paying themselves a minimal wage and keeping production costs to a minimum' (2006: 150).

In his interview, Loane wonders at the durability of so fragile an entity and concludes that the commitment to new writing 'about here' was one of the secrets of its survival. But, as Loane recalls, this emerged more through circumstance than from any strategic plan. Once they let it be known that they were interested in new plays, they were inundated by writers frustrated by the limited capacity of the building-based Lyric Theatre to entertain new work and this awakened them to the huge potential resource available to them within Northern Ireland. From this realisation flowed Tinderbox's policy of making work 'about here' – a term that was extensively discussed by the company and which related as much to the immediacy of presenting work in the audience's own voice as to any geographical frame of reference. This commitment to new writing would lead in 2004 to Tinderbox becoming the custodian of the Arts Council of Northern Ireland's *Sectoral Dramaturgy Scheme*, with a responsibility for the development and brokering of new plays throughout Northern Ireland (Luckhurst 2010). As Maguire concludes: 'Despite its inauspicious beginnings … the company has gone on to champion much of the new writing through which dramatic output from Northern Ireland has been reshaped' (2006: 150).

New writing for the stage has been coming out of the north of Ireland for at least a century, since the Ulster Literary and Group Theatres gave a platform to such prolific talents as George Shiels and St. John Ervine, whose work was also seen regularly on Dublin's Abbey stages. But the compression of hindsight condenses our understanding of this legacy. The comprehensive online *Irish Theatre Playography* reveals that in the eight decades of the twentieth century up to 1979, the average number of new plays from the north of Ireland was less than two. In the 1980s this rose to an average of more than six a year; in the 1990s, to more than nine. This trend can also be traced back to the popular success of the so-called 'Troubles Dramas' of the late 1970s and early 1980s. A decade of violence allowed dramatists a sufficient perspective on events to provide some measure of artistic and critical distance, and writers such as Martin Lynch, Christina Reid and Graham Reid (whose televised 'Billy Plays' starred a young Kenneth Branagh) increasingly captured the public imagination.

Tinderbox was in the vanguard of a cluster of small-scale companies who followed in the trail of these early pioneers and contributed to a rising surge in the output of new drama in Northern Ireland, partly through the introduction of more interactive modes of script development. In some cases this vogue for 'workshopping' work-in-progress may well have brought on writers who might otherwise have been overlooked, but in other cases such dramaturgical interventions proved problematic. This reached its most extreme form under the tutelage of Director Andy Hinds, whose workshopped version of Ken Bourke's *Wild Harvest* for Galway's Druid Theatre Company (1989), in which Loane performed, was almost unrecognisable when compared to the original script. This apparent dramaturgical democracy was intrinsically linked to the non-hierarchical spirit of independent theatre, and contrasted starkly with the autocratic literary management at the Lyric Theatre.

As Loane makes clear, Hinds was a major influence on Tinderbox's approach to new writing. The main vehicle for the showcasing of new work was their annual *April Sundays* programmes – rehearsed readings before a public audience – which grew out of two initial *Festivals of New Writing* in August 1989 and the Autumn of 1990. Of the 50 plays given public readings throughout this period, five went on to be given full productions by Tinderbox and at least six others were subsequently presented by other managements. Of nearly 140 new plays produced in Northern Ireland since 1988, Tinderbox has produced 29 (compared to 20 by the much more heavily subsidised Lyric Theatre) [4].

Tinderbox's commitment to new work has been complemented by the programming of more established works, but since 1990, when the company revived *Catchpenny Twist* by Stewart Parker (which Loane identifies as their breakthrough production), these too have tended to originate on the island of Ireland. Parker, who also wrote *Northern Star*, was a Belfast dramatist, who died tragically young in 1988 shortly after the success of the Field Day production of his play *Pentecost* that Tinderbox would go on to produce in 1994. In championing his work, Tinderbox made an important contribution to restoring his reputation in his native city. Similarly, when in 1991 they produced Robin Glendinning's *Donny Boy*, they were recognising an important playwright who was better known in Manchester than in his home country.

This 'permeability' of boundaries was also clear in their productions of *Someone to Watch Over Me* by Frank McGuinness (1995) and *Faith Healer* by Brian Friel (1996). Both playwrights are associated with Donegal, a part of the ancient province of Ulster, but contained within the boundaries of the Republic of Ireland. The poet Paul Durcan expresses this ambiguity with characteristic wit when he describes Inishowen, the peninsula at the top of Donegal that has been home to both Friel and McGuinness as 'the part of the South of Ireland/which is more northerly than the North' (1999: 158). The apparent blindness to political boundaries that Tinderbox's programme demonstrates underlines the difficulty of discussing their work in relation to the concept of Britishness (or indeed Irishness). In fact, artists in Northern Ireland often eschew any sort of national branding (*pace* Seamus Heaney's famous poetical protest at being included in the *Penguin Book of Contemporary British Verse*).

With *Independent Voice* by Gary Mitchell in 1993, however, Tinderbox introduced an important *new* voice to the Belfast stage that was unequivocally British. It was Mitchell's Abbey Theatre debut with *In a Little World of Their Own* in 1997 which brought his visceral vision of disenchanted working-class Protestant Loyalism to international attention, but Loane identifies this play together with the post-ceasefire play *Language Roulette* by Daragh Carville in 1996 as two of Tinderbox's defining moments. Between them, they represent the company's capacity to respond to the changing political realities around them, without becoming embroiled in the politics themselves. *Independent Voice* addressed the pervasive influence of paramilitary influence at the height of the Troubles, while *Language Roulette* was one of the first plays to confront the destructive legacy of three decades of violence on the young people who had become so alienated by growing up alongside it. Loane contrasts the ambivalent response to *Independent Voice* in Galway, which he suggests was complicated by residual political sensitivities, with the relative enthusiasm for *Language Roulette* when it transferred to the Bush Theatre in London. This, however, has probably more to do with the former play being performed before the onset of the Peace Process and the other after it.

The complexity of the Ulsterman's layered identity was well expressed by the poet John Hewitt, who was the subject of *The Green Shoot*, a biographical play produced by Tinderbox in 1999. He described himself in the *Irish Times* in 1974 as 'an Ulsterman of planter stock ... born in the island of Ireland, so secondarily ... an Irishman. I was born in the British archipelago and English is my native tongue, so I am British… I'm European. This is my hierarchy of values' (quoted in Warner 1981: 6). And yet it was ironically a Scottish influence through board member Mark Carruthers's vivid recollection of John McGrath's *Border Warfare* that finally brought the issue of national identity to the top of Tinderbox's artistic agenda. A prolonged discussion about a suitable Millennium production under the working title *North* in the late 1990s finally focused squarely on how to address similar issues for Northern Ireland.

As Loane explains, it was ironically the absence of an artistic director on Stephen Wright's resignation to join the BBC, combined with the advice of another board member about the potential availability of the Crumlin Road Courthouse that led ultimately to the decision to commission seven of the writers with whom Tinderbox had developed a connection (Daragh Carville, Damian Gorman, Marie Jones, Martin Lynch, Owen McCafferty, Nicola McCartney and Gary Mitchell) each to write a short play in direct response to the Courthouse itself under the collective title *Convictions*. Loane's vivid account of the decision-making process demonstrates what must surely be a pervasive characteristic of small-scale theatre – its counter-hierarchical and collaborative emphasis. The durability of Tinderbox can be traced to its readiness to pass the artistic baton from protagonist to protagonist.

The resulting event succeeded in integrating the imagination and creativity of many different artists (including the film-maker, Hugh McCrory, the composer, Neil Martin and the installation artist, Amanda Montgomery) and served, as Harvie has succinctly put it, to acknowledge 'the immense and inevitable significance of the past for the citizens of Belfast and Northern Ireland, [but to present] that past as not monolithic or set and therefore, within limits, as available for reinterpretation' (2005: 6). As one of the actors in the production, Vincent Higgins, put it: 'the production was of now. It was an Irish, Northern Irish, Ulster, nine and six counties piece' (quoted in Llewellyn-Jones 2002: 161). In saying this, Higgins highlighted how the inclusivity of *Convictions*, in terms of the range of voices it represented, potentially heralded the emergence of a more pluralist and integrated future sense of identity for Northern Ireland than the hierarchical one outlined by John Hewitt above.

Tinderbox's openness to so radical a site-specific experiment as *Convictions* derived partly from its lack of premises, but also from the success of *Northern Star,* which in 1998 the company had presented as a co-production with Field Day Theatre Company in the eighteenth-century Rosemary Street Presbyterian Church. The significance of the venue was not lost on Michael Billington who observed that 'short of seeing *Hamlet* at Elsinor you could hardly find a play that comes closer to home' (1998: 12). Hence, it was for a mixture of pragmatic and aesthetic reasons that Tinderbox presented their next two productions in Belfast's disused historic Assembly Rooms. *No Place Like Home,* which offered in 2001 an impressionistic account of the experience of refugees from West Belfast to Bosnia, was based on a text by Owen McCafferty, whose adaptation of Ionesco's *The Chairs* would be produced in the same venue in 2003, but like *Convictions* it adopted a highly interdisciplinary approach with significant contributions from the composer, Conor Mitchell; the choreographer, Sandy Cuthbert; and the visual artist, Amanda Montgomery, who had also worked on *Convictions.*

The second production to be staged in the Assembly Rooms (in 2002) was Tim Loane's own play, *Caught Red-Handed*. Having co-founded Tinderbox as an actor in 1988, Loane has also worked regularly with the company as a director and when his career took him into television, he became chair of the Tinderbox Board. But it is perhaps his return to the company as a playwright that has meant most to him. Set in Belfast in the future of 2005, *Caught Red-Handed* opens with a news report announcing that there is shortly to be a referendum on a united Ireland. The fine comic actor Dan Gordon took on the double role of the leader of the Alternative Unionist Party (a lightly disguised Ian Paisley) and a lookalike coerced into impersonating him. The knockabout slapstick style owed much to Dario Fo, one of whose plays (*Can't Pay, Won't Pay*) Loane had directed for Tinderbox in 1992, but the comic idiom allowed the play directly to address some of the unacknowledged taboos in Northern Ireland theatre (Grant 2004: 39–50). One scene in particular where audience members were invited to vote for or against a united Ireland challenged the liberal consensus that underpinned most local drama. While Loane is adamant that *Caught Red-Handed* (and its companion piece, *To Be Sure*, a satirical treatment of republicanism) deserve wider attention, he acknowledges that a local audience will inevitably be able to read it in greater depth. That perhaps is the unique selling point of small-scale theatre: the capacity to speak directly to a specialised audience, while retaining the potential to appeal to the world beyond. It is also an argument for a regional theatre company to resist being defined by its locality.

As Loane himself concludes, *Caught Red-Handed* highlights some of the key questions raised by this volume. It was Tinderbox's survival as a small-scale theatre company, in part because of its sustained commitment to new writing and the local voice, that allowed Loane to develop as an artist and provided him the platform for work that challenged some of the assumptions of Northern Ireland theatre. The concept of Britishness is also central to the play. The seemingly misplaced 'loyalism' that so mystifies outsiders in both Great Britain and the rest of Ireland is literally in the spotlight, and exposed to thoughtful but hilarious scrutiny. It is noteworthy that while Loane in his interview is clear about Northern Ireland's closer affinities with England than with the Republic, he illustrates this more in relation to negative experiences in Ireland than to positive ones 'across the water'. His position recalls Edna Longley's conclusion that:

> '"British" is only an allegiance, an umbrella for English, Scots and Welsh and some Northern Irish. Allegiance has cultural effects, and culture influences allegiance. Yet "Britishness" is not *opposite* to "Irishness". It is the affiliation whereby Ulster Protestants seek to maintain those aspects of their identity which are threatened by political Irishness'.
>
> (1990: 6)

The balance of forces bearing on theatre in Northern Ireland can perhaps best be understood with reference to 'cultural gravity' (Grant 2003: 150). This is the idea that cities like London and Dublin exert an influence in proportion to both their cultural mass and their distance from the subject of that influence. Thus, the cultural impact on Belfast of Dublin will almost equal that of London which though larger is further away. But it is significant that Loane refuses to be drawn into an explicitly political statement of allegiance. In this can be detected an important difference between Tinderbox and its illustrious predecessor, Field Day. While Field Day board member Seamus Heaney has famously argued that when it came to politics the company had less of a position than a 'disposition', its Irish nationalist credentials are undeniable. Tinderbox, on the other hand, appears quite apolitical, seeking to reflect rather than present the world around it.

In the interview that follows, apart from the issues of politics and identity that flow inevitably from the framing of the current volume in terms of nationality, two other key themes emerge. As is clear from the production statistics cited above, the small-scale theatre sector has for the last three decades been the principal engine of creative innovation for northern Irish drama and yet it depends on the flimsiest of infrastructures. As the Arts Council of Northern Ireland noted in their 1993 annual report, the early 1990s saw 'a remarkable rise in the number of young companies' (quoted in Byrne 1997: 77). A comparison between two surveys of small-scale theatre in Northern Ireland in the 1990s (Grant 1993, Byrne 1997) and the list of companies currently funded by the Arts Council reveals a remarkably consistent level of activity since that time, with about a dozen companies in each list. The last decade has seen significantly fewer new admissions to the sector, however, with the established names, often under new managements, tending to hog shrinking resources. Furthermore, a range of informal training opportunities such as the youth theatre and the university drama societies cited as major influences by Loane have given way to more rigid educational structures with the spread of university drama degrees across Ireland. While the additional resources that have accompanied these developments are to be welcomed, attention needs to be given to retaining the latitude necessary for the kind of initiative, enterprise and opportunism that shines through Tim Loane's account of the early days of Tinderbox.

Interview with Tim Loane

Grant:	You were a founding member and one of the first artistic directors of Tinderbox Theatre Company.
Loane:	One of many. Originally there were two, Lalor Roddy and myself. Stephen Wright was next to join. There were nine of us at one stage.
Grant:	Nine artistic directors?
Loane:	Yes, nine administrators, nine managers, nine egos, everyone did everything – or at least we tried to.
Grant:	That in itself says much about independent theatre. In those early days of Tinderbox to what extent were you aware of there being an increasing number of small-scale theatre companies across the whole country?

Loane: *Across the United Kingdom? No. As time went by we became more aware of what was going on elsewhere. But to begin with we were only really aware of other theatre companies in Northern Ireland like Charabanc or Replay or Field Day. I think they were the only three in existence when we started. There was something more anarchic about the way we approached the process of actually doing shows and becoming a proper company – probably a bit naive too. I always think it's ironic that the Arts Council had to give us money because they had asked to do something but hadn't paid us properly to actually perform, so Equity had the Arts Council over a barrel which is what turned us into a proper theatre company. It was* Catchpenny Twist. *We did the show and we were all on £50 a week because that's all we had. Then the Arts Council said great, you get us out of a hole by touring. So we toured* Catchpenny Twist. *The Arts Council lent us their van and provided a tour manager and covered some costs but they forgot to pay us properly as actors, so Equity was able to turn round to the Arts Council and say, with our assistance obviously, 'You can't do this'.*

Grant: *Obviously, Tinderbox was remarkably self-reliant, but in those days you just assumed that the Arts Council was the body that funded theatre.*

Loane: *There was very little local authority funding; none at all to begin with. We were just an annoyance to them. But from the very beginning we benefited from private sponsorship.*

Grant: *ABSA [5] had their incentive scheme then.*

Loane: *They did. Before the Arts Council came on board we were successfully getting sponsorship from local businesses. Small amounts but they made a massive difference.*

Grant: *And the Old Museum did provide a platform for the work.*

Loane: *It was crucial. And like Tinderbox, it was founded by individuals who wanted to do something* despite *the system, despite the Arts Council, despite the 'powers-that-be'. So the Arts Council was confused about how to respond. The Arts Council was a reactive body back then.*

Grant: *The core Tinderbox members had all come out of different courses at Queen's, long before there was a drama course there. What role do you think the Drama Society and also the wider connection with, say, ISDA [6] had?*

Loane: *In 1987 I was president of the Drama Society and ISDA came to Belfast in 1988, so even though it was an unpaid position I offered myself to be for all intents and purposes a professional organiser of the student drama festival.*

Grant: *One of the things that saddens me now about ISDA is that students tend to go for their own show and come straight back because they can't afford to stay for the whole event.*

Loane: *That didn't stop us! Everyone was aware that they were using their drama societies, particularly in Dublin, but also in Cork, as their drama training. I remember talking about the auditions they were going to and the theatre companies they wanted to work with. This opened our eyes to the possibilities that were on their doorstep, that were not available to us. It was only at the very end of our time at Queen's that I came to understand that our time in the Drama Society actually was our training, or rather the beginning of our training. If I had the chance to do it again, I'd take it much more seriously as that. But those in the South [of Ireland] did see that as their drama school because there was no drama school anywhere in the country.*

Grant: *So we have a generation coming out of Queen's in the late 1980s, the Old Museum there as a resource, and then other people like Lalor [Roddy] just turning up. Was he the only non-Queen's member?*

Loane: *No. There was also Miche Doherty, Angela McCloskey and Paula McFetridge. But there's no question that Lalor had a huge influence. I still remember the conversation with him, in a toilet as it happens, when he said 'we can do this' and we agreed to make a commitment to it for 12 months and to see where it led us.*

Grant: *Because of the ad hoc nature, nobody's thinking of archiving and legacy and all the rest, but it is striking just how quickly Tinderbox did become established. You mentioned the significance of the Arts Council needing companies to tour across the region.*

Loane: *There was definite pressure for that, but we had a genuine belief in the value of touring from our experience with other companies. I'd toured with Druid, and Lalor had toured with Charabanc.*

Grant: *Just looking at the early work, the fact that the first production was a Pinter double-bill followed by Edward Bond suggests an emphasis on British drama.*

Loane: *The first three plays were as British as you can get. Our only frame of reference was what was on the bookshop drama shelf. We didn't see that there was anything else for us to do. We needed to pick small cast plays that excited us. There weren't Irish plays, or at least we weren't aware of Irish plays that we should be looking at. To us in those days, theatre meant English. But then we stumbled on the idea of new writing. And I really mean stumbled.*

Grant: *Was Andy Hinds influential in that process?*

Loane: *Andy Hinds was very influential on me personally. His method of working with writers was not accepted by everyone in the theatre but I absolutely loved his approach. I met him in 1989. He gave me my first Equity contract for* Wild Harvest.

Grant: *And that was very much about his process of reworking the script.*

Loane: *Absolutely. Andy's approach in those days was all about devising. Whatever came out of the rehearsal process ended up on stage, so we would have been better perhaps starting from nothing rather than scripts.*

Grant: *Yet the writer has consistently been central to Tinderbox's work. How did the interest in Stewart Parker emerge?*

Loane: *Through meeting Lynne [Parker]. John Fairleigh [7] introduced us to her. We were aware of her, obviously through Rough Magic in Dublin, though we hadn't seen any of her shows. It was Lynne who said we should read* Catchpenny Twist. *She had directed a reading for us in the first Festival of New Writing –* Tantalus, *a play by Ken Bourke [8], and she suggested* Catchpenny Twist *would suit us age-wise and subject-wise. And it did, which moved into us into the area of being interested in revivals of significant Ulster plays.*

Grant: *There was also a Dublin connection, of course, with* This Love Thing *by Marina Carr that you co-produced with Pigsback Theatre Company [9].*

Loane: *Ah yes. I remember going to Dublin in the very early Tinderbox days to see one of the very early Pigsback shows,* East *by Steven Berkoff. So they were doing the same as we were. They were plundering the English back catalogue.*

Grant: *Did that dialogue with Pigsback not partly come out of ISDA?*

Loane: *They had been friends of ours since then. We had a shared history if you like. We were going to see their shows and they were coming to see ours. We thought: 'why not put our heads together and come up with something'; and then of course the only common ground we could agree on was that we liked doing entertaining plays in the theatre. That was it. So it was a play about nothing that mattered much.*

Grant: *Marina Carr had already enjoyed some success in Dublin [10].*

Loane: *We had been looking at young and interesting writers we thought we could connect with and Marina was up and coming – and young. It's a really bizarre thing when you think of it. It's tragic that the best that the combined ingenuity of two theatre companies could come up with was a frothy satire about love.*

Grant: *The highly interventionist dramaturgical approach that was influenced by Andy Hinds and that was to prove such a bone of contention throughout the project, presumably that was coming from the Tinderbox side?*

Loane: *Yes, and that really was an issue throughout rehearsals. The Tinderbox ones were constantly pushing the writer and pushing the director [Jim Culleton [11] from Pigsback] to push the writer to adjust things, to collaborate really, but neither Marina nor Jim were experienced in collaboration. It just wasn't their natural way to create theatre. So it was all quite uncomfortable.*

Grant: *Were there any subsequent connections with Dublin?*

Loane: *That was that, pretty much. It was great fun, but it's a shame we didn't find a way to create something with a bit more weight to it, that might have played to our strengths a bit more – in particular Marina's. I think it was a missed opportunity really.*

Grant: *Your next project shifted the emphasis firmly to Belfast with an exploration of the work of Thomas Carnduff, the* Shipyard Poet.

Loane: *Yes, that came out of our second Festival of New Writing when we did a reading of his play* Workers *(Byrne 2001b: 22–25). Fiona McMillan's [12] friendship with John McGrath had led us to that.*

Grant: *And then you produced the first Irish production of Robin Glendinning's* Donny Boy *[13].*

Loane: *At that stage we were reading newspapers looking for stuff. This was obviously before you could search them on the Internet. I remember Stephen finding the review from the Royal Court production of* Gibraltar Strait *[14] and I imagine he came across* Donny Boy *in the same way.*

Grant: *And then suddenly we get on to* Bright Light Shining *[by David Ashton],* Galloping Buck Jones *and* Independent Voice. *All premiers.*

Loane: Bright Light Shining *came through Stephen Wright's experience in the Bush Theatre. He applied for a 12-month position as assistant director. I think it was very good for him and very good for Tinderbox. He arrived back much more confident in his artistic interests. And it was soon after that he became the sole artistic director of the company.*

Grant: *And the link with Gary Mitchell?*

Loane: *That came out of radio drama after a conversation with Pam Brighton [15]. I was in one of his radio plays and had a conversation with him about writing a play for the theatre which he did within about a month.* Independent Voice *was one of the plays that defined the best of what we were capable of: by that I mean offering an independent voice to a writer and the facility to help them hone their craft in the early days of their career and give it a gutsy production behind it.* Language Roulette *[by Daragh Carville] was another example, as was* Second Hand Thunder *by Joe Crilly.*

Grant: *There's an interview in* Playing the Wild Card *(Grant 1993: 67) with members of Belfast's City Council's Youth forum who were clearly astonished at the immediacy of the impact the play had on them. They didn't expect a piece of theatre to speak so directly of their own lives.*

Loane: *We even took that show out to Kilcooley [16]! That was quite an experience.*

Grant: *After that the programming seems to reflect a change in emphasis. Where did the decision to produce* Pentecost *[by Stewart Parker],* Someone to Watch Over Me *[by Frank McGuinness] and* Faith Healer *[by Brian Friel] come from?*

Loane: *That was a purely commercial decision. The company went through a bit of soul-searching after* Independent Voice *and reckoned that some of the stuff we had done hadn't been that great and that audiences had been patchy. So we wanted to replenish our souls with stuff that we absolutely loved simply for the quality of the writing. I remember the board turning to Stephen [Wright] at the time, who had become sole Artistic Director and saying what would be one of your favourite plays. And he said* Pentecost *and they said 'Well do it!' And we said, 'But that's a Field Day play', and they said 'That was ten years ago. If you believe in it, do it!'*

Grant: *Those three productions really reflected the growing maturity of the company.*

Loane: *They did.*

Grant: *Whereas the earlier work still had that stamp of student energy, [Daragh Carville's]* Language Roulette, *though, in some ways was the high water mark of that period of the company's work.*

Loane: Language Roulette *hit something different again. It was to do with getting the right writer at the right time for the company, in the same way when we did* Catchpenny Twist *it was such a perfect signpost for us as a bunch of actors who weren't really sure what direction to go in. When it came to* Language Roulette *it was the right play for the company at the time and Daragh was the right writer as well.*

Grant: *I'm conscious that there's a parallel political history going on behind this:* Independent Voice *is done in the very early 1990s at a time of the intensification of Protestant paramilitary violence. Then you do these mature plays almost as a move away from a direct engagement with the violence. But* Language Roulette *is your first post-Peace Process play, or certainly post-ceasefire play. And that seems to be part of the theme of it as well.*

Loane: *It's post-ceasefire and it's 'pound for a pint' night which was an extraordinary combination! Part of what Daragh wanted to write about and what we wanted to look at was how all the young people just didn't give a shit. And the play was about young people today not giving a shit. So politically this was saying that this isn't political. You couldn't find a more political statement to make!*

Grant: *Which is precisely Hannah [Slattne]'s [17] argument now for the need for a new dramaturgy is that there is a need to address new themes, so it's interesting that you were beginning to address those changes as early as 1995. And then we come to* Northern Star *and* Convictions *which stand out as having that 'event theatre' quality. With* Northern Star *there is the added complication of the joint billing for Tinderbox and Field Day.*

Loane: *It all came out of a conversation I had with Stephen [Rea] in a car driving through the centre of Dublin one day and he mentioned something about* Northern Star *and I said 'chance would be a fine thing'. By that stage, Field Day hadn't produced for some time and their expectation of Arts Council funding had lapsed. And the next thing we know he is proposing a co-production between Tinderbox and Field Day! It is amazing how much had changed since the play was first done at the Lyric in 1984. That's why Stephen added one line ('It is new strung and shall be heard') [18] to the end of the play to make it optimistic, after agonising debate and discussion with Parker's agent. I think Stephen concluded that Parker was in a dark place and Northern Ireland was in a very dark place in 1984. It was not a play about optimism. Henry Joy McCracken's final words of hope are drowned out by the drums of war. So Stephen wanted to make the point that with a tiny change the play can be interpreted as a positive one.*

Grant: *Tell me about the origins of* Convictions *[in 2000]? You were by then chair of the Tinderbox Board.*

Loane: *For a time we didn't have an artistic director. That was where* Convictions *came from. Stephen left in early 2000. I still remember the panicky lunchtime meetings. What are we going to do and how are we going to do it. And it was Paul McErlean*

[19] who said if you're looking for somewhere interesting to do a play I've got the very spot.

Grant: To what extent were you conscious of building on the site-specificity of Northern Star?

Loane: It was an influence to the extent that we were aware of how successful that had been. We loved the idea of the venue meaning something. Do not underestimate the impact of Border Warfare. When Mark was talking about wanting to do North, he was very influenced by that. We were trying to find a way of encapsulating the spirit of the times. And then we went up to see the courthouse and came out saying: 'That was extraordinary! What do we do? How do we do it?' And I remember the final conversation when we nailed it – we spent many hours discussing it. We nailed it with red wine with Paula [McFetridge], Eamon [Quinn, general manager], me and Ophelia [Byrne, board member] at the table in Ophelia's house. And we nailed it – 'That's what it is!' But only after many, many hours of discussion.

Grant: Something that links Convictions with the next project, No Place Like Home [2001], was its interdisciplinarity. Owen McCafferty has talked to me about his excitement about the idea of an equal partnership of different kinds of artists that seems to have its roots in Convictions. The fact that there was the use of video, the involvement of a visual artist, and all of the journalistic research that fed into both. And then there was the use of another historic building, the old Assembly Rooms which was also to be the venue for your own play, Caught Red-Handed.

Loane: I'd been writing for television since 1996 and discussed the possibility of writing a play with Stephen [Wright] and Tinderbox had commissioned me to write Caught Red-Handed. It was one of the last things Stephen did before he left. So it meant that I was writing it in the year when we had no artistic director. It was a different departure in some sense for Tinderbox. I know Eamon [Quinn] was very keen on it from the outset. He could see it was going to work for what we needed it to do at that stage – not least that it was funny so would attract good audiences.

Grant: But it also cemented the company's sustained commitment to new writing.

Loane: What's interesting going back to the very beginning is that writers came to us. As soon as they felt that there might be someone else there – I'm thinking of people like Mark Patrick, Damian Gorman, Ken Bourke, Thomas McLaughlin and the like. And then we put a call out through a couple of journalists that we were looking for new writing and we were deluged with plays. I remember debating the precise meaning of 'plays about here' and Glenn Patterson [20] passionately arguing this was a legitimate aim. Plays like [John McClelland's] Into the Heartland and [Joe Crilly's] Second Hand Thunder and On McQuillan's Hill came out of that.

Grant: Certainly that was the ethos that you presented to the world.

Loane: That's how we earned our spurs. It's how we gained enough of a reason to continue. Had we not embraced the idea of new writing from here the company wouldn't *have continued in the same way. We answered a lot of needs of various people, not least ourselves as actors and directors.*

Grant: *The idea of 'Britishness' is an important theme for this book. As a Protestant from Cork, educated in Belfast who writes provocatively about the political scene here, what are your thoughts on that?*

Loane: *It's hard to divorce my own view of the world from my experience of Tinderbox but to put it in general terms, Northern Ireland has much more in common with Britain than it dares to admit; maybe even more than it has with the Republic of Ireland in many aspects of culture, like sport, newspapers, radio channels, TV programmes, which are mostly British. I've always maintained that. Culturally we've more in common. I'm not saying that's a good thing, but it's naive to ignore it.*

Grant: *It's undoubtedly true that where we've tried to create all-Ireland bodies for the arts that try and straddle the border, they tend to break down simply because the administrative structures are different.*

Loane: *Sure, but when I think of times that Tinderbox took shows to the Republic they were a terribly hard sell. There were times when we felt that Dublin, in particular, was not interested in what we had to offer – in what we had to say. And there were times we took shows to Cork and Galway and nobody came. I remember going to Galway with* Independent Voice *and the management refusing to pay us the agreed amount because so few people had turned up. They felt it wasn't the kind of play they'd wanted. And we said: 'Sorry this is a play that is pretty edgy stuff where we're coming from'.*

Grant: *I suppose, your main organisational reference points tended to be in Britain.*

Loane: *Equity was then British Actors Equity and still the Union office is in Glasgow. When we wanted to start a show we needed Equity contracts which meant Glasgow and ITC contracts which meant London. And Dublin had no role in that. The only connection with Dublin administratively was to apply for funding for north-south touring.*

Grant: *Given the volatile political climate throughout your time with Tinderbox, was the company conscious of always having to negotiate between notions of British and Irishness in their work?*

Loane: *This was rarely explicitly acknowledged. It's sometime said that fish don't know that there's such a thing as water. It's their natural element. So often what might seem from outside to be dominant issues, melt into the background when you're living with them all the time. But I think there's also a sense that art needs to transcend the day-to-day preoccupations of politics.*

Grant: *How far were you aware of the growth in the independent theatre sector in the rest of the United Kingdom? Were there companies you looked to in Britain – ATC and Paines Plough, for instance.*

Loane: *They were people we read about in newspapers, or whose plays we read. The main connection to England was through Dominic Dromgoole at the Bush. Stephen*

> *worked with him and that was a huge influence on us. We also learned a lot from the Belfast Festival shows. I remember seeing the National and the RSC every year. We got to watch actors like Alan Cumming, Fiona Shaw and Simon Russell Beale. Irish companies like Druid and Rough Magic did come occasionally, but it was the Medieval Players, Trestle and the like – English Theatre – that we got to see more often. Other than that, our main links were through the actors we worked with who were coming home from England or had worked in England at some point.*

Grant: *Apart from the Tricycle there isn't much regular dialogue between London and Belfast.*

Loane: *And the Tricycle is only interested if the theme suits them. Nick [Kent, director of the Tricycle Theatre, Kilburn] came over to see* Caught Red-Handed *on the strength of the reviews but I suspect he reckoned that nobody in Kilburn understands or gives shit about unionists. Although I wrote* Caught Red-Handed *and* To be Sure *for here and I made no concessions to anyone from outside here, I don't think either play is inward-looking. However, they do require a certain insider knowledge to 'get it' and the more knowledge you have on here the more you will get, so a local audience will definitely appreciate it more.*

References

Billington, M., 1998. 'He had a dream'. *The Guardian*, 18 November, p.12.

Byrne, O., 1997. *The Stage in Ulster from the Eighteenth Century*. Belfast: Linen Hall Library.

———, 2001a. 'Theatre – companies and venues', in Mark Carruthers and Stephen Douds (eds). *Stepping Stones: The Arts in Ulster 1971–2001*. Belfast: Blackstaff Press.

———, 2001b. *State of Play: The Theatre and Cultural Identity in 20th Century Ulster*. Belfast: Linen Hall Library.

Durcan, P., 1999. *Greetings to Our Friends in Brazil*. London: Harvill Press.

Grant, D., 1993. *Playing the Wild Card: Community Drama and Smaller-Scale Professional Theatre – A Community Relations Perspective*. Belfast: Community Relations Council.

———, 2003. 'A Romanian perspective on Brian Friel's *Translations*'. *Text & Presentation*, 24, pp. 149–59.

Grant, D., 2004. 'Breaking the circle, transcending the taboo', in Eric Weitz (ed.). *The Power of Laughter: Comedy and Contemporary Irish Theatre*. Dublin: Carysfort Press.

Harvie, J., 2005. *Staging the UK*. Manchester: Manchester University Press.

Jones, M. et al., 2000. *Convictions*. Belfast: Tinderbox Theatre Company.

Llewellyn-Jones, M., 2002. *Contemporary Irish Drama and Cultural Identity*. Bristol: Intellect.

Loane, T., 2008. *Comedy of Terrors*. Belfast: Lagan Press.

Longley, E., 1990. *From Cathleen to Anorexia: The Breakdown of Irelands*. Dublin: Attic.

Luckhurst, M., 2010. 'Dramaturgy and agendas of change: Tinderbox and the joint sectoral dramaturgy project'. *Contemporary Theatre Review*, 20: 2, pp.173–84.

Lynch, M. and the Charabanc Theatre Company, 2008. *Lay Up Your Ends*. Belfast: Lagan Press.

Maguire, T., 2006. *Making Theatre in Northern Ireland: Through and Beyond the Troubles.* Exeter: University of Exeter Press.

McCann, J., 2007. *Gathering Ground: Promoting Good Intercultural Practice Using the Arts.* Belfast: Tinderbox Theatre Company.

Moroney, M., 2001. 'The twisted mirror: Landscapes, mindscapes, politics and language on the Irish stage', in Dermot Bolger (ed.). *Druids, Dudes and Beauty Queens: The Changing Face of Irish Theatre.* Dublin: New Island.

Nesbitt, N., 1979. *A Museum in Belfast.* Belfast: Ulster Museum.

Urban, E., 2011. *Community Politics and the Peace Process in Contemporary Northern Irish Drama.* Bern: Peter Lang.

Warner, A., (ed.) 1981. *The Selected John Hewitt.* Belfast: Blackstaff Press.

Websites

cain.ulst.ac.uk (a comprehensive online archive of materials relating to the Northern Ireland Troubles)

www.irishplayography.com (a comprehensive online catalogue of new plays produced in Ireland since the early 20th century)

www.tinderbox.org.uk (the official website of Tinderbox Theatre Company)

Notes

1 http://cain.ulst.ac.uk/othelem/glossary.htm [accessed 28 May 2012].

2 The ancient province of Ulster consists of nine counties, but it is often used (particularly by unionists) to denote the 'six counties' of Northern Ireland. In this article Northern Ireland is used throughout, except where a broader (e.g. pre-partition) geographical description is intended, where the term 'north of Ireland' is employed. The Republic of Ireland is often referred to colloquially in Northern Ireland simply as 'The South'.

3 Other early members were Finn Agnew and Chris Glover (both Queen's graduates), Paula McFetridge (later to be Artistic Director of the Lyric Theatre and then Kabosh Theatre Company) who had attained her then all-important Equity card through work with the city's ground-breaking Community Circus and Miche Doherty, a member with Tim Loane of the Ulster Youth Theatre. Angela McCloskey, the company's first general manager, also had an Ulster Youth Theatre background.

4 www.irishplayography.com, a comprehensive online catalogue of new plays produced in Ireland since the early 20th century.

5 The Association for Business Sponsorship of the Arts, now Arts & Business.

6 The Irish Student Drama Association, which in those days included only Trinity (University of Dublin), Queen's and the University Colleges in Dublin, Galway and Cork.

7 Chair of the Tinderbox Board and founder of the Stewart Parker Trust which supports emerging playwrights.

8   Playwright who also wrote *Wild Harvest* and *Galloping Buck Jones,* which were produced by Tinderbox in 1994.

9   Renamed Fishamble Theatre Company, Pigsback was founded by Tinderbox's Dublin ISDA contemporaries in 1988 and has pursued a similar policy in relation to the prioritisation of new writing.

10   Carr's play *Low in the Dark* was premiered at Dublin's Project Arts Centre in 1989 and *Ulalloo* premiered on the Peacock Stage of the Abbey Theatre Dublin in 1991.

11   Member of Pigsback and now Artistic Director of Fishamble.

12   Early Tinderbox Board member from Scotland.

13   Premiered at the Manchester Royal Exchange in 1990 and given its Irish premier by Tinderbox in 1991.

14   A play by Hugh Stoddart about the killing of IRA activists given a reading in 1990 as part of the first Festival of New Writing at a time of high political sensitivity and attended by relatives of the dead.

15   English theatre director who first worked in Belfast in 1983 on *Lay Up Your Ends* with Charabanc and after working as a BBC drama producer set up Dubbeljoint in West Belfast in 1991 with Marie Jones.

16   A vast working class and hard line Protestant housing estate in Bangor, north of Belfast.

17   Hannah Slattne is Dramaturg with Tinderbox and also co-ordinates the Sectoral Dramaturgy Project.

18   The motto of the United Irishmen whose leader Henry Joy McCracken is the play's protagonist.

19   Tinderbox Board member.

20   Belfast novelist and Tinderbox Board member.

Chapter 3

Volcano: A Post-Punk Physical Theatre

Gareth Somers

This chapter discusses developments in the praxis of Swansea-based physical theatre collective Volcano; between the 1980s and early 1990s a variety of influences informed this initially unfunded company and helped them to form an influential corporal vocabulary of performance. Volcano (formed 1987) was one of a group of disparate and aesthetically diverse companies that emerged in the years between the 1970s and the first decade of the twenty-first century. These companies have contributed to a loosely demarcated and dispersed 'poetics' of British Physical Theatre, a category that is resistant to reductive definition but whose tropes have become increasingly orthodox components of British theatre culture.

British Physical Theatre emerged throughout the 1980s from seeds sown by avant-garde groups in the 1960s and 1970s. Conventionally its development is seen as a gradual assimilation and development of mime, theatre, dance and circus forms that, in combination with sociological and existential conditions, reflected changing visions of late twentieth-century British bodies (Govan et al. 2007: 158). Companies that encompass elements of this sort of physical theatre aesthetic include: RAT theatre (formed 1972), Cardiff Laboratory Theatre (formed 1974), Kneehigh (formed 1980), Brith Goff (formed 1981), Archaos (formed 1986), DV8 (formed 1987), Earthfall (formed 1989), Vtol (formed 1991), Para-Active (formed 1994), Frantic Assembly (formed 1994) and Gecko (formed 2001).

Callery sees its physical performance as originating from the use of the performer's 'self' as a material component of its corporal dramaturgy (Callery 2001: 4). DV8's Lloyd Newson has famously cited Grotowski's focus on dramaturgies of the individual's body as a key foundation of this process (Newson 1997: unpaginated). These tropes derive from the Grotowski traditions but also from the differing strands of French tradition developed by Copeau, Decroux and Lecoq. The influence of contemporary and postmodern dance theatre and hybrid companies like DV8, as Franc Chamberlain notes, added a dance-influenced vector to the ecology; this made three distinct sub-traditions within the broader ecology of British Physical Theatre (Keefe and Murray 2007: 119).

Meanwhile some 'director-less' groups like Volcano (initially at least) operated outside of such traditions and formed a collective aesthetic borne of a group subjectivity which is not easily classified within rigidly defined developmental trajectories. The aesthetic identities of these companies were shaped by their members' physical propensities, and augmented by serendipity and by a theatrical vocabulary that was partly assimilated from a variety of external sources. In order to augment other extant and 'official' histories of the company

I interviewed Steve Fisher, a founding member who worked exclusively from Volcano's formation at the end of the 1980s through to the early 1990s. The interview uncovers a distinctly post-punk sensibility within Volcano's early work; this is explored here, as are praxis traditions that reflect a fourth strand within British Physical Theatre. I will argue that from their early years in the 1980s Volcano developed an identifiably British post-punk, do-it-yourself spirit which was informed by a variety of external forces and was defined by the skills and limits of performers' bodies, aspirations and ideas.

Post-punk Alienation

Simon Reynolds argues that punk had already become its own parody by the summer of 1977 and was officially 'dead' by 1979 (Reynolds 2005: xvii). Nevertheless, the punk 'moment', even now, remains an enduring cultural influence. Like most youth movements, it was sometimes shallow, disparate and resistant to closed definition. Its heterogeneity still confounds narrow attempts to define it in terms of class identities and a single politics. Punk, much like Volcano's aesthetic, emerged from a concatenation of contradictory influences; in 1986 Paul Fryer argued that English punk was seen as a working-class expression of the streets, a reaction to inner city deprivation, desolated rural communities, poor education, increasing corporate centralisation and recession (Fryer 1986: 1). But he sees its reality as a predominantly white middle-class and primarily masculine movement (Fryer 1986: 1).

Simon Reynolds describes it as a fragile alliance between 'working-class kids and arty middle-class bohemians' (Reynolds 2005: xxvii). Cultural decline of socialist materialist discourse, the rise of feminism, Thatcherite valorisation of the free market and the ascendency of queer, gender and race politics, generated a complex mix of nihilisms and idealisms that would underlie post-punk ideologies and style. These initially combined with what Fryer sees as a Dada-like mix of art school sensibility and revolutionary DIY poetics (Fryer 1986: 1).

Demographic and ideological classifications are problematic though; punk was perhaps more than a youth cult or culture and was constituent of a broader cultural ecology: a complex structure of feeling. The heterogeneity of punk music alone establishes the movement as one which surpasses narrow definitions confined to the parameters of class identities and a single politics: the socialism of The Clash, for example, sits uncomfortably with the nihilism of the later post-punk Oi! Movement, the sexism of the Stranglers is antithetical to the radical veganism and feminism of the post-punk anarchist band Crass.

Post-punk style and attitude can be separated from differing combinations of ideology and self-interest that together instigated an 'alternative' movement wherein means of art production and distribution were reformed through co-ops and independent organisations. Post-punk culture legitimised conflict and tension so that even its sometimes overtly masculine image provided space for deconstruction and exploration. Gender confusion and feminism were key tropes in its aesthetic, and provided a stage on which feminism could contribute to deconstruction of its milieu. Lucy O'Brien notes that, 'it was during punk that the "sex wars" went overground, that the battle for territory on stage, on the street and in the workplace began to pierce the mainstream' (O'Brien 1999: 187). Raha states that 'many women in the seventies punk scene shied away from the feminist label and the punk label, too, in favour of a more individualistic and complex vision' (Raha 2005: 68).

In punk and post-punk culture, tropes of situationism, political montage, homemade clothes and the 'readymade' coalesced in an aesthetic field of self-production (cf. Sabin 1999: 1–12). These conjoined with the creative ignorance of the untutored. Serendipity and accidental design 'choices' embody the values of amateurism fundamental to British punk. The anarcho-pacifist band Crass, for example, wore uniform grey army surplus clothes, which became a signature 'uniform'; but this occurred because the band lived communally and one member had washed all their clothes at too high a temperature, dying all clothes a uniform colour (Berger 2009: unpaginated).

In the case of Volcano, as Fisher demonstrates in the interview below, instances of 'accident' and serendipity cohered with other punk tropes listed above; these contributed to an emergent aesthetic that would later (from the 1990s) contribute to a refined Volcano 'brand' informed by an increasingly commercial 'physical theatre market'. Meanwhile, in the late 1980s Volcano embodied a grubby sexually charged and ambiguous anger. In common with the more formally dance-trained arts collective DV8, they embedded tribal, aggressive and third-theatre tropes within their work. Fisher reveals below that, indirectly, and in some instances unconsciously, they articulated symptoms of, and responses to, demographic changes which accompanied Thatcherite free-market policies. These included the dissolution of communities, struggles to re-ascribe or supersede older regional and class identities and the effects of radical gender politics (Sabin 1999: 4).

Fisher voices the feelings of many of the children who grew up amidst these isolating social schisms, who against the backdrop of the Cold War seriously considered the possibility of life without future. The developing post-punk years were categorised by existential changes instituted by new representational technologies and a more flexible but less secure working culture. Later, in response to an increasing domination of global capitalism, the digital revolution and the birth of the Internet, post-punk culture has been seen as part of a network of generational responses to the alienating effects of postmodernity itself (cf. Moore 2010).

For Hebdige the punk subcultural style reacted to disenfranchisement by exploring their ability to affront and disturb the social order (Hebdige 1988: 18).

The Buzzcock's song *Boredom* articulates an early post-punk structure of feeling: 'So I'm living in this movie but it doesn't move me' (Buzzcocks: 1977). Both the visceral energy of punk and some early British Physical Theatre companies attempted to attack an accelerating cultural *anomie*: the 'self-absorbed withdrawal that numbs feelings of attachment to our milieu' (Miller 1996: 4). Animated bodies in Volcano's early productions channelled an anger which Fisher describes in the interview. The impact of these frenetic bodies was cognate with the distorted guitars and sneering vocals of punk music.

Post-punk Bodies

In a 1986 discussion between Bonnie Marranca, Gerald Rabkin and Johannes Birringer, the latter noted that: 'we live in a culture oversaturated with mass-produced images, technological practices, prefabricated consumption – our bodies fragmented in so many different pieces of reified techniques. I see this as an almost total depletion of human reality' (Marranca et al. 1986: 32).

Marranca in the same debate noted a developing absurd 'punk aesthetic' and suggests 'we're seeing the history of sexuality connected to the history of the world' (cited in Marranca et al. 1986: 19). For a post-punk cultural milieu, the body, sexuality, identity and their representations became performative-existential sites of cultural negotiation; the lyrics of X-Ray Spex's 1977 *Bondage Up Yours,* for example, combine images of sexuality, hegemonic restriction, festishisation and ownership of the body. Meanwhile, its visceral vocal delivery is more akin to a primal scream than to singing: 'Some people say little girls should be seen and not heard, but I think OH BONDAGE UP YOURS! 1-2-3-4!' (X-Ray Spex 1977). The name of lead singer 'Poly Styrene' depicts both the performer and the woman as an artificial, manufactured and unnatural product. This deconstructive matrix and its primal affect and de-familiarising effects are constituents of post-punk art. They bespeak to claim 'authenticity' within the intercises of cultural representation.

The 'defeminised' sexuality of Fern Smith's muscular and self-destructive physical persona in early Volcano productions speaks to these dialectics. Company founder Paul Davies describes Volcano's early work as:

> [a] certain kind of political intervention. (…) Class and sexual politics were the primary modes of experience and presentation. In one sense the issue was simply one of equality. In another sense there was an impatience and urgency about this work that bordered on the reckless.
>
> (Davies 2012: 1)

Post-punk art is often concerned with notions of authenticity and is often reactive to a sense of inauthenticity which is accelerated by mediatised modes of representation (Sabin 1999: 6–9). It reacts to the inauthenticity of what Heidegger might have identified as a loss of self, through capitulation to a formless theyness or alterity (Steiner 1981: 97). Heidegger saw authenticity (the attempt to claim one's style of being) as the route to avoiding the fallen-ness of *inauthenticity.* This paradoxically means that, existentially speaking, one must take oneself prisoner, because identity is always in the hands of the other: 'Bind me, tie me/chain me to the wall/I want to be a slave to you all' (X-Ray Spex 1977).

Paul Davies suggests that Volcano embodied a 'primitive urban theatre practice founded on the authenticity of the body' (Davies 2003: 2). This contentious notion infers engagement with modernism via a specifically postmodern romantic perspective. These inform the twin vectors of representational de-stabilisation and emancipatory authenticity that are reflected in a, perhaps very English, marriage in punk culture between a romantic expressivism in the radical tradition of Rousseau and deconstruction of the '[s]eemingly seamless text of the system of commodity signs [...] the resulting personal liberation is embraced in some quarters as an end in itself' (Carducci 2006: 126).

Unsurprisingly some vectors of punk and physical theatre attempted to reclaim or deconstruct increasingly mediatised bodies as Lucy O'Brien notes:

> Stories of race, class and gender were funnelled through post-punk culture, not just in agit-pop lyrics, but in the textures of the music itself; in the sound of clashing voices, stripped-down beats and fractured guitar. This idea is developed in the concept of embodiment which Lisa Blackman defines as the lived body.
>
> (O'Brien 2011: 28)

As Blackman points out though, our physical organic and psychological behaviours are always subject to mediation (Blackman 2008: 84). Whether bodies can be thought of as authentic or merely differently constructed is contestable. Nevertheless, personal expression provides a key trope of 'British Physical Theatre where the "experienced" or "lived" body is dialogic with the "trained"/"acculturated" body' (Govan et al. 2007: 167).

In the photostat program notes for their 1990 production of Tony Harrison's 1985 dystopic poem *V*, Volcano celebrate the possibility of 'a theatre which reinstates the danger, the confrontation and the excitement of live performance' (Volcano 1990: unpaginated). Robin Thornber in *The Guardian* described *V* at the Bolton Octagon as an 'explosion of energy' of 'sweaty muscularity' and said that it 'restored that edge of dangerous uncertainty to live theatre (...) it's not just exciting it's intimidating like no other verse in this country in this century' (Thornber 1990:32).

V's program notes outline the fundamentals of what they describe as a manifesto for the theatre company:

> THEATRE FOR THE NINETIES *Volcano* stands for the elimination of 'sloth and stale achievement' on the British stage. We have chosen to reject both the use of the script and work of 'The Dramatist'. Instead, through the manipulation of unconventional texts we hope to arrive at a theatre which is a true synthesis of language and physical dynamism.
>
> (V program 1990: unpaginated)

This manifesto is summative of Volcano's development throughout the late 1980s and reflects an anger-fuelled reaction to the British theatre establishment that echoed a wider post-punk sensibility.

A Very British Anger

Theodore Shank observed in 1994 that 'British theatre culture still contained an "official" culture consisting of the beliefs and behaviour of people who are perceived as having political and economic power (with) other cultures existing alongside the dominant one' (Shank 1994: 3). This critique engages openly with paradigms of 'Britishness'. Shank locates individuals and collectives who are non-English, non-white, or live outside southern England as predominantly othered by, excluded from or held in abeyance by a dominant theatrical economy. As a result, many theatrical and dramaturgical innovators in the British theatre ecology such as Volcano have come from the cultural cold, sometimes exhibiting frustration at their exclusion from mainstream culture.

Volcano's desire to develop their work in Swansea, away from the London-dominated theatre scene speaks against a British theatre mainstream defined in geographically and demographically hegemonic terms. These issues formed the starting point of our discussion:

Somers: *You mentioned that you felt excluded and alienated from the theatre scene?*

Fisher: *Theatres felt like an alien territory; an enclave of elitist culture, from which people like me had been consciously excluded. Paul, Fern and I were all angry for different reasons and it was the aggression which drew us together. Fern was angry about, amongst many things, I think, the framing of women as frail, weak and objectified in the cultural arena. Paul was a student of politics and I was motivated by a general left-wing, class-based dissatisfaction. We were angry with society, with audiences and with theatre itself that represented a culture we felt alienated from.*

Somers: *DV8's early works were also characterised by an anger, which Lloyd Newson notes was part of their 1988 physical theatre production* Dead Dreams of Monochrome Men: *'With Dead Dreams there was such a direct line between what we felt and what we showed: we felt angry, we showed anger immediately. And it got to a point where we burned ourselves out with that directness'* (Newson 1992: 11).

Fisher: *Yes, Newson's anger was connected with a queer politics; I think we were all loosely connected to a wider generational mood as well.*

Somers: *You have told me that anger proved a creative and uniting force which pulled Volcano together. Did you feel a connection to wider post-punk sensibilities?*

Fisher: *Although now it all appears, very obviously, part of a post-punk zeitgeist, it was not a conscious thing. Class was important then a battleground in many ways. Class sensibilities and certainties were fragmenting and could be seen everywhere. I was offered a place at Swansea University by a young radical academic named Paul Heritage. I had never really been to the theatre and, to be honest, I felt quite alienated from the major works we were presented with; they were all quite middle-class pieces. In the 1970s and early 1980s there seemed to be an unassailable gap between the classes. I remember reading Edward Bond's* Saved; *it had a different aesthetic and energy; crucially the play delineated a family structure and context which reminded me of my own upbringing. There was a pessimistic fatalism about the final scene – an overriding feeling of hopelessness. The majority of students at that time didn't know what it was to live in a house without books, without ambition and education. Bond spoke to that world.*

Somers: *The 'fury' of Steven Berkoff's early work upon theatre practitioners and writers of 1980s and 1990s has also been described by a number of people including Alex Sierz as influencing a new generation of theatre writers and makers (Sierz 2001: 26). Presumably this is true of Volcano as well? Your early productions* Greek, From My Point of View *and* The Tell Tale Heart *were all Berkoff plays.*

Fisher: *Berkoff possessed an aggressive exuberance. It was no coincidence that my first directing as a drama undergraduate was a Berkoff play, and that Paul Davies and Fern Smith staged Berkoff with the college drama society. This is how we first came to know of each other: our first shows were productions of Berkoff plays. Now, Berkoff's sexual politics seem dated and his performance style and choreography can look primitive, but one was aware of his exaggerated performance style; he brought together music hall, alienated anger and a rather refined French mime tradition. It was dating even then; but he was revolutionary and people forget that. I grew up in the Elephant and Castle and went to school in Bermondsey in South London. One or two of the streets I knew were mentioned in his plays. This identification was thrilling and affirming; working-class life, culture and even topography were not prevalent in most plays of the time.*

Somers: *Some of what seems now puerile also had an impact; he employed obscenities whose disrupting possibilities were also a feature of punk lyrics and publications (cf. Triggs 2006).*

Fisher: *Berkoff's aggressive working-class frankness was written from inside the culture. There is the scene on the bus in* East *in which Mike and Les are looking at a girl and they fantasise about 'having' her. Obscenity is used to express a tawdry sense of thwarted ambition; they see other people living those better lives and they don't know how to attain them. Sexuality, anger and stifled desire for social mobility were all wrapped up in those works; they are all about ownership, lust, desire and impotence. The point about that scene is that Berkoff writes about how moving from East to West London involved a massive cultural shift. Mike and Les are looking at what they can't 'afford'. Berkoff understood ironies like that: he employed phrases like 'he doth bestride the commercial road like a colossus'; it's not a dreary working-class drama written by a middle-class writer – he gives the protagonists a life (Berkoff 1994: 7). He collated the language of culture, grandeur and 'history', with prosaic recognisable settings and raised these working-class anti-heroes to a pantheon. It is facile in some ways, but the initial lines of East are highly significant:*

> *Les: Donate a snout, Mike.*
> *Mike: Okay, Les, I'll bung thee a snout.*
> *Mike and Les: Now you know our names (Berkoff 1994: 7).*

They were named and therefore they existed; its direct address was also really influential. Volcano's production of Greek in 1988 and the work onward was all about talking directly to the audiences – even touching them. The liveliness of the audience was essential; there is a living breathing relationship between performer, material and audience. This is a path that Berkoff set us off on. He breaks through the fourth wall to say 'you'd better stay awake 'cos I'm talking to you'. There can be a communal aspect to this idea, a notion of sharing with the audience, but we were making theatre in a time of divisions and fragmentation so there was something desperate in our approach.

Early Influences

Key to the development of Volcano's work was the nurturing influence of some figures outside of the English theatre and cultural hegemony. They worked within a Welsh avant-garde network. In 1991 the theatre coordinator of Cardiff's Chapter Arts Centre, Janek Alexander, included Volcano in a booklet entitled *Export Wales*; an internationally circulated calling card which David Hughes in 1994 identified as 'ostensibly defining a Welsh National Theatre made up of experimental groups' (cited in Shank 1994: 139). This dispersed association had been in development throughout the 1980s and before. Its artistic character can be contrasted with that of the official National Theatre of England, which, led by changes in the funding culture, began to incorporate more populist forms within its repertoire: in 1982, for example, it staged its first musical (cf. Eyre 1982).

Meanwhile, an internationally facing association of Welsh companies delivered predominantly experimental works to a limited number of exhibition sites. Practices and approaches of Grotowski and of the Odin Teatret informed the Cardiff Laboratory Theatre (a precursor to The Centre for Performance Research). The mixed media American performance art style of avant-garde work developed by Moving Being *circa* 1972–82 also influenced this Welsh scene. Hughes notes that all groups based at Chapter were situated somewhere on the continuum of these modes of physical and visual laboratory-based experiment.

Volcano, by contrast, brought their own aesthetic to this creative ecology when Alexander offered them the support of the building for their tour of *Greek* and later directed *V* in 1990. Politically speaking, Wales was acknowledging its own history and increasingly seeing the English language as a colonising impediment to its traditions of collective artistic practices, festivals, rituals and poetry. Companies like Brith Goff would take these nationalist concerns to the heart of their work. Meanwhile, the attraction of Wales for Volcano was its distance from the mainstream:

Somers: *How influential was Chapter and the Welsh physical theatre scene?*

Fisher: *It seemed important to be far away from London, we felt free there to make our own work in our own way. I wasn't overly aware of a Welsh physical theatre scene really. It was in the air and we became part of it. We were not overtly 'Welsh', in fact more 'Swansea' than anything. We were essentially opposed to what we saw as a cultural elite. Chapter was very important: a bohemian hub of excellence. It intimated an 'alternative' culture – far removed from the imposing structures of the theatre establishment – it was, after all, a converted school, set up originally as a collective of artists.*

Somers: *Did Janek Alexander influence your style of work?*

Fisher: *He was very supportive and he acted as a catalyst. He introduced us to people including Atalya from Seville and Branco Brezovec from Zagreb, and we learned from working with people and trying things. Brezovec directed us in collaboration with actors from Made in Wales in a Christopher Hampton play called* Savages, *in 1989, which was a kind of training in a way. Brezovec crashed different texts together and we were there just as actors but he didn't want acting or artifice but something more intrinsic to one's own personal gestural language. Until then we played 'ourselves' but we played 'Volcano' – we had a collective identity that was very empowering but of course sometimes overpowering.*

These moments of working with other artists had an impact on me. Janek was important as someone who had a perspective of the history and knowledge of various artists. Janek also acted as director/dramaturge for V, for which we felt we needed an external eye.

Somers: *Was that a learning process for you as well?*

Fisher: *Well, really at that time it meant he just joined the fray. At least that's my recollection but he had a very modest and quiet way of affecting things – in contrast to our more demonstrative technique – so maybe he 'directed' more than I recall. It was hard to direct us ... we worked by 'just doing it'... there was no great plan: we just got up and did it. I have a copy of the script for V. It has marginal notes like Paul jumps on Fern, Fern jumps on Steve, everybody stares and spits. We were discovering as we went along. We were not even tutored; we arranged our bodies in a straight line directly staring, shouting, speaking, spitting and running at the audience. There was nothing of the spiritual dimension of Grotowski or of the delicate whimsy of Complicite's early stuff.*

Somers: *Complicite seemed to take a French classical mime tradition to embody the 'Apollonian' vector of British Physical Theatre while you embraced a 'Dionysian' energy. Would you say there was something identifiably post-punk about the aesthetic?*

Fisher: *Yes, we were basically 'pogoing' and shouting. I see punk motifs now, just as I see the Welsh-scene influence in retrospect, though I was not conscious of either at the time. One of the precepts of punk was that training wasn't directly related to output (three chords and off you go). I was the only one of us with any formal drama training background. Paul studied politics and Fern studied psychology, we had met as students at Swansea University. But in my drama degree we received very little movement training; what Volcano did we made up ourselves. Philosophically we were of that post-punk generation. It was influenced by material loss and existentialism rather than the mysticism of the hippy era.*

Tropes of failure, physical endurance and anger categorised some of the new performance companies of the late 1980s and 1990s who displayed an assertive confidence and employed a postmodern and eclectic palette which valorised the sublimely flawed. Whilst Forced Entertainment knowingly counterfeited dilettantism and the virtuosic DV8 ran headlong into bodies or walls only to be defeated by physical matter and gravity, Volcano professionalised an unschooled amateurism. Punk tropes were also evident in Volcano's eclectic dramaturgy and theatricalism: performers often wore make up which combined tribal cyber punk imagery of Derek Jarman's 1977 cult punk film *Jubilee* with the geometric make up of nineteenth-century pantomime clown.

Fisher: *I remember sitting in front of a mirror with two fingers shoved into these little tubs of facepaint and slapping it on.*

Somers: *It reminded me of Hazel O'Conner.*

Fisher: *We didn't consciously play on those images but looking back you can't avoid the references; Adam Ant, David Bowie, Hazel O'Conner, even the earlier glam rock. They are all there with an attempt at classical Greek masks; we had black boxing boots, cycle shorts, zipped track suit tops … a uniform, not a costume. We wore vests, and we showed off our bodies.*

Somers: *A bit cyber punk, something more than human?*

Fisher: *Definitely something other and 'uber' stripped down uniform and masks. If you are going to set yourselves up against sloth and stale achievement on the British stage you had to have an appearance of vigorous otherness. We were a gang.*

Somers: *I remember the poster for V opened up like an old punk album cover complete with some diatribe in the middle.*

Fisher: *That show was very powerful because we had a kind of yearning for a British avant-garde where people discussed change and aesthetics and not just who they worked with or what funding they got.*

Somers: *You were consciously a 'self-othered' gang?*

Fisher:	*Yes, who engaged in a kind of localised appropriation of what Berkoff tried. It was great fun, we were aggressive and grotesque ... we did grotesque well.*
Somers:	*I think that there is a transgressive British grotesque tradition that is pagan and carnivalesque.*
Fisher:	*I agree and I think that it surfaces in punk.*

In the *Edinburgh List* of 1990, Sue Wilson writes that in Volcano's treatment of *V*: 'killing joke alternates with Verdi, Ballet with pogoing, assaults with embraces, Harrison's exploration of the conflicts between, classes, races, sexes, generations and cultures is given vivid vocal and physical expression' (Wilson, 1990: pagination unknown).

The eclecticism of Volcano's dramaturgy was cognate with that of Forced Entertainment: they attempted to 'discuss the concerns of the time in a language born of them' (Etchells 1999: 17). This generated a fragmented post-punk and postmodern vocabulary of performance (which was, under the influence of director and writer Spencer Hazel, a onetime collaborator with Volcano) taken up later by Frantic Assembly who cite Volcano as a major influence (Graham and Hogget 2009: 1).

Training

British Physical Theatre contributed to a change in approach to the actor in Britain, 'companies like Theatre de Complicite, Volcano theatre, and DV8 continue (...) to belie the popular conception that the English actor is dead from the neck down' (Jones 1996: 19). Some identified a disjuncture between vocal and physical expertise (e.g., Hudson 1991). Volcano's approach had developed outside of British actor training academies and, for some, their untrained voices then seemed an important part of an anti-'legitimate' theatre aesthetic providing a challenge to conventions of speech and correct diction; this rejection of conventional British theatre standards, unintentionally perhaps, reflects another post-punk trope exhibited by punk fanzines, which often left spelling and grammatical errors to further emphasise their rejection of mainstream (Triggs 2006: 73).

Somers:	*You have mentioned that initially you didn't have a formal training process, could you speak a little about your training and its development?*
Fisher:	*I'm not sure we were conscious of a physical theatrical training. We were not like dance people who were trained. The three of us had the fitness of youth. Paul was a black belt in karate, I did karate too and we spent a lot of time in the gym.*
Somers:	*Did you use karate because it had certain qualities that were instrumental to an aesthetic idea?*
Fisher:	*Well, we were doing it; therefore it got into the work really. Though, there is something about the balance of direct aggressive control in karate: it lends a certain stance and physical presence. It even affected the way we walked*

downstage to the audience. We were attracted to it for those qualities; we stood in rows pumping our legs and arms. We weren't skilled in any creative physicality – our training was exercise and karate. Beyond stamina and strength there was no real attempt at that time at developing a 'system'. Later we held workshops and realised we had to say and do things in them. At that stage we just did what we did; the physical aesthetic was to do with jumping, lifting, throwing, catching and running.

Somers: *But not, I'm sensing, as part of a Meyerholdian training or Lecoq style sport-influenced approach?*

Fisher: *(Laughs) No. Despite what some academics claim about the lineage of British Physical Theatre we hadn't heard of these people in the early days, or at least, we didn't sit in the rehearsal room thinking 'what would Meyerhold have done?'.*

Somers: *So Grotowski did not invent your brand of physical theatre?*

Fisher: *Not at all, we followed a series of old military training exercises; I think the military approach is unfortunately a very British way to think about this kind of work.*

Somers: *Jonathan Grieve of Para-Active said something similar to me once; he felt that the military training model was more suited to an English sensibility than for example a Mediterranean or Slavic collective approach.*

Fisher: *Well, it was our way. In the morning we did sit ups and press ups. We only realised that there was a wider world of training opportunity in 1990–91 when we went to Seville to have a residency with the Spanish theatre company Atalaya. They looked after us for a week in their ramshackle converted warehouse where they would frequently spend six months making work. They showed us their preparations; these comprised a complex set of vocal and physical exercises, like a performance in itself. This was about 40 minutes long; there were about 12 of them in the company. Then they invited us to reciprocate. We looked at each other and started doing press-ups and running on the spot. I realised then that we hadn't ever had to vocalise what we did. It was the energy of the company which people related to. We did, I guess, embody the punk aesthetic writ large – it's very hard to codify but I think that partially it means that our aesthetic was formed of our collective identity. We picked up skills and 'tricks' as we went. In 1989 at Edinburgh we got in with the Archaos circus crowd who had a similar anarcho-tribal feel to their work (they were playing to packed houses every day). We did a little pastiche of them in our show and they invited us back stage at the tent, we were the sort of company that people liked. We worked with a number of other actors and performers and gradually these collaborations altered and calibrated the work. Volcano has been great at collaboration over the last 25 years and this was the start of that.*

Nigel Charnock did some work with us. I worked with Carol Brown and Dynion Dance Company, choreographer Royston Muldoon and a lot of other great people. We developed through a fringe equivalent of the old rep-system sharing tricks as we went. We loved meeting acrobats for their skill. In Edinburgh we did some informal training with Archaos: their acrobats would share tricks and lifts etc.

Strangely it was watching the delicacy of another Welsh-based physical company Man Act that made me think about the possibilities of our aesthetic. We were in Edinburgh to perform our Greek, Tell Tale Heart *and* From My Point of View *trio, I remember a moment in the Man Act show when Simon Thorne and Phil Mackenzie came together in the centre of the stage. They reached out to each other, slowly, grasped hands and then lowered each other to the floor, very slowly descending, arching backwards. Phil had worked with Lindsey Kemp who was known for working with slowness. And this was something we didn't do. We didn't work with slowness or with delicacy like that. Phil wouldn't have done karate, he would have used Tai Chi or a similar 'soft' martial art.*

Somers: *How did the devising process work?*

Fisher: *We spent hours in a room with gym mats on the floor practicing jumps – we just wrestled and tried stuff. We looked for intuitive ways of moving the body particularly in lifts. We often hurt ourselves. I remember dropping Fern as we tried an ambitious jump and catch in* Greek *once in the students' union poly at Elephant and Castle: I leapt and cracked my head on the air-conditioning, I was virtually concussed and we carried on. I crept off to the back stage area, checked myself out and tiptoed back on. The tension of the potential for disaster or danger was always there.*

Sexuality

In the late 1980s, AIDS, Clause 28 and a reactionary call to return to traditional values lent representations of homosexuality, like those of DV8's *Dead Dreams of Monochrome Men*, radical political bite. Meanwhile, the sexual politics of Berkoff's works were becoming problematised: Peggy Butcher asks of Volcano's *Greek* in *Time Out* in June 1988: 'I wonder to what extent a play in which phallic images are paramount, can effectively question the violence it portrays?' (Butcher 1988: pagination unknown).

In 1991 Melanie Hudson's review of *Medea Sex War* tellingly entitled 'Theatre for Body Builders' describes a problematic sexual politics embedded within the spectacle of performative display. *Medea Sex War* combined a text by Tony Harrison with Valerie Solanis's 1968 feminist SCUM manifesto. Hudson describes the tension of an uneasy dialectic between hegemonic, transgressive and coercive aspects of sexually aggressive spectacle:

The paradox of the evening is that the Villain of the piece, Hercules (Stephen Fisher), is a prime representative of a type also pilloried by SCUM; the woman hating, narcissistic body-builder who worships all things material – in particular his own muscle, it is his final act of slaughter which allows SCUM to suggest why tragedy itself may be an inherently male form – the male loves death – it excites him sexually. And yet the production itself by its very attractiveness invites us to join in Hercules worship of muscle and so implicate us in the result.

(Hudson 1991: pagination unknown)

Betty Caplan in *The Guardian* of the same week illustrates another layer of complexity:

Here there are only losers interchanging the main parts of the two women Angela Bullock of the Kosh and Fern Smith appear to be as angry and destructive as the men if not more so. Paul Davis and Stephen Fisher (Jason/Hercules) seem somehow more vulnerable. Jason even allows a bare quivering midriff to show. He longs to win the Golden Fleece and become rich and desirable to women. It makes you realise how outmoded good old hetero-sex has become.

(Caplan 1991: pagination unknown)

Representation of the male as sexualised object became contentious in physical performance in the 1990s. Fiona Buckland notes in 1995 that homophobia in dance (and in physical theatre) meant that: 'Compared to the female figure, the male figure in dance is still invested with power, but the range of expressions which can be represented by men is restricted at one end of the emotional spectrum' (Buckland 1995: 375).

Frieze magazine suggested in 1995 that the ambiguous alchemy of transgression and conformity within tropes of camp and body building was a 1990s trend which engaged with these strata of performance (Savage 1996: 413). DV8 sought to carve physically articulated space for what would become known as a 'queer' aesthetic. For Volcano though, representations of feminist informed male heterosexuality proved problematic. Jason's availability as viewed subject challenged heterosexual conventions of male as viewer, rather than as subject of voyeuristic spectacle, while Hercules' display allowed the viewer to gain some voyeuristic sense of control over his misogyny; however, both characters and performers invite audience approval and thus request endorsement of their virtuosic physicality by dint of the commoditisation of their body's capacities to generate spectacle. Fisher reveals that the political complexity of these sexual politics began to cause him some personal discomfiture:

Fisher: *We had become successful and were starting to attract relatively lucrative funding streams compared to the poverty of our early days. I began to ponder the fine line between leftist and rightist politics. Initially what I considered to be a group physicality borne of disenfranchised anger had developed into adoration of the physical form.*

During a performance of Greek *in Rhyl, seeing a woman in a wheelchair and a Vicar wearing a dog collar clapping enthusiastically, I felt some sense of irony … I thought we were talking to the disaffected and angry youth, but by then we were talking to middle-class theatre lovers. Also the irony of displaying my 'perfect'*

body to a wheelchair user made me believe that I had become part of the same
elitist and aggressive process of representation that I had always been opposed to.

'Your Future Dream is a Shopping Scheme!' (Sex Pistols 1976): The 1990s

Do-it-yourself culture and Berkovian rage gave way in the 1990s to a mood of jaded acquiescence, to commoditisation and to 'irony' which blurred lines between nihilism and its critique. In the 1990s, post-punk culture took a new turn with Cool Britannia which led to the branding of In-yer-face Dramatists, British Physical Theatre, Brit-Artists and Brit-Pop bands. British Physical Theatre became a familiar umbrella term and many of the companies already mentioned in the introduction to this chapter became large, core-funded interests. The British theatre ecology, as Baz Kershaw notes, became increasingly 'consumer led' from the late 1980s as: 'Theatres were integrated into the bourgeoning service, tourist, heritage and "hospitality" industries and in the process its audience were refashioned as customers' (Kershaw 2007: 194).

Branding of arts leisure and products became a ubiquitous feature of this ecology. In 1988 *The Observer* ran an article entitled 'Style People out of Date' in which they describe the mood of the time as one of ubiquitous obsession with '*style* over *content*' (Savage 1996: 239–41). In this environment, originality became an 'essential selling point' and market forces lead companies to cease to experiment but instead to reproduce elements of their own previous successes. Artistic attempts to negotiate these issues became increasingly paradoxical: the issue is embodied in two sections of Volcano's 1990 program where post-punk sensibilities embedded in Harrison's 1985 poem collide with 1990s 'Cool Britannic' materialism.

> Harrison's poem revives an old debate about distinguishing between cultural practices, and the relationship of these practices to class and power. It has been our unfortunate experience to have lived in an epoch in which 'The Right' has successfully manoeuvred this debate off the political agenda. In place of culture, just as in place of society, we are offered supposedly equal opportunity to consume just as much or little as our pocket affords. This social fantasy is alarmingly similar to both Eliot's 'list of culture' and the now popular post modernists' happy grunt of relativist delight. Ostensibly Thatcherism, Eliotean Conservatism and Post modernism all give up on culture in preference for their respective delusions of the market, the tradition, and the academy.
>
> (*V* program notes 1990)

Elsewhere the program requests 'sponsorship for their 1990/91 program of work' (*V* program notes 1990). This does not imply hypocrisy; it merely illustrates the problematic nature of a desire for authenticity that exists 'outside of' postmodernity or consumer culture. Fisher infers that like punk itself British Physical Theatre also died shortly after its conception:

Somers: *At what point does increasingly popular art which is organic, counter cultural and responsive to its time become a product?*

Fisher: *You make me think about the nature of our identity within the 'scene'. The term physical theatre became passé quite quickly. People soon started teaching elements of it as if it were a vocabulary of tricks. It then loses authenticity. Fern and I created/ discovered/found a kind of lift which is often used now, but then we just worked out what specific bodies could do together. Moves were developed from our own physical propensities. Physical theatre is now an accepted model but to us, the medium was partly the message and we were part of the medium. It was partly this change from authenticity to awareness of a market which eventually led me to leave the company.*

Volcano, as I remember us, were much more like a group, a tribe, than a 'company'. Perhaps that was partly why the 'form' that I thought we worked on seemed at the time to be 'of us'. It was our work; it didn't have a formula, initially that was great. After a while for me it became restrictive.

Conclusion

A combination of post-punk tropes cohered in the early work of Volcano: aggressive 'honesty' combined with a sometimes camp theatricality framed the physiques of the performers within a distinctly 'Low Fi' mise-en-scène. They were paradoxically macho, gender-transgressive, failing, virtuosic and seductive. They 'sampled' from the cultural archive and exuded an identity-forming tribal aggression. They accentuated symptoms of alienation through aesthetic sartorial and counter-institutional theatrical strategies that were directed at constraining socially conditioned models of English/British class and sexual role ascription. They challenged many conventional approaches to theatre-making.

The formative years of British Physical Theatre, the 1980s–90s, after the first pioneering wave of the 1960s and 1970s was categorised by post-punk do-it-yourself culture. People made their own garments in response to corporate homogeneity, but it was also a time when marketing gained ascendance; others started to wear labels on the outside of their clothes, as street fashions became high-street fashion, so counter culture, with the ascendancy of the free market, became shop-counter culture. Fisher charts Volcano's negotiation of these vectors of cultural development as concomitant with a cultural move from Punk 'anger' towards the 1990s 'cool' and branding for success.

Speculation as to whether such developments might be considered authentically punk is perhaps unproductive. Carducci notes that in 1979 Hebdige argued that rebellious youth subcultures appropriate certain consumer goods to construct autonomous identities, inscribing new, oppositional meanings onto them. However, he later revised his position to acknowledge the power of commercial culture to reintegrate counter hegemonic styles into the system of consensus (Carducci 2006: 116).

But Cartledge notes, band managers like Malcolm McLaren and Bernie Rhodes of the Clash were more concerned with raiding culture to sell 'style' rather than to provide symbolic resistance to consumer models (Sabin 1999: 149).

Thus, issues of aesthetics and materiality's stand at the centre of dialectics of 'the body', creative expression, authenticity and the manufacture and dissemination of artistic product. The concern that experimental art might become a mere repository of research which effectively supplies mainstream movements with novel but sanitised tropes may be a universal one, or a more specific symptom of a pragmatic capitalist British theatre ecology.

Volcano theatre and their compatriot companies have continued to negotiate these difficult issues during the 20 years that have elapsed since Fisher's departure. But in 2013 as I write, young disenfranchised theatre makers are once again leaving universities to enter a financially desolate artistic landscape and theatre ecology, where funding and support structures have corroded. Some of these young people may find ways to negotiate their own alienations and existential trials in order to speak to the current times in a language borne of their own experience.

References

Berger, G., 2009. *The Story of Crass*. Oakland, CA: PM Press.

Berkoff, S., 1994. *Plays 1*. London: Faber & Faber.

Blackman, L., 2008. *The Body*. Oxford: Berg.

Buckland, F., 1995. 'Towards a language of the stage'. *New Theatre Quarterly*, 11: 44, pp. 371–80.

Butcher, P., 1988. *Time Out*, Pagination unknown.

Buzzcocks, 1977. *Spiral Scratch*. New Hormones Records UK.

Callery, D., 2001. *Through the Body: A Practical Guide to Physical Theatre*. New York, NY: Routledge.

Caplan, B., 1991. 'Medea sexwar'. *The Guardian*, Pagination unknown.

Carducci, V., 2006. 'Culture jamming: A sociological perspective'. *Journal of Consumer Culture*, 6: 1, pp. 116–38.

Keefe, J. and Murray, S., 2007. *Physical Theatres a Critical Reader*. London: Routledge.

Craig, E. G. and Walton, J. M., 1983. *Craig on Theatre*. London: Methuen.

Davies, P., 2012. 'Physical theatre: History, process and development'. http://www.volcanotheatre. co.uk/128/resources/essays-and-articles.html (accessed 3 August).

Etchells, T., 1999. *Certain Fragments: Contemporary Performance and Forced Entertainment*. London: Routledge.

Eureka, 2012. http://www.eureka.co.uk/ (accessed 3 August).

Eyre, R. (dir.), 1982. *Guys and Dolls* (slide program). UK: National Theatre.

Fryer, P., 1986. 'Punk and the new wave of British rock: Working class heroes and art school attitudes'. *Popular Music and Society Paul*, 10: 4, pp. 1–15.

Govan, E., Nicholson, H. and Normington, K., 2007. *Physical Theatres. Making a Performance: Devising Histories and Contemporary Practices*. London: Routledge, p. 158.

Graham, S. and Hoggett, S., 2009. *The Frantic Assembly Book of Devising Theatre*. London: Routledge.

Guattari, F., 1989. 'The three ecologies'. *New Formations*, 8, pp. 131–147.

Hampton, C., 1974. *Savages*. London: Faber.

Hebdige, D., 1988. *Subculture: The Meaning of Style*. New York, NY: Routledge.

Hudson, M., 1991. 'Medea sexwar'. *What's on in London*, 8 May.

Jones, N., 1996. 'Towards a study of the English acting tradition'. *New Theatre Quarterly*, 12, pp. 6–20.

Kershaw, B., 2007. *Theatre Ecology: Environments and Performance Events*. Cambridge: Cambridge University Press.

Marranca, B., Rabkin, G. and Birringer, J., 1986. 'The controversial 1985–86 theatre season: A politics of reception'. *Performing Arts Journal*, 10: 1, pp. 7–33.

Miller, W., 1996. *Durkheim, Morals and Modernity*. Montreal: McGill-Queens University Press.

Monk, C., 2008. '"Hey you, standing there, what you got to stare at?" The post-punk female in British film'. Unpublished conference paper at *1970s British Culture conference*, University of Portsmouth (UK), July.

Moore, M., 2010. 'Postmodernism and punk subculture: Cultures of authenticity and deconstruction'. *The Communication Review*, 7: 3, pp. 305–27.

Newson, L., 1997. 'DV8 Physical theatre 10 years on the edge: DV8 physical theatre, interview with Mary Luckhurst'. http://www.dv8.co.uk/about_dv8/interview_bound_to_please_ten_years_on_the_edge (accessed 2 August 2012).

Newson, L. and Meisner, N., 1997. 'DV8 Physical theatre'. http://www.dv8.co.uk/about_dv8/interview_dance_dancers_strange_fish (accessed 2 August 2012).

Nilan, P., 2007. 'Youth Culture', in Poole, M. and Germov, J. (eds). *Public Sociology: An Introduction to Australian Society*. Crows Nest: Allen & Unwin.

O'Brien, L., 1999. 'The woman that punk made me', in Roger Sabin (ed.). *Punk Rock So What? The Cultural Legacy of Punk*. London: Routledge, pp. 186–98.

———, 2011. 'Can I have a taste of your ice cream?'. *Punk and Post Punk*, 1: 1, pp. 27–40.

Observer, 1988. *Style people out of date*, 25 September.

Raha, M., 2005. *Cinderella's Big Score: Women of the Punk and Indie Underground*. Emeryville, CA: Seal P.

Reynolds, S., 2005. *Rip It Up and Start Again: Post-punk 1978–84*. London: Faber.

Sabin, R., 1999. *Punk Rock, So What? The Cultural Legacy of Punk*. London: Routledge.

Savage, J., 1996. *Time Travel: Pop, Media and Sexuality 1976–96*. London: Chatto & Windus.

Sex Pistols, 1976. *Anarchy in the UK*. EMI records.

Shank, T., 1994. *Contemporary British Theatre*. Basingstoke: Macmillan.

Sierz, A., 2001. *In-yer-face Theatre: British Drama Today*. London: Faber and Faber.

Steiner, G., 1981. *Martin Heidegger*. Paris: Flammarion.

Thornber, R., 1990. 'V'. *The Guardian*, 21 May.

Triggs, T., 2006. 'Scissors and glue: Punk fanzines and the creation of a DIY aesthetic', *Journal of Design History*, 19:1, pp. 69–83.

Volcano Theatre, 1990. *V program notes*.

Wilson, S., 1990. 'V'. *The List*, 1, July.

X-Ray Spex, 1977. *Oh Bondage up Yours*. Virgin records.

Chapter 4

Tiata Fahodzi: Second-Generation Africans in British Theatre

Ekua Ekumah

Femi Elufowoju Jr. founded Tiata Fahodzi, a combination of a Yoruba Nigerian and a Fanti Ghanaian term which translates as 'Theatre of the Emancipated', in 1997 to rectify an imbalance he felt existed on the British theatre landscape. In the 1980s and 1990s, specifically in London, the works of an unprecedented number of companies and black playwrights became more visible, albeit on the fringes of the theatrical landscape. Second-generation migrants of British Caribbean heritage largely dominated this boom later known as a Black British Theatre movement (Macmillan 1999). The Caribbean domination was due to the fact that playwrights and performers of Caribbean extraction made up a greater percentage of Britain's black population during that period. However, an African presence did exist, consisting mostly of West Africans who also migrated to Britain in the post-war years, but their cultural presence was minimal in post-war black British theatrical movements. By setting up Tiata Fahodzi, Elufowoju created a platform for British West African communities to add their voices to the black British experience, thus changing and broadening what has since remained a constantly evolving black British stage. In its two decades of existence the company has secured a niche in British theatre, penetrating the theatrical landscape in especially the last decade.

This chapter traces the strategic journey of the company from the periphery to what is arguably off-centre through an examination of the shifts in the company's mission from formation and its aesthetic and artistic philosophy under Elufowoju's leadership. The company has moved from primarily 'magnifying the voice of the West African on the British stage' (programme notes 1997) at its inception, to producing work 'sourced from within British African communities' for an 'all inclusive British audience' (company publicity notes 2007). Their current byline 'Tiata Fahodzi Africans in British Theatre' (company website 2009) highlights the emergence of a new generation of West African British theatre makers and the inevitable sociocultural challenges they have faced and adjustments they have made.

Starting out as a devising company, Tiata Fahodzi's maiden production *Tickets and Ties* (1997) explored the lives of West Africans living in London. The result of a social experiment, this was Elufowoju's attempt at telling the story of his African migration; following in the steps of many migrant companies and dramatists such as Tara Arts, Michael Abensetts and Mustapha Matura. Theatre Royal Stratford East produced *Tickets and Ties* and supported Elufowoju in exploring whether there was, in fact, a demand for a company that catered specifically for the stories of West Africans in Britain. The success achieved by

Tiata Fahodzi that attracted a new diverse audience of West Africans into the theatre was proof enough for Elufowoju to set up the company and later embark on a tour of Sweden. Elufowoju's vision at the inception of the company was simply to provide a platform for an expression of his cultural identity at a time when the issue of ethnic minorities had found its way, for a number of reasons, onto the political agenda in Britain. Firstly, Tony Blair's New Labour government, elected into power in 1997, inherited a legacy of minority inequalities in housing, employment, education and healthcare from Margaret Thatcher's and John Major's Conservative governments. The disadvantages suffered by Britain's immigrant and minority communities from the 1940s, the policies put in place to address them and the minority communities' racialised and radicalised reactions are well documented (cf. Proctor (ed.) 2000; Patterson 1965; Fry and Gilroy 2010).

Given the number of significant political, cultural and social events at the time of its founding, Tiata Fahodzi's entry onto the British theatrical scene was timely, politically and culturally. The decline of many black-led theatre companies at the end of the 1980s such as Staunch Poets and Players, Carib Theatre and Black Mime Theatre fragmented the cultural affinity that once existed in black British minority communities (BMEs). The often-documented history of the Windrush [1] generation and their West African contemporaries speaks of the difficulties these migrants faced on their arrival in Britain. The arriving migrants found themselves the major catalysts for historical changes in the racial and cultural landscape of Britain to date [2]. Deirdre Osborne's comprehensive article *Writing Black Back* (2006: 13–31) charts the historical presence of black people in the British Isles. Dating back to the first millennium, it is not the first to document evidence of a black presence on the British Isles that predates slavery. Osborne's account positions this fact critically against the derogatory representation of black identity on the stage. She cites 'imperialism and, its major consequence, racism' as being responsible for suffocating or distorting 'the existence of [a] sustainable and autonomous black theatre in Britain' (Osborne 2006).

The newly arrived migrants found ways of defining their identities in their new environments, the stage being one of these outlets. Errol John, Wole Soyinka and Barry Reckford led the way in theatre accompanied by novelists George Lamming, Edward Kamau Braithwaite and Derek Walcott amongst others who were beginning to penetrate the British literary world by writing about characters and identities firmly rooted in their home nations with a strong sense of self, countering the derogatory representations and definitions from outside of this migrant community. This eclectic group of migrant playwrights looked to Britain as the 'mother country'. Yvonne Brewster describes them as not dealing 'with the concerns of the new immigrants but rather with the culture and society out of which these *privileged young black men* had ventured in search of learning' (Matzke and Okagbue 2009). The next wave of migrant playwrights such as Mustafa Matura, Alfred Fagon and Michael Abbensetts opted for a renegotiation of the migrant identity by preoccupying themselves with writings about the challenges and hostilities immigrants faced settling into Britain whilst looking back to their home nations. Osborne writes particularly about these writers' use of what Braithwaite terms 'nation language', a notion explained further by Lynette Goddard in reference to Matura.

> Matura writes with warmth, humanity and humour, celebrating his Caribbean cultural heritage and broadening British theatre aesthetics by representing West Indian characters speaking in their own accents and articulating their own styles and customs as a political resistance to the dominant conventions of the English stage.
>
> (Goddard 2011)

Yvonne Brewster's article *Black British Theatre in London 1972–89* provides a rather personal perspective of a black British theatrical trajectory that she witnessed as a practitioner. Her insight into the companies that flourished including her own Talawa Theatre Company shows how government and funding bodies such as The Greater London Council (which was abolished in 1986) and the Arts Council supported and sustained culturally specific theatre in Britain. The Greater London Council proved to be a lifeline for minority communities particularly in the 1980s, a period framed by the aftermath of the Brixton riots. Onyekachi Wambu reports that:

> In the 1980s Britain and its institutions started to open up to black Britons. The decisive incident was the 1981 Brixton riots, and the publication of Lord Scarman's report investigating the causes of it. Scarman identified the causes as police relations and school exclusions. Investment in black community groups was one of the solutions. This investment … led to the support of many black institutions and artists.
>
> (Wambu 2011: online)

Margaret Thatcher's Conservative government, the recession that hit the British economy in her first term, and the resultant rising unemployment and robust move towards privatisation in her bid to improve the economy had a rather negative impact on black British communities. Jatinder Verma states categorically that Margaret Thatcher sanctioned the racist sentiments of Britain whilst her government was in power 'in her election speech, when she first came into power, which was in 1979. She talked about the natives of Britain feeling swamped by alien cultures' (Verma 2012 quoted in *Margins to Mainstream*). As Lynette Goddard argues: 'The boom of black theatre in Britain and the start of its demise coincide directly with the beginning and the end of Margaret Thatcher's time as Conservative Party Prime Minister' (Goddard 2007: 28).

The arrival of New Labour and the sociocultural tensions surrounding the murder of Stephen Lawrence in 1993 and New Labour government's policy on ethnic inequalities transformed the political landscape. According to Blair:

> And I want above all, to govern in a way that brings our country together, that unites our nation in facing the tough and dangerous challenges of the new economy and the

changed society in which we must live. I want a Britain which we all feel part of, in whose future we all have a stake, in which what I want for my children I want for yours.

(Blair 1997: online)

Blair's New Labour engaged with 'difference' in its many forms and demonstrated its commitment to minority communities in Britain by implementing a number of reforms and new initiatives, particularly within the Arts Council of Britain, which funded previously sidelined minority communities. Alex Sierz explains: 'New Labour's financial generosity meant that all cultural institutions, including theatres, had to deliver on social policies: their mission was to create wider audience access, greater ethnic diversity and more innovative work' (Sierz 2011: 2).

Tiata Fahodzi benefitted from being in the right place at the right time under New Labour. This company has not had an easy ride to its current position in British theatre as Elufowoju observed at the Eclipse Conference on 'Developing strategies to combat racism in theatre'.

Enough cannot be said about the struggles endured by black arts organisations in getting their work seen and programmed nationally. Initially getting Tiata Fahodzi's work programmed was a nightmare and we were under no illusion that it was going to be easy. Besides we were aware that venues had their pockets to watch and we were a new company with a bizarre name, led by a young 'ambitious' black director with no track record or qualitative value attached to him. No one wanted to touch Tiata Fahodzi with a barge pole. Anyone who'd take us on at that stage would be taking a great risk.

(Elufowoju 2001 quoted in Eclipse Report)

The establishment of Tiata Fahodzi was a direct response to the absence of West Africa in British theatre. The company began with the very specific agenda of making visible and audible the migratory presence of West Africans in Britain. Prior to the formation of Tiata Fahodzi the notion of a black British theatre movement was linked mainly to Caribbean experience in Britain. New Labour policies, funding councils' support and Tiata Fahodzi changed this narrow definition and restored a sense of collective black consciousness as Paul Gilroy observed:

[S]hared experiences of 'race' and social class in the first generation led to the territorial and previous social status of Caribbean immigrants becoming irrelevant: they were seen as 'West Indian' and working class by the white majority. The consciousness of this in the second generation gave rise to the new identity, self-consciously both black and British, lacking the strong links with Caribbean places that the first generation had felt.

(Gilroy ctd. in Dabydeen et al. 2007: 47)

While historical records such as Septimus Severus, the famous Libyan-born Roman general, coming to 'Britain c. AD 210' (Niebrzydowski 2001; cited in Osborne 2006: 13) show the presence of black people in Britain, there was little understanding of cultural differences in African diasporic communities. Among the group are West African immigrants, many of whom came to Britain as their nations' elites to attend the top universities in Britain in the 1920s. Subsequent waves hereafter, like their first generation counterparts with a distinctly West African ethos, were largely invisible in a Caribbean dominated black British theatre until Tiata Fahodzi began to address them as a specific cultural constituency. Since then plays such as Roy Williams' *Fallout* (2003), triggered by the stabbing of Oluwadamilola, and Bola Agbaje's first play *Gone Too Far!* (2007) have tackled West African diasporic experiences in Britain.

Expanding the Aesthetic Landscape of Black British Theatre

Tiata Fahodzi's aesthetic at its inception was rooted in West African performance practices, tilting later towards modern Nigerian theatrical conventions. In the resulting syncretic form of storytelling, music and dance were combined with Western conventions of the 'well-made play'; artificial plotting and the build-up of suspense leading to a climactic end, and elements of naturalistic drama. The syncretic model is described by Christopher Balme (1999) as 'one of the most effective means of decolonising the stage, because it utilises the performance forms of both European and indigenous cultures in a creative recombination of their respective elements, without slavish adherence to one tradition or the other' (Balme 1999: 2). Tiata Fahodzi began by staging panoramic views of West Africans in Britain as in *Tickets and Ties* (1997), a devised piece by the company, scripted by Sesan Ogunledun and Femi Elufowoju Jr. In every respect syncretism was a logical process for the company as it sought to define its West African and later Nigerian identities within British theatrical and cultural landscapes.

Within a relatively short period Tiata Fahodzi transformed itself in response to the rapid sociocultural changes then happening across Britain. By the early 2000s the company's aesthetic focus was to make its work more 'inclusive' to a British audience or reducing the 'exotic' elements that characterised its previous productions, a condition imposed by its funders. This was the company's third aesthetic shift, resulting in what Homi Bhabha would describe as 'a third space' (cited in Rutherford 1998: 211) or, in other words, the creation of a politicised hybrid, inclusive syncretic theatre in which all sections can dialogue. These aesthetic and strategic shifts were not only logical, they also reflected changes within the company's own cultural constituency for by then and as Hall puts it succinctly, 'young black cultural practitioners and critics in Britain' were already 'increasingly coming to acknowledge and explore in their work this "diasporic aesthetic" and its formation in the postcolonial experience' (Hall 1994: 402).

Tiata Fahodzi's first play, *Tickets and Ties: The African Tale (1997)*, evolved through a series of devised workshops. Scripted by Elufowoju and Sesan Ogunledun, it explored the experiences of an extended family of West Africans living in London. The play operates on a central narrative around which various sketches representing the spectrum of the lives of West Africans living in Britain were presented. Borrowing heavily from his Nigerian cultural 'baggage', Elufowoju made use of traditional Nigerian theatrical practices such as storytelling and music, combining it with naturalist Western conventions to tell the story of West Africans in the diaspora. A naturalistic setting of home was critiqued through the clever use of props; suitcases and tea chests, an iconic image in most African and African Caribbean migrant homes, were used as furniture and also as a constant symbolic reminder of an 'other' home. The play's strategic inclusion of a historical account of an African presence in Britain dating back to the Roman era was an attempt to interrogate the perceptions of Africans in Britain. Elufowoju and Tiata Fahodzi were at this stage planting the seed of 'syncretism', which resulted in a particular aesthetic that resonates with the African diasporic community. The production made a mark; firstly, it identified theatre practitioners born or living in Britain who had a strong sense of their West African heritage and secondly, it brought West African audiences into the theatre on a large scale.

The company moved from Theatre Royal Stratford East to the Oval House, where it produced three shows, *Booked* (1999), *Bonded* (2000) and *Makinde* (2001). This small but reputable theatre was not a producing house at the time, but was supporting and developing new writing in black and Asian communities. With the theatre's support, Tiata Fahodzi entered into creative partnerships with other theatres in London and secured funding from the then London Arts Board and the Arts Council of England that enabled the company to embark on a national tour of Britain in their three-year residency. The three productions leaned specifically towards a Nigerian aesthetic as opposed to the collective West African voice that the company addressed originally. Elufowoju's Nigerian cultural capital influenced the ideological content of the company's work, a subject he elaborates on in the interview with this writer: 'I see myself, first and foremost as a Nigerian: and that affects absolutely everything that I do' (Elufowoju 2011).

By now the company had found a niche in the market and were quite happy to continue down that exotic route of difference. Elufowoju started to feel the limitations of the company's remit and took the first steps in establishing a foothold on the British theatre landscape by looking outside London to the regions with their production of *Bonded* (2000). For the company touring was and is still crucial to introducing and sustaining an African theatre and drama presence in Britain. Tiata Fahodzi's subsequent productions, and even the highly acclaimed productions from 2006 onwards such as *The Estate* (2006), had not managed to translate the London success into regional bookings and a national tour. The company's success was essentially limited to London. The next major challenge for the company was to repeat its successes in the regions.

Another strategic change was in how the company branded itself. In trying to broaden the appeal of the company's work to attract mainstream British and West African audiences, the company changed the spelling of its name from 'Tiata' Fahodzi to 'Teata' Fahodzi, to make the pronunciation easier for those unfamiliar with the Nigerian polyphonic spelling.

The company's by-line also changed to reflect the widening, diverse audiences attending the company's performances. Looking back, Elufowoju observes that the difficulty the company faced during this transition: 'was something we waged war with, and we tried to compromise the ambition of the company by inserting the word "British" West African into our by-line' (Elufowoju 2011). Clearly, the company was, at this stage, unsure of its own identity and what it wanted to project. The company's innocent attempt to be recognised and included within the British theatre landscape resulted in the company relinquishing its identity and, in typical postcolonial construction, redefining itself through the master gaze. As Ngugi wa Thiongo cautions, 'Eurocentrism is most dangerous to the self-confidence of Third World peoples, when it becomes internalised in their intellectual conception of the universe' (Thiongo 1993: 17). Tiata Fahodzi viewed its place within British theatre as outsiders looking in, seeking acceptance from the centre, its vulnerability evidenced in the fundamental changes to its name and by-line. At this point, what was important for the company was a platform and getting as many people as possible to see the work, by any means necessary.

Tiata Fahodzi's production of *Abyssinia* (2001) by Adewale Ajadi, which targeted the Ethiopian community in Britain, and the production of *Sammy* (2002), charting the life of the legendary performer Sammy Davis Jr, provoked questions about the company's mission and artistic philosophy. Following a reflective two-year period away from the theatre scene, Tiata Fahodzi returned in 2004 with a new appendage to the Tiata Fahodzi brand with the creation of *Tiata Delights,* 'the first ever festival of play readings by Africans in Britain' (Goetz and Kell 2007). The company made new writing central to its existence and capitalised on the current trends of the previous 10–15 years of new writing in British theatre (Sierz 2011; Billington 2007, 2009). The company thus redefined its artistic philosophy on the two vital roles it provides, making theatre and developing new writings. The festival of play-reading provided a much-needed platform for showcasing numerous unsolicited scripts from playwrights within the African community who saw Tiata Fahodzi as a gateway to placing their stories within the public domain to the notice of a wider audience, theatre industry and potential employers. The indisputable success of *Tiata Delights* is evidenced in the number of plays that started off as performed readings that later became full productions in mainstream theatres in London: Talawa and Soho theatre co-produced Michael Bhim's *Pure Gold* (2007), Royal Court produced Levi David Addai's *Oxford Street* (2008), Ade Solanke's *Pandora's Box* (2011) from *Tiata Delights 08* was produced at the Arcola Tent in May 2012 to great critical acclaim, to mention a few of the successes.

The strategic partnerships and collaborations between Tiata Fahodzi and established theatre houses and companies have continued particularly with the Arcola Theatre, Soho theatre and the Almeida Theatre. All three have hosted the festivals and supported the company's productions: the Arcola theatre played host to *Tiata Delights 04* and to Tiata Fahodzi's production of Ola Rotimi's African classic *The Gods Are Not To Blame* (2005) and hosted Elufowoju's final production for the company, Joe Penhall's *Blue* Orange (2010).

Soho Theatre, known for producing new writing and developing writers, as part of its Writers Centre hosted Tiata Fahodzi's *Tiata Delights 06* and *07*, as well as joining forces with the New Wolsey Theatre Ipswich to produce one of Tiata Fahodzi's box office successes *The Estate* (2006) written by Oladipo Agboluaje. Soho also hosted Fahodzi's 10th anniversary triumph *Joe Guy* (2007) by Roy Williams and the equally successful prequel to *The Estate, Iyà Ilé* (2009). This partnership and the calibre of playwrights the company has nurtured and collaborated with did not only raise the company's profile substantially, its impact on mainstream theatre audiences was becoming obvious. At a time when the Soho Theatre was referred to as 'the edge at the centre', this once voiceless company from the periphery was taking strides towards the centre and causing the 'centre' to take notice, a reflection of its mission statement about 'producing theatre sourced from people living within British African communities, aimed at an all-inclusive British audience' (Geotz and Kell 2007). During this period, partnerships between Tiata Fahodzi and the Almeida theatre were also taking place. Almeida hosted the company's *Tiata Delights 08* and in 2010 a full-length performance reading of Michael Bhim's *The Golden Hour* was co-presented by Tiata Fahodzi and Almeida Theatre. In these ventures Tiata Fahodzi presented itself successfully and boldly and penetrated Almeida, a mainstream theatre that serves a particular white middle-class community.

In 2009 with the launching of what proved to be the most critically acclaimed box office success for the company thus far with Agboluaje's *Iyà Ilé*, Tiata Fahodzi changed its by-line again to signal a change in direction and format by defining itself with the sobriquet, 'Tiata Fahodzi Africans in British Theatre' (Company Website 2009). This proclamation is significant in many ways; the company had come full circle in the kind of productions it staged. A large proportion of the productions had a Nigerian perspective, but they also had a universal appeal that spoke to an 'all inclusive British audience' too. The heightened dramatic moments that have since come to define Tiata Fahodzi productions are very far removed from naturalism, but perfectly in sync with traditional African storytelling. The productions are a very specific engagement with 'home' that is immediately tangible in the atmosphere. The cultural specificity of such audience-driven productions has been analysed by Sierz who argues that 'Experiences such as this suggest that the audience is a vital element in the creation of meaning. It is even tempting to say that the meaning of a play lies in the experience of the audience' (Sierz 2011: 6).

The Interview

Ekumah: *How did Tiata Fahodzi come into existence?*

Elufowoju: *The company was set up initially to redress the imbalance that was pretty evident about 12, 13 years ago of the landscape of British theatre, which had a considerable critical mass of work, coming from the black community, deeply rooted within* first to second generation Caribbean artists, living and working in the United Kingdom.

When I was given the opportunity to stage a play of my choice on the traditional British theatre stage, Theatre Royal Stratford East, I was pretty aware at the time that it was a huge opportunity to try and almost explore, as a litmus test, whether there was room, whether there was a demand, whether there was a presence, whether there was relevance in putting together a collage of stories which reflected the lives of Africans.

When all those questions were answered in the affirmative, it became the company's central mission statement to produce work that emanated from West Africans for West Africans in West African bubbles of London.

Ekumah: Can you briefly talk me through the ideological trajectory of the company from its inception to what it is now?

Elufowoju: Yes the mission statement initially was geared towards a West African community, bringing West African work to the British stage. Through the years we realised that our community is wide and that it's limiting to segregate ourselves and limit the vision of the company. And that is why we broadened it. And even after broadening it, to take on Africa, we still wonder whether we are serving that mission statement thoroughly, because it's very difficult to cater for absolutely everyone. And then there were challenges to the statement that we were faced with.

Ekumah: Challenges from where?

Elufowoju: Challenges in terms of our audiences... People would make a comment, and you respond to the comment. At the time, I was very much of the opinion that African theatre within the mainstream was non-existent. So there was that political thing that we wanted to confront.

It was important that the press about Nigeria, in terms of the cultural and intellectual capital that we were putting out there, was positive. And so by putting on these plays and putting on display, actors from a particular heritage were illuminating the wealth of experience, of heightened experience within the theatrical form... Just so you know, Tiata Fahodzi is now based at the Africa Centre. See this is movement. Tiata Fahodzi is now The Africa Centre!!! We are at the heart of theatre making!! (The company have since moved from the Africa Centre).

Ekumah: Yes indeed, but if I may take you back to the beginning, can you explain how the company was structured?

Elufowoju: Well, originally, I was the founder artistic director and I had no boss. Self-imposed dictator. There was an autonomy that I had as the founder, and it goes without saying that was only because of the way the company was formed. We bought the entity of a company off the shelf at Companies House.

Initially, the company was not legally constituted. We did not have a board of governors who were signing the cheques. Then the company became legally *constituted. We had a board of governors appointed to ratify absolutely every decision I made.*

Ekumah: *When did this happen?*

Elufowoju: *Between 2002 and 2004 the company underwent a major organisational change, in terms of whom I was answering to; the company now employed me. As Artistic Director my appointment had to undergo due process. I had to be reviewed, bi-annually, by the board, who had to give me a start appraisal.*

Ekumah: *Did that make any major changes to the way you worked?*

Elufowoju: *Yes, administratively it did. Things did not change for a while, not until we had our first administrative director, Susan Marnell. Before, we had an administrator who was responsible to me. However, an administrative director was responsible to the board. Financially, the company became a bit more stable. Everything had to be accounted for. And we had to have quarterly accounts, half year and annual accounts. And we had an auditor; it just changed the spectrum of everything. So in terms of a tier, if you were to root and branch the company, there was the board at the top, I was the artistic director and underneath me slightly to the right was the administrative director, and then there were other auxiliary roles which sprung from that.*

Ekumah: *As Artistic Director of Tiata Fahodzi, did you feel there was an aesthetic/philosophy for small-scale British theatre and did the company contribute to the notion (if any) of a small-scale British theatre aesthetic/philosophy?*

Elufowoju: *Equity convened a conference, about small-scale, middle-scale theatre, and we were working in 'small-scale theatre' only because that was the definition and category that we fitted into. But it is actually a state of the mind.*

    It's small scale in terms of how we perceive the capacity of the company, but in terms of the ambition, it's middle scale, it's top notch, so why are we being defined by categories in that way?

Ekumah: *What is the place of small-scale, middle-scale companies in the country?*

Elufowoju: *I am going to say that there is still this slight industrial snobbery on the kind of work that is happening in marginal and in fringe venues where funding is negligible, or non-existent. And there is a spotlight on middle-scale theatre companies that can produce and have got the financial backing to produce twaddle, a lot of bad products, but still put them on in theatres because they've got some semblance of a brand which will dictate market forces. They've got a star name and they've got a star director or they are just rich enough to be able to put the show on. It's an indictment of the industry that that kind of segregation, demarcation is allowed or exists but there is nothing we can do about it.*

Ekumah: *But you are doing something about it by making ...*

Elufowoju: *No but what I did about it was always saying, we are not small scale. That is a mentality. Because, if you say to yourself, I am small scale, then that mental incarceration will keep you locked up from making any further growth. And we've said, ok, we may be small scale in name, but our aspirations are far greater than that.*

Ekumah: *What ideological positions/structures do you think drive 'Britishness' and how has Tiata Fahodzi responded to or challenged these both in content and aesthetics?*

Elufowoju: *With the whole British thing, for us, it was always about finding compatibility with the British stage. We started with West Africa, and the ambition to tell stories from the whole continent kind of evolved with the years and the age of the company. So at the very initial stage, what was British about our work was the impact and influences of being second generation Nigerians, Ghanaians, Sierra Leoneans and Gambians; finding how those influences and elements of our own formative upbringing met a synergy with what our parents' understanding of bringing us up should be. Their own sensibilities, our own stories, and how they connect with an all-inclusive British audience … we wanted to ensure that we were sharing our heritage, in a way, which conformed to Western concepts of how British theatre should be received. So we were talking about finding a medium of expression, which was palatable and accessible for non-West African theatregoers. But purposefully and primarily, to encourage our communities to connect with British theatre and acknowledge, reflect, connect and affirm what they knew was a celebration of their lives on the British stage. So the Britishness is actually that. If there is a canopy, with British written all over it … I think first and foremost, what is British about it and what makes the work feel integral for a British audience is the approach to the work, the understanding that the audience have of the work and the people facilitating the work.*

Ekumah: *And when you talk about facilitators you mean your actors, writers…?*

Elufowoju: *Yes, the actors, directors, writers of the work are all working in Britain due to certain circumstances. And they range from being born here to being brought here, immigration, and in some cases, I would say, necessity-asylum seekers. But I am sure there is some kind of academic notion of what Britishness actually means. It was something that we seriously waged war with and I know we tried to compromise the ambition of the company by actually inserting the word 'British' West African (into our publicity). I remember a contemporary of mine having a stand-off with me and saying, 'what is British about the work?'*

Ekumah: *So with this in mind, you were making a big statement then about the company when you declared, 'Tiata Fahodzi Africans in British theatre'.*

Elufowoju: *Yes that was me appeasing such contemporaries… The postcolonial rage that we have inherited; I don't have that as a chip on my shoulder, in terms of my approach to my work.*

Ekumah: *How do you see yourself; as an African in Britain, a Nigerian in Britain or a British Nigerian?*

Elufowoju: *I don't see myself as British Nigerian, although that is the perception that people have of me; they call me 'oyinbo dudu', which means 'white black man'. I see myself, first and foremost, as a Nigerian; that was very much because of my formative upbringing. The bulk of my upbringing and education or intellect, my philosophy and the capital of my African intellect and sensibility were ingrained while I was there, so coming back to England, a Nigerian, and that affects absolutely everything that I do, and say, although with inflections and…*

Ekumah: *It is filtered.*

Elufowoju: *Yes, it is completely filtered, by the virtue of the place I am residing in. But ask anyone about how they see me; they say 'oh, he is British Nigerian'. I was called a Nigerian Englishman recently.*

Ekumah: *I think this combination of British and Nigerian has served the company well, and I am talking specifically about the* Estate *and* Iya Ile, *two landmark productions in terms of the company's trajectory.*

Elufowoju: *Yes,* Iya Ile *was nominated for an Olivier Outstanding achievement in an affiliate theatre, which is very humbling in terms of where the company started and where it got to under my leadership. We recognised the potential a particular writer had, and we gave him the opportunity to create. We threw the limited funds we had at the idea to grow. So we bred it. We capitalised on it and we had to claim it. It was the best thing to happen to Nigeria, abroad. Culturally.*

Ekumah: *How would you describe your theatrical aesthetic?*

Elufowoju: *Well for me aesthetics … has been dictated by the role I am playing at that particular moment … as a freelancer, my aesthetics will vary, according to the piece of work in front of me. If it's a classical piece of work, within the canon of European theatre, my aesthetics are slightly dictated by convention, however, I would love to believe that I have built up an ability to approach the work differently from other people of my generation and my contemporaries, in a way that the experience will be seen as radical, and I will use the word radical, a radical interpretation of the traditional form of the particular work. By the virtue of the fact I am an African, and I am bringing the wealth of my experience, in countering worldviews or encountering a set of circumstances that are ingrained in the play in a different way. Aesthetics is talked about as something that can be seen, and felt by the audience; something that has an impact on their experience of the art form. I come to it with an understanding of what that narrative is, making sure that my interpretation is robed and festooned with my unique approach to telling stories, as an African man, but also making it clear and accessible to an all-inclusive and embracing audience from all over.*

Ekumah: *Now the reason I ask that question is because of someone like Peter Brook, he has a particular aesthetic. What is that underlying aesthetic factor for you?*

Elufowoju: *Maybe I don't have one. I would like to think that when you come and see a Femi Elufowoju Jnr production, that the one thing that you would definitely recognise as his brand is the fact that there are very fluid transitions between scenes. And that there are no dressing room moments where there is a blackout and you are sitting there. I think that every moment in the theatre has to serve the story, regardless of whether or not you are having a costume change or the environment is changing around you. That is not really an aesthetic, it is more a working method. I wouldn't really want to be renowned for an aesthetic, I would love to be renowned for having a working method that works. And continually works with different art forms.*

Ekumah: *Can you now explain your rehearsal practice, with regards to form, structure and space? Are you using your specific performance practices to articulate your African Diasporic heritage?*

Elufowoju: *I don't. It depends on the play. I always have a week of dissecting the play with the company; … We talk about the physical and emotional journey of the characters and that is when we get up on our feet.*

Ekumah: *Could you tell me a bit more about how you use space.*

Elufowoju: *I'm always conscious of spatial awareness. I often talk about actors understanding their environment, to be so unnatural to your audience; it is perfectly fine to be natural with those who you are working with on stage, but to have a very unnatural relationship with your audience is the key thing that I strive for. So that is what I talk about all the time, in actors, characters defining their environment and locating themselves within that environment which is natural for the world of the play, which they are standing on, and not for us the audience…*

Ekumah: *In your role as Artistic Director, the final artistic decision on commissioning playwrights lies with you. Can you talk me through that process?*

Elufowoju: *I commission the playwrights; I make suggestions to the board the writers I would love to see form the vision of the company. The board members are very supportive, and that is what they are there to do. They challenge my views too. With every play there is the potential to produce; and if we don't have a producible play then we have to look elsewhere, which means forking out extra cash. So I have to be absolutely sure. They trust me.*

Ekumah: *How do you work with the writers?*

Elufowoju: *One of the new things in our budgetary guidelines, when new writing became a central ambit for what the company does, was the role of a dramaturge. So I always want to be able to ensure that the company was able to attach a dramaturge to a writer. Writers get a chance to do a lot of research. Drafts are read all the time, we don't just read the play, we've got to listen, to hear it. So we do a series of readings, trial and errors and move on to another draft if it doesn't work.*

Ekumah: *So you sound like you're working in much the same way that some of the other more established theatre houses function, such as The Royal Court, Soho Theatre, etc. Did you pick up ideas from them or did this formula just evolve?*

Elufowoju: *The one thing that I learnt when I was at the Royal Court as an associate director was that writers are really a different breed. There are some really responsive writers and some that are really cock sure of their writing but would respond positively to criticism. And there are other writers who go 'don't know what you are talking about mate'. I have been very fortunate to work with writers who get it and work towards fulfilling the brief. And there are some writers, who unfortunately won't get it. And I learnt how to tell a writer that we are not going to produce their play … if the play doesn't work and you are absolutely sure that your audience are not going to get it, then there is no point.*

Ekumah: *Being the only African British theatre company in the mainstream, did you feel pressurised to look at issue-based subject matters that affect the African community in Britain or do you tell the stories you want to? I am talking about responsibility versus your own taste.*

Elufowoju: *I have never actually been fuelled by my own agenda. Because there is always public money involved. The company is a regularly funded company. I always think about the community and the audience. That was one of the many things that gave me a buzz. Trying to find the right play for our audiences especially as we only produced a play once a year, the period between a play closing and the next one opening is a good 12 months. The culture of audiences going to the theatre goes stale between the two points and you need to really galvanise them to come out again, so you have to make sure it is the right kind of work. Especially if you are saying it is the kind of work that emanates from the community.*

Ekumah: *How do you go about doing that, making sure the play is what the community wants?*

Elufowoju: *Well, we never really know what the community wants, we see what is happening around us, and we always have auxiliary projects, like readings and concerts, and we do a lot of ambassadorial work. We attend seminars, and I want to do more of them and become more associated with such things.*

Ekumah: *I am interested in the kind of partnerships you established for the company, it's a central structure in placing the company where it is currently.*

Elufowoju: *There was a paranoia that no one wanted to talk to us or work with us and the board said to me, 'Femi, you need to go out there and make those connections. Talk to David Lang, Spacey, some people in the early days did not want to know, then they see the shows and think hang on … this might be good for the DNA of our company'. And that's what happened there. We were able to prostitute ourselves really.*

Ekumah: *What compromises did you have to make for the greater good of both companies involved?*

Elufowoju: *I would say money. Forking out most of the money, because they knew that their brand in itself was sexy, and that was all they needed to bring. I mean there was financial support, but we had to do a lot of compromises. It was like a switch, we had to work with them in kind, beef up the bill, those kinds of compromises. There was a lot of playing the game, and now, I refuse to play the game... I can actually put my foot down and say I am not playing that game. I will not let my integrity be trod on.*

Conclusion: Theatre of Transitions and the Dramaturgy of Tiata Fahodzi

The positive response to the company's production suggest that the company and Agboluaje, one of its key playwrights, have identified and filled a void regarding African diasporic identity on the British stage. Through a process of redefinitions and repositioning Tiata Fahodzi stayed true to its aesthetic style, allowing the nuances of black diasporic cultures and mainstream British society to co-exist. The company exudes an air of confidence that comes from an awareness of its acceptance by mainstream audiences. This is an unconscious recognition that audiences of different kinds will engage with different works. Tiata Fahodzi has claimed its own space and position; it has retained its own identity whilst sharing public space with other British theatres.

The statement 'Tiata Fahodzi: Africans in British Theatre' is a bold statement about a once marginalised community striding into the centre. The emancipatory slant in the company's latest mission has been achieved through several transitions. Its repertoire reflects the company's journey, a body of work coming from a community that is perceived as 'other' is now visible, centralised, and by claiming both their Africanness and their Britishness is constantly negotiating that hybrid identity of Africans in the diaspora [3]. Tiata Fahodzi has made the case for diversity and integration in British theatre. The initiatives such as the Eclipse Report, the Whose Theatre Report and the Black Regional Initiative in theatre were all set up to work towards these goals. The company has not only laid claims to creating a theatre that focuses on sociocultural transitions from one stage to another, it also traces a clear historical spectrum in the development of BME theatres.

References

Addai, L. D., 2008. *Oxford Street*. London: Methuen Drama.

Agboluaje, O., 2006. *The Estate*. London: Oberon Modern Plays.

Agboluaje, O., 2009. *Iya Ile (The First Wife)*. London: Oberon Modern Plays.

Ajadi, A., 2001. *Abyssinia*. Unpublished script.

Ashcroft, B. et al., 2006. *The Post-Colonial Studies Reader*. London: Routledge.

Balme, C. B., 1999. *Decolonizing the Stage: Theatrical Syncretism and Post-Colonial Drama*. Oxford: Clarendon Press.

Bhim, M., 2009. *The Golden Hour*. Unpublished play.

Billington, M., 2009 [2007]. *State of the Nation: British Theatre since 1945*. London: Faber and Faber.

Blair, T., 1997. 'New Labour because Britain deserves better'. http://www.labour-party.org.uk/manifestos/1997/1997-labour-manifesto.shtml (accessed 19 May 2012).

Brown, H. et al., 2001. *Eclipse Report: Developing Strategies to Combat Racism in Theatre.* A one-day working conference held on two consecutive days at Nottingham Playhouse, 12 and 13 June.

Dabydeen, D., Gilmore, J. and Jones, C. (eds), 2007. *The Oxford Companion to Black British History.* New York: Oxford University Press.

Elufowoju, F., 1998. *Booked.* Unpublished script.

——, 2000. *Makinde.* Unpublished script.

——, 2002. *Sammy.* Unpublished script.

Elufowoju, F. and Ogunledun, S., 1997. *Tickets and Ties—The African Tale.* Unpublished script.

Fry, P. and Gilroy, P., 2010. *Staying Power: The History of Black People in Britain.* London: Pluto Press.

Goddard, L., 2011. *The Methuen Drama Book of Plays by Black British Writers.* London: Methuen Drama.

——, 2007. *Staging Black Feminisms: Identity, Politics, Performance.* Hampshire, NY: Palgrave Macmillan.

Goetz, K. and Kell, T., 2007. *Tiata Fahodzi Tenth Anniversary All African Stars 08 Souvenir Programme.*

Hall, S., 1994. 'Cultural identity and diaspora', in Laura Williams (ed.). *Colonial Discourse and Post-Colonial Theory: A Reader.* London: Longman.

McMillan, M., 2004. 'Rebaptizing the World in Our Own Terms: Black Theatre and Live Arts in Britain'. *Canadian Theatre Review,* 118, pp. 54–61.

McMillan. M., 1999. 'Ter speak in yer mudder tongue: An interview with playwright Mustapha Matura', in K. Owusu (ed.). *Black British Culture and Society.* London: Routledge.

Matzke, C. and Okagbue, O. A. (eds), 2009. *African Theatre: Diasporas.* Oxford: James Currey.

Nu Century Arts and The Octavia Foundation, 2012. *Margins to Mainstream: The Story of Black Theatre in Britain.* Documentary film.

Ogunledu, S., 1999. *Bonded.* Unpublished script.

Osborne, D., 2006. 'Writing black back: An overview of black theatre and performance in Britain'. *Studies in Theatre & Performance,* 26: 1, pp. 13–31.

Patterson, S., 1965. *Dark Strangers – A study of West Indians in London.* London: Pelican.

Proctor, J. (ed.), 2000. *Writing Black Britain 1948–1988: An Interdisciplinary Anthology.* Manchester: Manchester University Press.

Rotimi, O., 2005 [1971]. *The Gods Are Not to Blame.* Oxford: Oxford University Press.

Rutherford, J., 1998. 'The third space: Interview with Homi Bhabha', in J. Rutherford (ed.). *Identity: Community, Culture, Difference.* London: Lawrence & Wishart Ltd.

Sierz, A., 2011. *Rewriting The Nation – British Theatre Today.* London: Methuen Drama.

Thiong'o., N. wa., 1993. *Moving the Centre – The struggle for cultural freedoms.* Nairobi & Portsmouth: East African Educational Publishers & Heinemann.

Tutton, M., 2012. 'Young, urban and culturally savvy, meet the Afropolitans'. http://edition.cnn.com/2012/02/17/world/africa/who-are-afropolitans/index.html?hpt=iaf_t3 (accessed 25 July 2012).

Wambu, O., 2012. 'Black British literature since Windrush'. http://www.bbc.co.uk/history/british/modern/literature_01.shtml (accessed 20 May 2012).

Williams, R., 2007. *Joe Guy.* London: Methuen Drama.

Notes

1   In June 1948, the ship SS Empire Windrush docked at Tilbury in Essex, England carrying on board 492 immigrants from the Caribbean, who were responding to the call to rebuild Britain after the Second World War. This arrival marked the beginning of post-war mass migration into Britain from her colonies. This generation of migrants later became known as 'The Windrush Generation'.

2   David Upshal's BBC 4 Documentary series *Windrush* (2008) was made to commemorate the 60th anniversary of the arrival of the Windrush generation in Britain. It chronicles the arrival, the racial divisions, the rebellions in order to gain recognition and the search for a British identity by a generation and its descendants who have changed the face of Britain since 1948.

The following books provide further reading on the Windrush Generation:

Wambu, O. (ed.), 1998. *Empire Windrush: Fifty Years of Writing about Black Britain.* London: Victor Gollancz; Phillips, M. and Phillips, T., 1998. *Windrush: Irresistible Rise of Multi-Racial Britain.* London: Harper Collins; Dabydeen, D., Gilmore, J. and Jones, C. (eds), 2007. *The Oxford Companion to Black British History.* New York: Oxford University Press.

3   See Taiye Taukli-Worsonu (2005) and Mark Tutton's (2012) articles that introduce and further the discussion of the term 'Afropolitan', a combination of the words African and cosmopolitan that could be applied to the hybrid nature of the artistic and aesthetic philosophy that now drives the work of the company.

Chapter 5

Keeping It Together: Talawa Theatre Company, Britishness, Aesthetics of Scale and Mainstreaming the Black-British Experience

Kene Igweonu

Introduction

Indeed, twenty-first century diasporic communities, particularly in their second generation of immigration and beyond, tend to be vibrant, adaptable, and predisposed to intercultural solidarities.

(Knowles 2010: 54)

Contemporary British theatre, like the society itself, is a mélange of peoples and cultures that often operate on a platform of *multicultural* exigencies, thus making it difficult to achieve a genuine inter-dependence of cultures or 'intercultural solidarities', to borrow Ric Knowles's term. Because most diasporic communities tend to operate on the margins of British society, their theatres also play from those margins, often as a way of serving their respective peoples and cultures. This negates the inherent inclination of the diasporic communities represented *in* these marginal performances to engage with other cultures in Knowles's intercultural solidarity in order to better negotiate their place in the British society to which they belong. As a black-led theatre company, Talawa's ideological stance is encapsulated in the vital role the company plays in negotiating black-British experience on and off the stage. However, the company owes its success in this role to its responsive and nuanced treatment of the issues involved. For instance, writing in his seminal work on the company, Victor Ukaegbu acknowledges this when he notes that:

Talawa fulfils its ideological brief without being propagandist or moralist, its performances reject a simple analysis of problems, opting instead for a more objective interrogation of the issue(s) in question.

(Ukaegbu 2006: 131)

It is, therefore, this aspiration of engaging society in a continual process of negotiation that is not based on antagonism that stands Talawa Theatre Company apart as a unique black-led theatre company in Britain today.

This view, that Talawa engages the British society in negotiating the experience of black peoples, has clear resonance with Knowles' position in *Theatre & Interculturalism*, where he articulates his commitment to '…theatrical attempts to bridge cultures through performance, to bring different cultures into productive dialogue with one another on the stage, in the space between the stage and the audience, and within the audience' (2010: 1). According to Knowles, a necessary first step in bridging cultures and bringing them together in this productive dialogue is to recognise the flexibility that makes a culture vulnerable to other cultures around it. Following from this recognition, however, is the fact that while cultures are not impervious to change, *black culture* has to be enacted constantly in its different manifestation as it negotiates its place among other cultures.

> It begins with the assumption that culture – the fluid, day-to-day, lived realities of specific peoples in specific places and at specific times – exists only insofar as it is enacted, performed into being by the daily and (extra-daily) ritual and performance activities of individuals and communities as they negotiate their place in the world.
>
> (Knowles 2010: 1)

Consequently, it is this process of enactment that provides the space in which intercultural solidarities are manifested. As a black-led theatre company, Talawa not only sets out to perform the black-British experience into being through its productions, but also to provide the *space* (literally and ideologically) for these negotiations to take place.

In the rest of this chapter, I examine the idea of Britishness as articulated by Talawa, as well as their place within the mainstream British theatre establishment as a company that straddles both the small- and mid-scale theatre spaces. The discussions that unfold in the rest of this chapter are interspersed with excerpts of an interview [1] I had with Patricia Cumper who was Artistic Director of Talawa Theatre Company from 2005 to 2012. The structure adopted in presenting the chapter creates a reading frame of two interlinked parts in which a critical discussion followed by an edited transcription of the interview is used as a way of contextualising the thrust of the argument.

Talawa Theatre Company

Talawa Theatre Company was founded in 1985 by the quartet of Yvonne Brewster, Carmen Munroe, Mona Hammond and Inigo Espejel to serve particularly as a *black-led* theatre company, in response to what they perceived as the lack of representation and creative opportunities for actors of black and ethnic minorities in Britain. In a conversation about Talawa's founding quartet in a recent interview, Don Warrington describes them affably as a 'bunch of feisty women' (Allfree 2011: 52) who felt that 'there was nothing out there that represented them' (Allfree 2011: 52). Consequently, from inception, Talawa's principal objective was to provide a viable platform for nurturing and showcasing black talents, giving voice to the black-British experience and cultivating black theatre audiences, as well as developing mainstream audiences for black work.

After 25 years of existence Talawa Theatre Company is unarguably the most successful black-led theatre company in the United Kingdom today. With over 40, including many award-winning, productions to its name, the company has come a long way in helping to redefine the idea of Britishness, particularly what it means to be black and British. The variety of work produced by Talawa in their first 25 years of existence is vast and eclectic, and ranges from great African and British classics to new writing and plays by award-winning writers including C.L.R. James, Derek Walcott, Michael Abbensetts, Wole Soyinka, Patricia Cumper, Mustapha Matura and Michael Bhim. Talawa's history is framed on either side by their production of C.L.R. James' *The Black Jacobins* in 1986 and their most recent production in the form of their 2011 offering of George C. Wolfe's *The Colored Museum*. While this chapter does not set out to offer a discussion of Talawa productions [2], it will return briefly, as part of my examination of the company's ideology in relation to the notion of Britishness and small-scale theatre and the significance of the first production in framing their ideological stance.

Till date, the company has had a total of four artistic directors, arguably five if one considers Ben Thomas, a veteran actor with Talawa who was appointed as Acting Artistic Director following the sudden resignation of Paulette Randall in 2004. From the company's inception in 1995, Yvonne Brewster served as Artistic Director before handing over to Randall in 2003. However, the period between 2003 and 2005 marked one of the most difficult times for the company. Talawa had spent about four years negotiating the acquisition of a £9.5 million building in Westminster, London, to house the company's work in what would have become the first major venue programmed by blacks. However, the Arts Council of England withdrew the £4 million funding support which led to the eventual collapse of the project. Consequently, the Arts Council pledged to invest at least £3.5 million of the fund originally intended for the building in funding black and minority ethnic artists to develop new spaces, however, the Council never followed up on that promise (Iqbal 2011). It was in the midst of this turmoil that Patricia Cumper was appointed as Artistic Director of Talawa Theatre Company in 2005. Taking over just after the resignation, in 2004, of Randall as well as seven other staff and board members (Iqbal 2011), Cumper made tremendous progress with the company and rescued it from near total collapse and from being placed under administration. She finally stepped down as Artistic Director in 2012. Asked to speak about her bequest to Talawa as she prepared to hand over to Michael Buffong in the spring 2012, Cumper recalls this difficult period in the company's existence:

> It's actually stabilising the company because when I took it over they were about to get rid of it. They were […] telling us, 'you write the letter we'll sign it, you are going to go away'. I had to put together a business plan for [the company's recovery] and then continue to drive it through to see what else we could do to build our credibility. I think the fact that I'm handing over something that's got three years funding guaranteed, and that we are still part of what we call the national portfolio organisations – where Nitro is falling away [originally founded in 1979 as the Black Theatre Co-operative], Collective Artists

are falling away, Tiata Fahodzi has got small – and we managed to hold on to that, to me is quite important.

(Cumper 2011)

A confident Cumper equally goes through a long list of other achievements, including Talawa's consistency in showcasing high-quality black talents through its major productions and commissions, facilitating the development and promotion of work by black, Asian and minority ethnic (BAME) artists through initiatives such as Flipping the Script and Talawa's Writers' Group, the company's annual showcase of new writings. She also talks about the immense success of Talawa's annual summer school which she describes as 'phenomenal!' (Cumper 2011). All these point to the fact that, as Artistic Director, Cumper was able to move forward one of Talawa's principal objectives – of empowering and giving black directors, writers and actors a voice. Cumper is pragmatic and recognises that, as she puts it:

[…] the productions are not the most important thing, but they are a line through all the other things that you want to achieve in terms of providing opportunity and providing a kind of intellectual continuity. So there is a lot of below the line work that goes on in the developing of writers and other practitioners that we have done.

(Cumper 2011)

This is because, in addition to its determination to be recognised as a company that is consistent in producing challenging, innovative and entertaining work, Talawa prides itself on its ability to continually produce a good number of talented actors, writers, directors, designers, technicians, marketers and theatre administrators who go on to build successful careers within the wider British theatre and entertainment industries. It is such achievements, as Patricia Cumper argues, that demonstrate Talawa's recovery since 2005 and its continual growth in significance, influence and contribution to contemporary British theatre and identity.

Negotiating Britishness: Small-Scale Ideology, Mid-Scale Politics

Talawa is one of several touring theatre companies that emerged in Britain within the last three decades. On the black and ethnic minorities' scene, the emergence and, particularly, demise of such companies was prevalent. The growth in the number of small-scale theatre companies during the early years of that period was often in response to ideas associated with postmodern avant-gardism in theatre making, and the new audiences that an increasingly multi-cultural British society provided. Thus the new companies that emerged in this period found a ready-made set of ideological, philosophical, cultural and racial concerns to which they could subscribe in order to define their identities and the aesthetics that would inform their work. Writing about those early years McMillan observes that:

The renaissance of a black arts movement in the 1980s signified the coming of age of second-generation blacks who had grown up in Britain and were exploring questions of identification and representation. Could being black and British be reconciled, and what did this mean?

(McMillan 2006: 55)

However, the renaissance and 'coming of age of second-generation blacks who had grown up in Britain' was, in essence, a reflection of the aspirations of black peoples living in Britain in general, led primarily by Caribbean émigrés. Lending his voice to this development, David V. Johnson argues that:

The history of black people on the British stage and their contemporary presence was seldom profiled or rarely discussed in the mainstream. The main change to this was in the development of black theatre companies in the 1980s. Talawa Theatre Company emerging in the midst of this and later becoming the longest running of these companies can be seen to have lent itself to the task of beginning to redress the balance.

(Johnson 2001: 4)

Whereas, as McMillan observes, black-British people were beginning to explore questions about their identity in the 1980s, Johnson goes further to acknowledge the significant role played by Talawa in negotiating those questions. Johnson's observation is shared by Cumper who concedes that the current generation of black-British people have grown with 'a strong sense of their Britishness' (Cumper 2011). However, she is quick to add that despite seeing themselves as being 'absolutely British', they are still not exempt from some of the questions about their identity that mark the renaissance of the 1980s. According to Cumper, the current generation of black-British people continue to re/define their Britishness as part of ongoing conversations surrounding identity, representation and belonging in British society.

A key defining feature of the small-scale touring theatre companies that emerged during this period in the 1980s, and the ones that followed them, is the experimental nature of the work they undertook and the way they worked in small venues and spaces. Till date, small-scale theatre companies continue to be defined by their experimental approach, choice of materials/content and the size and nature of the venues in which they play. Crucially, they provide the space for new audiences to experience theatre, as well as a space for nurturing young creative talents on the subsidies they receive from various sources, particularly the Arts Council.

As I have already indicated, the space occupied by small-scale touring theatre companies is one that is in constant flux with several companies failing to survive beyond their first few years of existence due to several factors, mainly financial. However, rather than disappearing off the scene, some of these companies merely changed their focus to ensure they continued to exist, while some of those that were successful, artistically, financially and administratively, often transform to become part of what could be referred to as a British theatre establishment. The sort of transformation suggested here has a lot to do with the companies finding creative means of meeting the ever-changing funding priorities of major benefactors such as the Arts Councils, in order to secure their continued support. These priorities are often predicated, among others, on factors such as the demographic reach and impact of the theatre companies on their local and cultural communities, as well as the nature of production and development work undertaken by these companies, some of which work within a particular cultural aesthetic. To meet some of these demands, theatre companies are forced to make strategic changes that often result in ideological shifts, which may inadvertently impact on the aesthetics of scale they adopt for their productions. In most cases this forces theatre companies to remain small scale in order to survive. However, it is in successfully navigating these changing demands, and yet being able to retain their ideological stance as a mid-scale theatre company that stands Talawa out.

Talawa definitely falls within the category of companies that have become part of the 'establishment' in their 25 years of existence. From its inception the company ideologically identified itself as one with clear ambitions to be mid-scale. However, the exigencies of public funding has seen them straddling the gap between small- and mid-scale theatre space; engaging in experimental and developmental work on the small-scale, while producing major shows that sits comfortably within the mid-scale. Talawa's tenacity in holding on to the mid-scale goes back to its very beginning as a theatre company. As already indicated, Talawa signalled its determination not to be classified as small-scale with their inaugural production of C.L.R. James' *The Black Jacobins*, a play about the Haitian revolution of 1791–1804, as its first major work in 1986. With its large cast and ambitious scale, producing *The Black Jacobins* was a major political and ideological statement by the then nascent Talawa Theatre Company, and served as a deliberate attempt by the company to stake its place within aesthetics of scale operating in British theatre. The production served as a strong signal of the company's mission to mainstream the black-British experience, speaking about which Cumper points out that:

> One of the things that the founder of the company, Yvonne Brewster, felt very strongly about was that what we were not going to do was be pushed into studios and small venues – to be seen as an experimental theatre company. She wanted to occupy the mainstream.
>
> (Cumper 2011)

In addition to Brewster's desire to render an 'authentic' version of a play that was first performed in London in 1935, with roles designated for black actors played by 'white Englishmen blacked up' (Brewster 2006: 88), her funding application to the then Greater London Council made her aspiration for the company very clear.

> The application also made clear this would have to be a large-scale production using at least 25 actors with a rehearsal period of no fewer than seven weeks ending in a

three-week run at the 400 seat Riverside Studios main auditorium. This may not seem overly ambitious today in our brave new world, but then it was virtually unheard of for a black theatre company, especially one with no track record at all, to expect to be funded to the tune of £80,000 for one production.

(Brewster 2006: 88)

Evidently, *The Black Jacobins* is a testament to the company's ideological stance on producing mid-scale work that spoke directly to the mainstream. Consequently, as indicated in my introduction, the significance of this first production in framing Talawa's ideological stance cannot be underestimated.

Talawa's political will and tenacity in those early days was matched by audiences who according to Cumper saw their patronage of Talawa as a 'political act' (Allfree 2011: 52). This was during a decade marked by a phenomenal rise in political awareness by black people in Britain as evidenced by the Brixton riots of 1981 and 1985, which took place against the backdrop of the perceived inequalities experienced by black people in Britain at that time. In the Interview with Allfree, cited above, Cumper acknowledges that, 'During the 1980s, attending a Talawa production was […] a "political act"' (Allfree 2011: 52). This is because the company provided the political platform for black people, not only to ask questions about what it means to be black and British but to situate their experience, culture and history as one that is contemporarily and quintessentially British, along with those of other communities represented in the Union. Moreover, this development is rendered all the more remarkable by the fact that as an agent of political awakening Talawa's influence was not limited to blacks who were born or grew up in Britain, but encompassed all black peoples living in Britain and beyond at that time. This is a fact acknowledged by the American born playwright and critic, Bonnie Greer, who in an interview with Nosheen Iqbal of *The Guardian* recalls that:

Talawa's 25th coincides with my own 25th anniversary living in London. And Talawa was one of the reasons I moved to the United Kingdom: I wanted to be a part of it, to work with the sparkling array of black directors and actors employed by these theatres.

(Iqbal 2011)

Talawa's broad-based appeal to blacks in general, due to the political space that it provides for them, is a result of a deliberate policy by the company not to be seen as representing a Caribbean or African aesthetic, but one that is black-British. This policy was effectively instituted by Brewster during Talawa's early years as a way of undoing a pattern that begun to emerge following the company's successive production of three Caribbean plays: *The Black Jacobins* (1986), *An Echo in the Bone* (1986) and *O Babylon!* (1988) (Brewster 2006). Cumper argues that situating the company as black-British rather than Caribbean or African allows it to root back to both cultures, as well as to stake its presence in Britain in order to proclaim its Britishness and that of those it represents. Whilst Talawa remains content to operate in the small-scale, the vision and sheer doggedness of its leadership over the years has meant that the company is now firmly recognised as a mid-scale, instead of a small-scale, theatre company. However, as a company, the founding vision and philosophy that situates Talawa within the realm of a small-scale company has remained unchanged throughout its 25 years of existence.

The rest of this chapter is divided between the transcription of my interview with Cumper and a concise conclusion in which I sum up my key argument regarding Talawa's role in negotiating Britishness. The transcription that follows has been split into two separate subheadings, 'Black-British or British Theatre? Ideological Position on Britishness' and 'The Aesthetic of Small- and Medium-Scale British Theatre'. This approach has been adopted in order to further unpack the interview and present it topically in a way that helps to better contextualise the arguments I have offered throughout this chapter. In the first part Cumper discusses the notion of Britishness, the place of black peoples and cultures in contemporary British society, and the role of Talawa as a company that represents the aspirations of black-British people and that provides the space for intercultural and multicultural solidarities to forge new creativities. It starts off with Cumper commenting on an issue that is aptly recognised by Deirdre Osborne who argues that:

> While the staging of plays by black British dramatists in mainstream London theatres might reveal an increasingly contested sense of the 'mainstream' and revisions of what has been perceived as the traditional theatre market, traditional theatrical hegemonies remain evident. White men continue to remain at the helm despite the forays into cross-cultural programming with 'new' writing.
>
> (Osborne 2006: 28)

Under the second heading, Cumper emphasises Talawa's enduring link to the idea of a small-scale British theatre, in terms of their developmental and educational work in small and new venues, while simultaneously fulfilling their founding philosophy of mainstreaming the black-British experience by ensuring that all their key productions are mid-scale.

The Interview

Black-British or British Theatre? Ideological Position on Britishness

Igweonu: *In terms of describing ethnic minorities' theatre in Britain, do you think we should still be talking about them as black theatre, black-led theatre or simply as British theatre?*

Cumper: *Ideally I would love for it to be British theatre, but we also have to accept the fact that although the weather has changed, the climate hasn't. [...] I am not just talking about race or ethnicity, but also about gender. I think there are changes that still need to be made, and so companies like Talawa continue to need to exist. I don't personally understand why anybody would question the fact that Europe and Africa have been closer together than any other two continents and that the conversation between them, culturally, has been one of the most exciting. It's been painful and it's been difficult, but it's been one of the most exciting. You can't right now sit on a more interesting place than that sort of interface. That's what drama loves; being right on those margins and looking at all sorts of ideas. So that's how I feel about it. I think there may come a time when we are simply accepted as part of that [British theatre, as opposed to black-British theatre], but I don't think it's now.*

Igweonu: *Does being funded by the Arts Council allow you to do the kind of work you want to do?*

Cumper: *No, it's constantly a fight. I mean, what happens is you are expected to do X amount of work, you are funded to do half of X, and what you have to do is make partnerships and find funding in order to do the work. That is the deal that you make and it's frequently an uncomfortable one especially, for example, if they are calling it 'black'. What happens is, I'm going to get an audience that is, in London for example, more Nigerian than it is Caribbean. So how am I going to find a public that goes across those two? That is not necessarily an easy thing to do. I'm looking at a burgeoning black middle class, but I'm also looking at the fact that the majority of the people that I want to bring in wouldn't pay £12, £15, £20 to come to the theatre to see the kind of work that we are presenting.*

But I think the fundamental thing that hasn't been taken on board by venues, and I know the Arts Council is concerned about this, is that they think they have to do the same programming and advertise it different. I think what they need to do is go to that audience and ask them what they want to see and then programme differently. And that's a huge mind shift for a lot of the theatres. Every story reaffirms a set of core values; if you go to a Harold Pinter or to a [Alan] Bennett [award-winning English playwrights], you are part-bound to a particular narrative, and if you are in the audience being uncomfortable with this Oxbridge kind of narrative coming at you, then why should you come back?

Igweonu: *You spoke earlier about the changing demographics of black people in London, and the kind of work that mid-scale companies like yours do to nurture young talents. How would you describe Talawa's contribution to this matrix and the notion of the mid-scale British theatre?*

Cumper: *You know, the one thing we've done is survive. On the other side of it, I think we have to say that we've worked quite hard. We started from Yvonne [Brewster] to make sure that in terms of our finances and our administration the company was tightly run, so whatever happened, everything was entirely transparent. We've been always entirely transparent with what we are doing and I think that is one of the things that help our funders to trust us. The other thing is that we make a case for the work that we do and the stuff that we want to do that isn't about anger, and it's not about opposition. It's actually about saying 'this is where we are and this is what we do'. Sometimes it's a very hard position to hold because sometimes you are very angry. There is no polite way to say it, a lot of the time black practitioners come in here [Talawa] and they finally have to put down the burden of representation... and come as a performer and artist and whatever else, and we try and support that or work with that as far as we can. The funders know they are not serving wide enough audiences, so a company like ours would be allowed into all sorts of spaces because what we do is allow them to think that they are interacting with different audiences. [...] We constantly look at what we are doing and make sure the administration is pretty sharp, and then we just fight it [using the artistic and ideological vision of the company].*

Igweonu: *On a more general level, is there an ideological position or structure that drives the notion of Britishness in contemporary theatre, and how would you say Talawa responds or contributes to such an ideology?*

Cumper: *What is fascinating, it does seem to me, is that most of the mainstream theatre – mid scale and above – that I've seen is very much about an English audience saying to itself 'we're terribly clever, we're terribly verbal'. And there is a kind of tacit assumption that if you are in the theatre with me you are essentially middle class, and you are probably slightly left leaning. So there is a kind of picture of what theatre is, and it defines a particular narrative that the British have about themselves, about being clever and verbal, and liberal. That also makes it class-based, as well as terribly middle classed. When you have a company like Talawa coming in [...] it's not quite the same. What we literally are is the upstart in that space, we tend to mediate and speak the critical language of the venues that we go into. But what we are also doing is trying to continually bring in all the other things about us into that space. Sometimes I think we are used as a safe way of doing that [of bringing the black-British experience into mainstream spaces]; they are not sure about having a black production in the building, but 'it's all right if Talawa is there' because we can mediate in that way.*

I still feel, to some extent, this company is essentially powerless. We are constantly negotiating our presence with the funding bodies, with the theatres, and that, at this point, is what our role is. But there will be a point at which they will say 'right we want to do a project with Talawa, what is the project?' Rather than the other way around, 'oh, that's quite a nice project, ok we'll do it with you'.

Igweonu: *In their book* Windrush: The Irresistible Rise of Multi-Racial Britain, *Mike and Trevor Phillips write about how the Empire Windrush generation helped to redefine what it means to be British to include not just black people but other races as well. In what ways have Talawa contributed to further redefining the idea of Britishness?*

Cumper: *It's something that we actually talk about, just internally, a lot. It's a bit like the cross of Saint George. When I first came back here [from Jamaica] in the early*

1990s, to me it [the Saint George's cross] literally just meant BNP [British National Party]; it meant racist. How do you claim that back and make that part of your heritage without feeling a slight sense of [indignation] every time you see it? When you think about it, Saint George was Turkish. Even Morris dancing comes from Moorish dancing out of North Africa. So if you think about all of those things, then it's about embracing that sense of what Britishness is in all its complexities. It's about settling people's feeling so they don't get defensive or worried about it, but actually celebrate and enjoy it. I think it is one of the things we try and do, but it's never easy.

[That is why Talawa was deliberately set up], not to be a sort of African or Caribbean company. It was to be a black-British company, and that allowed us roots back to everywhere, and even to stake our presence here. What is fascinating to me when you see a lot of the younger practitioners – and when I say young I mean from sort of mid-1930s down – they have a strong sense of their Britishness. Whereas maybe for me and, certainly, Yvonne's [Brewster] generation, it was 'I'm a Jamaican coming in here'. They [younger practitioners] are absolutely British but they are still defining that Britishness as well and I think that's the conversation we are part of. It [Britishness] is constantly under discussion, it's entirely fluid, and I don't think it's been defined yet. Just a bit like claiming the mainstream, I think claiming Britishness is very important for the development of the work.

The Aesthetics of Small- and Medium-Scale British Theatre

Igweonu: *In our earlier exchange you indicated that Talawa is considered a mid-scale theatre company as opposed to being small scale. How does the classification system work?*

Cumper: *It's about how you negotiate your relationship with the Arts Council. So they [the Arts Council] will give you different levels of funding according to what scale they think you are. One of the things that the founder of the company, Yvonne Brewster, felt very strongly about was that what we were not going to do was to be pushed into studios and small venues – to be seen as an experimental theatre company. She wanted to occupy the mainstream. Now, to be mid scale is to be anywhere between a sort of 200 seater to a 600 seater [theatre]. It's not [the same as] the huge theatres but it has enough presence… So we define ourselves as mid-scale simply because what we don't want to do is to allow ourselves to be seen as sort of experimental or working studios, or not working with ambition. We have all the usual financial constraints but we try to work in those venues [mid-scale venues], which is why we create partnerships with West Yorkshire [West Yorkshire Playhouse in Leeds], with Young Vic [Young Vic Theatre in London] and places like that.*

Igweonu: *In a recent interview with the Metro you stated that the work you do at Talawa, and in black-British theatre generally, can no longer be considered fringe theatre but mainstream due to the cultural diversity of the British society. Can you elaborate on this point as it touches on your earlier comment about Yvonne Brewster wanting Talawa to occupy the mainstream from its founding?*

Cumper: *A part of that is about saying something in the hope that it will come into being. You know that it's an argument that's being made by the diversity section of the Arts Council. It's also an argument being made by the black, Asian and minority ethnic (BAME) companies that, essentially, if you want to have new ideas, fresh ideas, new influences, new energies coming into any art form, you look as widely as possible. We actually represent those influences coming into the society so we'll be 'grit in the oyster'. It's an idea that we present a lot.*

   Outside of London we are not hugely represented. I mean, in London I think your visible ethnic minorities, as we are described, are like 40% of Londoners. Certainly [this ratio is down to] 10%, 12% or even 2% in some of the places that we tour to. A lot of the time people from minorities know the majority better than they know themselves because we have to live with them, but what we [people from minorities] also know is ourselves [in ways the majority does not know us]. We [Talawa] look at things through a different lens and it's that lens that Kwame Kwei-Armah [acclaimed British playwright and director] talks about a lot that I think is the most interesting thing about the work we do.

Igweonu: *Let us return, for a moment, to the idea of a mid-scale British theatre. Would you say there is an aesthetic or philosophy that drives mid-scale British theatre?*

Cumper: *I think the most important thing about being that size is the slightly uncomfortable relationship I was telling you about, the quality of the work that needs to be presented, and the size of the audience. For example, I always use Stratford East [to illustrate] because they have a 450-seater [theatre], they produce big musicals and that kind of stuff, but they need additional subsidy just to be able to continue to work. So mid-scale theatre is always, practically, going to be subsidised theatre, and it's always going to be that theatre through which things pass to go other places. It may be where things start, but it's always going to be something that needs additional support around it. For example, with Talawa, so many writers, actors, directors and all kinds of people have started, been nurtured, done their initial work [with the company], and then gone on to other places. That is the importance, I think, of mid-scale companies. Talawa has a complete duty to 'push the envelope' as much as it can, and to make sure that it provides opportunities for as wide a range, and as a targeted a range, of people as it possibly can… 'Yes we need support, but actually we are part of an ecology and we create and offer all sorts of things within that environment'.*

Igweonu: *Think back to the period before Talawa became recognised as a mid-scale theatre company, to when you were seen as small-scale. Was there a philosophy at that time that is, perhaps, different from what it is now?*

Cumper: Yvonne [Brewster], from the very beginning, had the ambition that she would be going into decent-size theatres; she never ever saw herself as small-scale. The first thing she did was The Black Jacobins, which is a cast of thousands [figuratively speaking]! And I think what happens is of necessity, what you [Talawa] do is, you do one big show and then you do smaller developmental shows or studio-based shows because you can take the risk. You can go to the Riverside [Riverside Studios in London] or Drill Hall [The Drill Hall theatre in London] – do something smaller, but the ambition has always been to operate at that level [mid scale]. The theatre that was going to be built would have been, I think, a 270–300 seater that would then fall to the small end of mid scale [negotiation to acquire the £9.5 million building at Westminster, London, collapsed after the Arts Council of England withdrew its £4 million support for the project]. That was always the ambition [operating in the mid scale]. The sense was, I think, a particularly immigrant sense of 'no, you are not pushing me out into the corner'. We are happy to work in that way [as small-scale theatre] but in terms of how we represent ourselves through our major productions, we've always wanted to go mid scale and we try and push harder if we can.

Igweonu: Would you then say that is one of the major contributions that Talawa continues to make to small-scale British theatre today even though you don't consider yourself small scale?

Cumper: Absolutely, I think what we are is a conduit where people can come from small scale all the way through [to mid scale]. We do work on the small scale with all the developmental work that we do. It's just for our main productions, just out of sheer cursiveness we are staying mid scale so that we can say 'this is why we get the money'.

Igweonu: With mid-scale companies like Talawa reaching back into the small scale as part of its philosophy, is there still a space out there for companies that just want to remain small scale?

Cumper: Oh yeah, I think so. We've got a company called Custom/Practice with Rae Mcken and Suba Das [Custom/Practice is a London-based theatre company founded in 2009 by artistic directors Rae Mcken and Suba Das]. They do classical theatre techniques that work with BAME practitioners to tell particular stories; they are a small-scale theatre company. Tiata Fahodzi can produce mid scale and below [Tiata Fahodzi is a London-based theatre company founded in 1997 by Femi Elufowoju Jr, with Lucian Msamati as its current artistic director]. There's the Arcola [Arcola Theatre in Hackney, London] led by Mehmet Ergen. What I would like to see more than anything though is a small-scale space programmed by black theatre makers. I think that would be really, really interesting.

Igweonu: Is such a space still something Talawa is best placed to champion and possibly provide?

Cumper: I don't know. We'll have a new artistic director next year so he'll decide [Michael Buffong took over as Artistic Director from Patricia Cumper in early 2012].

But there is something called Sustained Theatre. Their London Hub is a whole bunch of companies including dance, circus and theatre companies, and the money that should have gone into Talawa's theatre will create, hopefully, a number of spaces around the country. [The London Hub is a cooperative that works to unite leading BAME artists and companies to ensure the UK arts and cultural landscape reflects the diverse, rich and vibrant talents of contemporary British society] [3]. But interesting to me is that the London Hub kind of think 'well, we don't need rehearsal space, we actually need a space to programme' and I think that might be the next thing that happens, I hope.

We [Talawa] are a gypsy company in that we move from venue to venue and, although we have something of a following, it's always as if with every production we are almost starting from scratch, and that's labour intensive. I think a small-scale theatre that actually allows people to go from acting, directing, writing to programming and producing would be a fantastic thing because too few people are producing.

Igweonu: *For the first time in its 24-year history, Talawa will have a man [Michael Buffong] as its artistic director. What does Michael's appointment say about Talawa from 2012, in terms of its driving ideology? Should we expect a change of direction or ideology?*

Cumper: *That's interesting because somebody asked me to contribute to a book on black women theatre makers, and I realised that of the 40-something productions that we've done, only four or five of them have been by women, and maybe three of them by black-British women – if I count myself and I'm sort of marginal. So I realise that race seems to trump gender in a lot of these decisions. That was interesting for me because I always saw these two as things that I was really passionate about [that is, issues of race and gender]. Race really did seem to be the more important one. In a strange way, because the company is settled and mature, [it needs to] have somebody like Michael come in, who is entirely about making good work – that is his passion, he's got that. He's created that feeling for himself, people respect him, he will make the partnerships, and it's all about making good work. But actually, he represents the next stage.*

When I got through, I think they [Talawa] needed somebody who could argue the case, who'd be fairly steady – I think that's why I was chosen. At this point, I think that foundation is in place and what needs to happen is a sort of theatrical pyrotechnic – really impressive shows, pulling in good people and just literally pushing the company up in terms of public [perception] so that you think of Kneehigh [theatre company based in Cornwall] or Punchdrunk [a London-based experimental theatre company], or any of those companies. Talawa is [among them as] one of those companies still experimenting with things and being innovative. I'm not particularly worried about that [the appointment of Talawa's first male artistic director]. I think it's a good natural progression.

Conclusion

As Britain's premier black-led theatre company, Talawa embodies the aspiration of the current generation of black-British people who consider that their cultural identity is neither marginal nor entirely diasporic, but *indigenous* to contemporary British society (Osborne 2006). This stance does not seek to negate the influence of the diaspora in shaping how black people in Britain see themselves today. On the contrary, it recognises that Britishness is not a fixed concept but the creation of an unremitting process of negotiation spurred by intercultural solidarities. In this respect, Talawa has successfully served in two very important roles; as a theatre company that represents the black-British experience to mainstream audiences, and that equally curates the processes involved in continually negotiating their place within the British society as whole.

References

Allfree, C., 2011. 'The big interview, Talawa Theatre Company: From feisty to philosophical'. *Metro*, 13 October, pp. 52–53.

Brewster, Y., 2006. 'Talawa Theatre Company 1985–2002', in Davis, G. V. and Fuchs, A. (eds). *Staging New Britain: Aspects of Black and South Asian British Theatre Practice*. Brussels: Peter Lang, pp. 87–105.

Cumper, P., 2011. Personal interview by Kene Igweonu [audio/mp3] at Talawa HQ, London. 20 October.

Iqbal, N., 2011. 'Talawa Theatre Company: The fights of our lives'. *The Guardian*, 29 May. http://www.guardian.co.uk/stage/2011/may/29/talawa-theatre-company-25th-anniversary (accessed 27 October).

Johnson, D. V., 2001. 'The history, theatrical performance work and achievements of Talawa Theatre Company 1986–2001. Unpublished PhD Thesis. Warwick: University of Warwick.

Knowles, R., 2010. *Theatre & Interculturalism*. Basingstoke: Palgrave Macmillan.

McMillan, M., 2006. 'Rebaptizing the world in our own terms: Black theatre and live arts in Britain', in G. V. Davis and A. Fuchs (eds) *Staging New Britain: Aspects of Black and South Asian British Theatre Practice*. Brussels: Peter Lang, pp. 47–63.

Osborne, D., 2006. 'Writing black back: An overview of black theatre and performance in Britian'. *Studies in Theatre & Performance*, 26: 1, pp. 13–31.

Ukaegbu, V., 2006. '*Talawa* Theatre Company: The "likkle" matter of black creativity and representation on the British stage', in Godiwala, D. (ed.). *Alternatives Within the Mainstream British Black and Asian Theatres*. Newcastle: Cambridge Scholars Press, pp. 123–52.

Notes

1   In presenting excerpts from my interview with Patricia Cumper, I have included commentaries in my own words [in square brackets] where necessary to help clarify some of the references to people, companies and other relevant points.
2   For a comprehensive discussion of Talawa's major productions see Ukaegbu, V., 2006. 'Talawa Theatre Company: The "Likkle" matter of black British creativity and representation on the British stage', in Godiwala, D. (ed.). *Alternatives Within the Mainstream British Black and Asian Theatres*. Newcastle: Cambridge Scholars Press, pp. 123–52.
3   http://thelondonhub.com/ (accessed 2 November 2011).

Chapter 6

Agitation and Entertainment: Rod Dixon and Red Ladder
Theatre Company

Tony Gardner

At the time of the interview with Rod Dixon, Red Ladder has been functioning as a company for 44 years, and for all but three of those years under its current name and with a strong sense of continuity even in the face of its sometimes radical changes in personnel, finances, organisational structure and of course audience tastes and expectations. Indeed, the extraordinary resilience of the company is matched only by the frequency with which its members have needed to negotiate upheavals and crises driven by both internal and external pressures. It serves in many ways as an object lesson in self-reinvention as a survival strategy for small-scale companies. How the company has achieved this repeatedly but without losing sight of its core principles or identity is quite remarkable, and allows us today to recognise Red Ladder as essentially the same company as it was in 1971 when it changed its name from the Agitprop Street Players that first appeared at the Trafalgar Square Festival of 1968, reflecting very closely the political turmoil and newly invigorated activism of that watershed year.

Its fellow companies and peers such as CAST (Cartoon Archetypal Slogan Theatre), 7:84, Belt & Braces, The General Will, Monstrous Regiment and others provide compelling historical examples of performances that engaged directly with the politics of a particular era, as carefully documented in Catherine Itzin's *Stages in the Revolution* (1980), Andrew Davies' *Other Theatres* (1987) or Sandy Craig's *Dreams and Deconstructions* (1980). Red Ladder was certainly motivated in its early years by these same political convictions, but it has also managed to outlive these companies by dint of its commitment to reflecting the changing circumstances of its audiences and the larger communities in which they are embedded, as well as a less ideologically constrained set of principles. This was in large part due to the early decision to base the company in the north, and especially Leeds, where they have been both witnesses to and participants in the vicissitudes of the region as it progresses towards a post-industrial future. At certain times in its history, the company has been so absorbed in this political and cultural transformation of its locality that it has fallen somewhat from the larger theatrical map, although without disappearing from it entirely. For more recent members of the company such as Rod Dixon, who joined as Artistic Director in 2006, the perception was that Red Ladder had simply 'gone under the radar' through the 1990s while it focused on community engagement projects and the evolving multicultural politics of the area, and needed to be reintroduced once again to a larger audience. The fact that Dixon regarded this as being first of all a *theatrical* audience is made very clear in the interview, as is his perception that this was merely a restatement of the company's founding principles.

The agitprop techniques learned in the early years and applied in all types of non-theatrical settings – from factory gates to social clubs – were balanced from the start with a delight in theatricality, large-scale spectacle, sweeping historical perspectives and popular forms of entertainment, as seen in the ambition of pieces such as *Strike While the Iron is Hot* (from 1974), musicals about the weaving industry and the Chartist movement (*Taking Our Time*, 1978), the steel industry (*Nerves of Steel*, 1979), nuclear power (*Power Mad*, 1979), as well as pieces about the National Health Service (*Bring Out Your Dead*, 1983 and *Safe With Us*, 1985), the Holocaust (*Preparations*, 1983) – not to mention the brewers, coal miners, police, CND activists, the homeless and so on, who all received dedicated treatments in the first half of the 1980s. As John Hoyland (who scripted the first Agitprop Street Players piece *The Little Artist*) explained of the period, the interest in Agitprop grew out of a recognition that the politics of the left needed to address cultural as well as economic and social contexts, and explore 'the application of the imagination to politics and the application of politics to the imagination' (cited in Itzin 1980: 39). A dynamic tension between these two core concepts – politics and the imagination – has continued for much of the company's history, with the balance shifting in different phases of work, and even individual productions. In the early years, for example, Hoyland goes on to observe that:

> The general feeling of the Red Ladder people at that time was that they did not come out of the theatre tradition; they did not see themselves as theatre workers for a long time. […] The main impetus was political rather than theatrical.
>
> (cited in Itzin 1980: 43)

Despite this, the sketches and short plays created by the company in those years frequently borrowed from the language of popular entertainment and even historical music hall forms, such as in *The Rose-Tinted Spectacles* created for touring to Tenants' Associations (from 1968/69) that mixed broad comedy and drag acts with exhortations to political action. There was a certain scepticism also from the trades union and labour movement about the effectiveness of this type of approach rooted in working-class culture and theatrical tradition, and the company has frequently moved in and out of the orbit of such official organisations for this and other reasons. It is therefore a challenge at times to pin down the precise nature of the company's political convictions through the subsequent decades, while the theatrical exuberance and breadth of stylistic choices evident in the early years has been a recurring feature of their work.

Red Ladder's major project of 2012 brought this into especially sharp focus. *Big Society!* was written by Boff Whalley, created in collaboration with pioneering political musicians Chumbawamba, and featured comedian Phill Jupitus in the leading role as manager of an Edwardian music hall venue facing hard times. It was presented at the Leeds City Varieties Music Hall (former stage for Charlie Chaplin, Buster Keaton, Harry Houdini among many others, as well as the BBC's *The Good Old Days* from 1953) to mark its reopening after a painstaking refurbishment and recreation of the original 1865 interior. Citing

John McGrath's *A Good Night Out* (1981) as a significant influence, Whalley explained this turn to virtually antiquarian nostalgia as follows:

> In an era when the musical is dominated by Lloyd-Webber opera-lite and lowest-common-denominator West End rock band bio-cliches, it seemed fitting to rediscover the world of Music Hall, so often swept under the carpet of cultural snobbery. In response to the not-forgotten rallying-cry of 1970s agit-prop – from the theatre of those such as 7:84 and Dario Fo – Red Ladder and Chumbawamba have grasped the chance to bring the form of Edwardian mass entertainment into the forum of radical politics.
>
> (Whalley 2012: 2)

The biting political satire that attempted to puncture the Conservative Party's recent 'big society' rhetoric with frequent, although oblique, reference to current events sat sometimes a little uneasily alongside its fond tribute to the music hall tradition, and especially its northern variant, as 'recreation grounds for the working class [...] regularly packed to the rafters with bawdy, uncouth audiences and bawdy, uncouth performers' (Whalley 2012: 3). Music hall favourites such as *It's the Same the Whole World Over* (with lyrics that complain 'it's the poor what gets the blame, it's the rich what gets the pleasure, ain't it all a bloomin' shame?') were set next to original songs such as *We're Not In This Together* as well as *Big Society!* itself, with its mocking refrain: 'We're all in this together! All you little people sing along, We're all in this together!' The point is here rather bluntly made, and indeed the production attracted some criticism for lacking political teeth, or a clearer relationship between the conceit of the music hall as a microcosm of the country and the reality of contemporary politics against the backdrop of the global financial crisis. Michael Billington in particular noted that it wasn't 'quite the sabre-toothed satire I had been hoping for' (Billington 2012).

Such confusions of political meaning or intent can easily be exaggerated, however, as in many other respects Red Ladder continues to occupy an unapologetically radical territory that has been mostly abandoned by their peers. Or rather, the company has decisively re-occupied it in recent years as part of Rod Dixon's stated intention to 'put the red back into Red Ladder'; only this is not the colour of the Labour Party or even of international socialism, as the company's formal, organisational affiliations remain decidedly ambiguous. There are some historical reasons for this that deserve a little more scrutiny, as they help to explain how the company has been able to survive for so long despite its dependence on public funding. It received its first Arts Council grant (of £4000) in 1973, and since then many of the challenges that it has faced have resulted directly from this dependence on public bodies including regional arts boards, county and metropolitan councils, specialised providers such as youth services and so on.

A decisive moment in the company's history in this respect was 1985–86, when it was pushed by its funders into reorganising itself from its initial 'socialist collective' with its flat hierarchy, and instead adopt an official company structure with an appointed

Board of Directors and – critically – an artistic director as well as a new set of formally articulated company policies. There is no doubt that, without this sea-change at the height of Thatcherism and Conservative power across the country, the company would have fallen gradually by the wayside. As it happens, the result appears to have been a decision to allow the company to be squeezed into the margins, but with a radical re-appraisal of this marginal position as a new site for continuing activism and community engagement. Following this period, Red Ladder's politics shifted decisively towards feminism, multiculturalism, equal opportunities and the micro-politics of everyday life, and the creative practice became dominated by work with and for young people. The new artistic policy of the mid-1980s under the artistic directorship of Rachel Feldberg spelled out these aims, and included as priorities:

- To create an artistically exciting socialist feminist theatre.
- To take this work to audiences who would not normally see theatre, young people 14–25 and the adults who work with them. To perform on their own ground and places where they normally meet, rather than in theatre venues.
- To make our work accessible to all young people and in particular to reach young people for whom there is little or inadequate provision; young disabled people; Black young people (within which we include Asian and African Caribbean teenagers), young people in inner cities and isolated rural areas.

(Pal 2008: 94)

The consequences of this shift are documented in detail by Swati Pal in her research into the company's work from the 1960s to the 1990s. In a context where 'political energy became colossally fragmented' (Pal 2008: 52) right across the small-scale theatre sector, Pal traces the company's journey towards increasing engagement with particular communities in the region, specifically young Asian women, and away from general touring or modes of production addressing broader audiences or plays concerned mainly with class politics. This may have represented a type of retrenchment in the face of the politically hostile environment in the 1980s, but it also signalled an extremely productive and creatively adventurous period, despite the relative narrowness of scope in the company's work. Red Ladder turned to the younger generations as a means of exploring the politics of the future, and there they discovered a fertile new territory and a wide-ranging programme of interventionist performances, most notable among which were *On the Line* (1986), a devised work toured to youth clubs exploring racist attitudes, *Bhangra Girls* (1989) created specifically for young Asian women's groups, and a series of works for the young disabled that integrated British Sign Language (e.g. *Listen* by Philip Osment in 1992). This strand of work was intensified with the appointment of Kully Thiarai as the new artistic director from 1994, with a new mission statement for the company that made explicit its commitment to young people as well as a renewed emphasis on touring beyond the region:

Red Ladder is a national touring company recognising that investment in young people is an investment in the future and is dedicated to:

- Creating and providing artistically excellent high quality theatre for young people who have little or no access to, or experience of, the theatre;
- Touring new work nationally which, through exploring issues specifically designed for young people, is pure theatre; [...]
- Developing new writing and other theatre skills.

(Pal 2008: 131)

The emphasis here on nurturing skills as well as developing a new touring programme of "pure theatre" was emblematic of the company's renewed focus on empowering young participants by providing access to the means of theatrical production, defined in quasi-political terms. Fostering independent creative output serves here virtually as a strategy for resistance against the otherwise wholly consumerist culture of late capitalism that both defines and excludes these communities from meaningful production. For this and other reasons, as Pal notes, 'Red Ladder is perceived as one of the foremost youth and community development theatre companies in the country' (Pal 2008: 167), and this continues today under Dixon's artistic directorship with the Red Grit project, in which young people are provided with professional development opportunities, including the chance to tour work of their own making under the company's banner. As Dixon explains in the interview, creating new work with young people as well as for them remains an important commitment for the company and a sign that its politics, while not exactly utopian, continues to be distinctly optimistic in outlook.

The official recognition of Red Ladder as a training agency in the 1990s also meant that this strategy of diversification secured new income streams, especially through its traineeship programme for Asian women that was focused mainly on stage management and administrative roles. However, it also occasioned one of the difficult episodes in the company's recent history. In particular, the financial stability of the company was put into question by Dixon's decision to close the Asian Theatre School and concentrate instead on reinvigorating its touring programme. Started as a joint project between Red Ladder and Bradford's Theatre in the Mill in 1997, the various activities associated with the Asian Theatre School represented a significant element of the company's regular funding. Dixon explains the complex circumstances surrounding his decision in detail in the interview and the figurative mid-life crisis that it precipitated around the celebrations of its 40th anniversary. This exposed, among other things, the sometimes difficult fit between the company's continuing dependence on public funding and its oppositional politics of resistance and protest. The prospect of the company finally disappearing after this funding cut appears to have been a very real one, and perhaps surprising given the reaction by other small-scale organisations in the region and beyond who experienced similar losses as the country's austerity programme first began to bite, and yet rebounded with almost a sense of defiance (Sheffield's Third Angel and Forced Entertainment spring to mind here).

The Interview

Gardner: *When you first joined Red Ladder as Artistic Director in 2006, it already had almost 40 years of continuous history as a company. How conscious were you of needing to engage with or otherwise account for this legacy of work when mapping a future direction for the company?*

Dixon: *Like many of us, I thought Red Ladder had gone, been lost to all of us, like 7:84, Belt and Braces, CAST [1], and companies like that. I was working as Acting Artistic Director of a sweet little theatre in Plymouth called the Barbican Theatre and I was trying to programme work that was more diverse in flavour for that very predominantly white city down in the South West, and I came across a play called* Silent Cry *written by Madani Younis. It had Asian Theatre School written on it, but it also had Red Ladder and on the strength of that I booked it. It was a piece about death in police custody and it was young and it was quite a naive piece of writing. He is now Artistic Director of the Bush so he won't mind me saying it. It made me realise that Red Ladder had very cleverly gone under the radar for the last couple years. I had heard of them as a student and as a leftie I had always wanted to be interested in their work, but like a lot of students all I really knew about was the paragraph here and there in most textbooks and that's all there is. Plays like* Strike While the Iron is Hot *(1974), which is a really early piece of work. I met Kath McCreery who came to see* Big Society! *and she was in Red Ladder from 1969 to 1974 so there are lots of stories to tell there. Whereas John McGrath (7:84) wrote down everything and I am reading his works again now, revisiting* Naked Thoughts That Roam Around *[2], and I listened to Kath and realised that actually an awful lot of what Red Ladder was doing was pre-dating 7:84.*

It has almost gone down as a myth now, but I said in the interview that I was going to put the red back in Red Ladder. It could have either got me the job or not got me the job, it's the stupid thing you say when you are nervous and it had been quoted back to me by the board so it must have happened. When I looked at the work before 2006, it was high production valued, quality work for teenagers that I respected, but I knew that what I didn't want to make was high quality production work that went into youth clubs to 14 year olds who would then not want to go and see it the following year because they were 15, and that is the handicap of that sort of work. I didn't want to be rebuilding our audience every year and I felt that is possibly why Red Ladder had disappeared as they had been pigeonholed by the Arts Council, and that is the dangerous thing when you want to change direction. But the board were behind me, they wanted to see the politics come back in but the words 'political theatre' make audience run a mile. So you are going to have to make work with a political heart but that is still entertaining, is still good writing, it isn't polemic.

Gardner: *And you joined the company shortly before its 40th anniversary, when presumably you needed to realise plans that were already in place to mark the occasion and celebrate the company's past, as well as define its new agenda?*

Dixon: *I had a shaky start in 2006/07; in that transitional moving away I had to make work that was covering both camps. The first piece of work that I inherited was called* Kaahini. *It was a piece of work made in 1997, about an Asian woman, to celebrate the beginning of Asian Theatre School (ATS), because ATS was targeting Asian women. Wendy Harris had then appointed Madani (Younis) to run the ATS, and I picked up the move of ATS into Freedom Studios, which is a big one. It meant that the £85,000 we were getting a year for ATS went with them but it didn't go until this year. The Arts Council had to take that money back off us to give to ATS/Freedom Studios to plug that gap. It makes sense, but it is still a bit of a shock to lose £90,000. Madani has gone on to be Artistic Director at the Bush which is an interesting appointment as he has never directed in London so maybe that is good for London. Mark Shenton, in* The Stage, *has bewailed the recent comments by David Hare that the Bush is no longer a Fringe theatre. He talks about two tiers of theatre, those that can afford it and those that can't, and that the Bush is pushing over towards the bourgeois and the ticket prices are £24 and it's a business like everything else. Wendy picked up on all the work that Kully Thiarai had done when promoting the ATS as certainly a niche area that is needed in the theatre that is different from Tara Arts and different from all the other Asian companies.*

          So in 2006, I wanted to move the work away from what I saw was good work for teenagers but kind of worthy. I wanted to make work where the teenagers would come with their parents or grandparents. In other words, making work that addressed some of those important social issues but wasn't issue-driven. The work used to be booked by youth workers, but the first question wasn't who is the writer but what is the style, what is the issue, what are we delivering on their programme of social medicine, which I am not very interested in.

Gardner: *The spinning out of ATS from the main company was one of many organisational upheavals that Red Ladder has faced over the years. Could you comment on the transformation of the company's structure in the mid-1980s, why it happened and what its impact has been?*

Dixon: *Red Ladder was no longer a collective, and we were forced into becoming a hierarchy (in 1985). I still know artists who worked with Red Ladder then who were angry, and angry with Bernard Atha, the Chair of the company's Board of Directors since 1976. He is an amazing man with a strong political heart, a very clever politician in that he has survived New Labour – still old Labour – and was mayor of Leeds. There are famous pictures all through Leeds City Council of mayors with their Mayoresses, and there is Bernard with Nelson Mandela, how good is that? The company had that forced upon them, they hadn't paid their income tax, which is great, but not very sensible within a capitalist reality. That was the way Bernard dealt with the Inland Revenue and the Arts Council, he forced the company into a hierarchy so we had our first artistic director. It is really interesting reading John McGrath's writing now about how he headed up a left-wing company and was uncomfortable in the dictatorial role he had to take on as writer and director, and that the work suffered sometimes major bust-ups. That is the problem with the left, we are so pious. Possibly, in our understanding of how we run ourselves, we shoot ourselves in the foot.*

I am most excited about the Occupy movement and the activist movement since Reclaim the Streets, because consensus is now the way things work, it is painfully slow but it does mean that you can have a flat structure. We try to operate like that now within Red Ladder, but it is just the two of us … so a flat structure of two. There is just myself and Chris Lloyd, a producer, who came on board as general manager. Very quickly I realised we didn't want a general manager, but wanted someone with more of a producer's head. Consequently he has been the one who has brought in Jane Verity, who is our freelance press officer, and you saw the coverage we got for Big Society!, *which was remarkable, bloody terrifying but remarkable. That is the kind of strategy a left-wing company has to be part of, they can't just sit back and say we don't want to be part of this system, we are in it, we can chip away at it from the inside.*

Gardner: *It's very striking how much of the same political rhetoric surrounding funding for the arts with which Red Ladder was forced to engage in the 1980s is alive again today for the company. It's also remarkable how newly topical the campaigning pieces about NHS reform such as* Bring Out Your Dead *(1983) and* Safe With Us *(1985) have become. Was the taste for this kind of public politics lost in the company's forced transformation from a collective to a hierarchy?*

Dixon: *The last piece of work when we stuck our heads well and truly above the parapet was* Ugly *(2010), and again some people hated it and some people loved it. And I mean hated it to the extent that they would write me an A4 length email, but that is what theatre is about for me, about provoking conversation. I am proud of the fact that we are back where we were without it being a retrograde step. Some of the early work might have been a bit polemical and a bit embarrassing, I wasn't there so it is arrogant of me to say that. I think that is what I meant when I said let's put the red back in Red Ladder: let's go back to where we were, but for a twenty-first-century audience.*

It is like we have gone up a spiral staircase: down here were the working class Tories like John Major and Margaret Thatcher, and we go up the spiral staircase to the public school educated Blair, and then we go further up the spiral staircase and there we are with the Eton crowd and we are safe in their hands completely, as long as we work in Tesco for free. We haven't moved. I switched on [BBC's] Question Time the other night, as I wanted to see Owen Jones and I couldn't bear it. *The first question was about unemployment and the first person answering that question was Ken Clarke, talking in exactly the same way about unemployment as Thatcher did. So we have to address an audience that is in the same place.*

I think Rachel Feldberg [3] made the decision that actually maybe we were banging our drum on deaf ears, and to change our direction. We had been strongly feminist. I am the first male artistic director ever, actually, because all artistic directors had been women, and Chris Rawlins and all the rest of them were part of a collective. [Rachel's] decision was to go towards teenagers and hard-to-reach youth, so taking work into estates – not schools, not theatre in education. That has always been the misunderstanding: that we are a T.I.E. company because we work with teenagers. I think that was a very wise move at the time, particularly as Thatcher was gunning anything with the word 'red' in it; if she could defeat the miners my god she could trample all over us. To go slightly underground was good, but also this is where I guess the social issue foreground was what Wendy Harris picked up, and then Kully Thiarai started taking it into the Asian projects.

Gardner: *And so, partly as a strategy for survival, the company began to develop a different type of micro-politics, focused instead on gender, sexuality, cultural identity, but there was also an effort to create new international links?*

Dixon: *It was very hip in the 1990s, and schools were going on about multiculturalism and everybody was going on about saris, samosas and steel bands but they weren't actually talking about multiculturalism. I think Kully was probably reacting strongly to that and trying to investigate racism not just cure it. There was a bit of work in Canada. When I first arrived I had already made a connection with the West Bank in Palestine with a company called Al Harah (which means 'neighbourhood'), linked to the Freedom Theatre in Janine – but not linked, because it is not possible to travel from Beit Jala to Janine in one day because of the checkpoints. I was working with an artist called Sammy Metwasi, for whom we managed to get the Arts Council funding to come over for a year [4]. He is a very good director, a very good performer and so we were working very hard to build something. My first three-year plan was to aim to go to Palestine in 2010 and then the Gaza thing happened and the funding disappeared. The only people who would have funded it were Jordanian Arabs, and apparently the British Council said it was just too politically hot.*

This was less about [political] internationalism and more about educating our home audiences about the truth about Palestine. This was a difficult one in Leeds given its population, and Bernard pointed that out to me very early on in discussions but agreed that work had to be done. We abandoned it in the end, I'm afraid. I also naively tried to pull a political fast one by introducing the company to Julia Pascal, who is a Jewish writer but very pro-Palestine, and they said we can't work with a Jewish person. The Arabs would not fund anything. I said: 'you are not in Palestine, you are in Britain, can we do this as there is no way that this dispute is going to end unless we try to bring people to the table?'

Gardner: *Alongside this international outlook has been the company's commitment to Leeds and the region, where it has been based almost since its beginning. Has there ever been a temptation to move the company elsewhere, or are the roots here now too deep-reaching?*

Dixon: *Actually we haven't been doing so much work in Leeds. We'll make it here, but then get in the van and tour it somewhere else. That was something I recognised when I got here in 2006: there wasn't a Leeds presence. It was the first night that I got here. I was helping the company do a get out. I arrived in production week of* Worlds Apart, *which was a very interesting experience as Wendy had already left and a visiting director was working with the writer Mick Martin and all of the actors. So I arrived in production week and the situation was difficult. As I was helping them do the get-out outside the Carriageworks, a very drunk man came up to me and said, 'Fuckin 'ell Red Ladder, you're still going!' And I just thought: brilliant, the local people really know who we are. He didn't actually, he just happened to be from Wortley and lived across the road from the van ...*

So, I thought, since Asian Theatre School is leaving, we have to replace it with a training company that is Leeds based. We can't put £80,000 into it, but we will do something that is low key but does actually train people. So that's where we started out. Being true to making theatre for young people, the first Red Grit project was a selection of 10- to 19-year olds who then devised a piece of work with the promise that one of them would be given a job and that we would tour that piece of work. What a risk that was. That was in 2007. So from 2006 onwards we decided that we have to engage with Leeds somehow, so we thought: let's give someone a job. The piece of work they devised was so abstract and so absurd and teenagers loved it, but theatre buildings hated it. School parties came and loved it, teachers didn't. It really was absurd. It was about being trapped in a subconscious world. David Toole was in it, who is now in DV8 Physical Theatre and is a remarkable mover, and Stephen Mosley who has gone on to work professionally. I am really proud of that. We have actually produced a professional artist out of Red Grit, haven't done it since because I have been scared of that risk. It's funny about risk, how risky can you be? You are a business whether you like it or not and if you screw up the company will go down and I feel that is what happened to 7:84 England. 7:84 Scotland, on the legacy of The Cheviot, the Stage, and the Black Black Oil, *ran and ran and ran. But 7:84 England screwed up a few times, made some poor shows. That takes us right back to this present argument, that Mark Ravenhill is saying we have a right to make work that doesn't attract audiences. Why have we got that right? I am not sure if we have. It is arrogant. Howard Barker says the same thing. I am uncomfortable with that.*

Gardner: *Have the recent funding decisions, and particularly the loss of a significant source of income for Red Ladder, affected this attitude to taking such risks when it comes to programming work? How does the recent return to larger-scale theatre and musical pieces such as* Big Society! *fit into the picture here?*

Dixon: *Our programme for the next few years is busier than ever. I don't want to play into the Tories' hands by saying that maybe artists do work harder if they have less money. It's that classic thing: if you want the rich to work harder you pay them more, if you want the poor to work harder you pay them less. But to a certain extent* Big Society! *didn't come out of that, it is part of a series of three. In 2008, when I think the work finally had my stamp on it, we had* Where's Vietnam *that Alice Nutter wrote for us for our 40th anniversary. It sold out for four nights in West Yorkshire Playhouse, then* Forgotten Things *written by Emma Adams, about teenage suicide but also about Alzheimers. After that Boff Whalley (of Chumbawamba) said that he was writing a play called* Armley – The Musical *for the West Leeds Festival, with two days to rehearse it for two performances on Sunday afternoon outdoors. So Boff wrote the play and it was an incredible powerful comedy about the asbestos disaster in Armley. There was a factory in Armley that pumped out asbestos like snow into the atmosphere and kids were making snow balls out of the stuff and a lot of people got cancer and died. A woman whose husband died in that factory took them to court and of course it turned out they were owned by an American corporation who could afford to just go 'Fuck you'. So it was a classic working class struggle. So Boff wrote a comedy, can you imagine! A comedy about that! It was a musical and it had songs.*

    We played it outdoors at Armley Mills to an audience of Armley people and I was singing a song called 'Snow in July' which was funny but also exactly about the incident. Everyone was laughing and I was playing up to the gags and I look down and there was this front row of elderly local people, stony faced with tears in their eyes. Afterwards they all came up to us and thanked us for telling their story. Some of them had never been to see the theatre in their lives. Boff and I thought in the pub that we had something. Alex Chisholm from the West Yorkshire Playhouse was there and she shouted out 'He's behind you!' and she was not working class at all. So me and Boff thought, what about an adult pantomime? When the adults get the chance to shout out and it's light entertainment, not very deep. So he wrote a play called Riot, Rebellion and Bloody Insurrection. *It was incredibly light and the bourgeois didn't like it. They thought it was trivial, which it wasn't. It encouraged that raucous, low, common, popular and base behaviours. Which is just what we want in the theatre, it is too polite. The Arts Council didn't like it, they kind of sniffed at it. An improvement of that was* Sex & Docks & Rock n Roll, *which was a rock 'n' roll play about a real dispute in Liverpool about a dock strike where the trade union, the National Union of Seamen (N.U.S.), also John Prescott's union. There is a long history between John Prescott and Chumbawamba since the glass of water incident. The baddie in* Riot & Rebellion… *was clearly John Prescott, the dispute in 'Sex & Docks…' was where the N.U.S. let down the workers. What happened in the dispute was that the workers went on strike while on board ship, which is a hanging offence even now because it is mutiny. The N.U.S. wouldn't support them, so they set up their own union called the National Seamen's Reform Movement (S.R.M.) which was much more anarchist and much more left-wing. And we played that in Liverpool, sold out, and there were members of the S.R.M. who remembered it. It was rock 'n' roll. Songs were great and we are going to do it again at the City Varieties next January. Boff wrote that from America so he never actually saw it until the last night. And then we wondered what would be next. We'd done a pantomime, a rock 'n' roll left-wing trade-union-attacking pantomime.*

Gardner: *It seems clear that the germ of the idea for* Big Society! *was in this newly revived commitment to politically engaged popular theatre forms, and with it the attempt by the company to appeal to new types of audiences. The decision to explore historical music hall conventions and traditions seems to follow logically from this.*

Dixon: *Peter Sandeman from Leeds City Varieties [music hall] invited us to perform there when it was refurbished, and we started thinking about making a music hall piece. Boff had been reading about the music hall, the* real *music hall. The Northern and Scottish music hall was really dirty, really lewd, but also highly political and anti-establishment, and the police were called night after night after night to Northern music halls because of the riots that would start outside. That's what we want to do, and Boff said we need a [star] name because we couldn't do two weeks at the City Varieties and expect to fill it without one. So we approached Phil Jupitus because we had a sense that possibly he had the right politics and he totally did and the rest is history. And interestingly, again the bourgeois was saying these things about it. I say the bourgeois, but I know the Arts Council assessor is a very middle-class man. Michael Billington said 'it's not very savage, is it?' It wasn't ever meant to be savage. It was meant to be a good night out and people emailed me and said that although they agreed with the reviews at first that it wasn't very political up front, in the light of two days later or three days later it seemed really political and really submissive.*

   Particularly that old musical song 'The Same the Whole World Over' – taking it and modernising it so it's about stealing a bottle of water, you know post-riots, was very contemporary. If you go down the route of being on the nose, which we talked about, we were going to black up the piano player and make the statement about, the historical politics as well as today's politics, but then we just thought that would be too on the nose, too left-wing – too Mark Thomas, bless him, too Billy Brag. All the Tories in the audience would just walk out, but I had Tories emailing me saying they loved it. I don't believe in party politics at all and Red

Ladder actually has never really been biased towards party politics. We never have. We're not flag wavers. We're pure anarchists and we actually don't believe that party politics work. So the piece had to be political but apolitical as well.

The piece toyed with those pantomime traditions that bourgeois people aren't comfortable with because they're too low – popular and base. It's what working class people go and see once a year, pantomime. They don't go to the theatre other than pantomime. We were trying to use those devices and those worlds, subvert them and modernise them for adults. The Telegraph *said it was 'brainless', which is hilarious, but you know the* Financial Times *liked it…*

Gardner: *There's a definite sense there of a return to Red Ladder's roots in highly theatrical, often musically driven political work, going back to the early days as the Agitprop Street Players, and also a recognition of the pendulum swing of political realities in the country that Red Ladder has experienced directly.*

Dixon: *Billington said that connecting 1912 to 2012 was ridiculous, but we wondered why. The argument was that there was manufacturing industry then, and plenty of jobs. But there was a police force that would still beat the shit out of you. There was an Edwardian cabinet, all Eton-educated and very wealthy. You know, it's exactly the same as 2012. It's not about jobs, because jobs aren't the answer, jobs are wage slavery as we Marxists know. I think the last few shows, those Chumbawamba shows, really are a hark back to 1969, 1974. Kath McCreery came and saw the show, she is one of the very first members of Red Ladder. She said it's absolutely what we should be doing and yes it harks back to her work but it doesn't at the same time. The banner, by the way the escapologists held up during the show – 'Workers will never be free while women are in chains' was from* Strike While the Iron is Hot, *and Kath was delighted that we were using it.*

She also said it doesn't always have to be musical and sing-along, and actually the next piece of work we're making is called The Thing about Psychopaths, *which Ben Tagoe is writing. He is a local writer from Wakefield, just been on the BBC Writers Academy. Kath was saying that the work right at the beginning was pure activism. To give one example: they found out that some workers had occupied a factory that made aeroplane parts for civil aviation. The management had got a very lucrative deal to build parts for war planes that were going to be sold to a real dubious dictator, in somewhere like Indonesia. Where they all, most likely, were going to be used against civilians, so the workers occupied the factory and refused to make those parts. The dispute was about a month in when they contacted Red Ladder through the unions. They agreed to support the workers, but only if they invited the management in. Red Ladder did a play about the dispute and about where the planes were going to go. Then they had a post-show discussion, as all Red Ladder used to have. The post-show led to a series of discussions that actually ended the dispute and they cancelled the order. Amazing. That is where we want to go back to. Now workers aren't occupying factories like they did in the 1970s, but students are occupying UCL. I am really excited that the radicalisation of young people is really strong and we should capitalise on it. You know it's all about being organised. That early work is something that I'm really interested in recreating.*

Gardner: *Would you ever be tempted to shift from national touring to a more permanent base, for example on the model of the Tricycle Theatre with its similar commitment to political dialogue with its audience? As a strategy for expanding and securing the company's future?*

Dixon: *No, we still want to be a national touring company. The Arts Council has only left us enough money to tour one show per year. We can't do that. Venues only have a certain amount of space within their program for touring material. So we've got to have at least two shows a year to put out, otherwise we'll disappear again. Although I want to continue to play non-theatre venues like working men's clubs, I don't want to do that exclusively. That's what Red Ladder did before me. We exclusively played youth clubs. So you disappear from the theatre map and you can't do that. If you are going to be taken seriously by the theatre industry you've got to work also in theatres. So we're going to do both, and have a strong regional presence. Community plays are an important part of it. We want to do three over the next few summers. Trevor Griffiths has written an amazing piece of work called* March Time, *which is a film screenplay that he and I are going to adapt for the stage. It's set in 1927, with the hunger marches set off after the General Strike. As they march down though the country to parliament, you go through the decades, from the 1940s to the 1980s, and they get to Parliament Hill and there are 700 activists from time who've walked through. So Walt Taylor, the Luddites, everybody is there. We could make a piece to work in a vast space like a warehouse or the Round House, and the audience could become the march at the end of it. So that piece of work is vast. We haven't got any funding for it. I don't know how we're going to pay for it, but I'm desperate to do it.*

Gardner: *Apart from that, what else might the future hold for Red Ladder as it evolves once again in response to changing fortunes?*

Dixon: *David Peace (who wrote* Damned United, Red Ridings) *is writing a book at the moment about Bill Shankly, and he's going to work with us to turn the final section of that book into a play called* Red or Dead. *And the play isn't going to be about a football manager. It going to be about what happens to you when you are a socialist, but you become lionised and then you retire, which you think is the peak of your career. When you have nothing else to do, you've been tossed aside and you don't know what to do with your life…*

Promised Land *is sports book of the year for 2011. It's quite ironic because I said I'd never do anything for the Olympics. I used to be an athlete, a dead serious runner, but I don't like Lord Coe, I hate him with a passion. I was running on the track in Sheffield in 1980, 1979–80 before the Olympics and Peter Coe, Lord Coe's coach came on and asked us to get off the track, because Seb wanted to train.* Promised Land *is about the Jewish experience of being a Leeds United supporter. Anthony Clavane's book,* Promised Land, *is semi-autobiographical, but he and Nick Stimson have attempted to turn it into a piece of music theatre. Well theatre with music. Boff's going to write us a serious piece of work about Tom Maguire, who was a socialist in Leeds in 1890 who led a gas strike. Avaes Mohammad is writing three plays. He's a northern Muslim writer but he now lives in Turnpike Lane and he's researching extremism with Thornaby mosque. So he's writing us a play about 9/11 and 7/7 and then the present day. Alice Nutter still wants to write for us but we don't know what yet. We're researching a play about working class suffragettes who took all the brunt of it all. It was the working class suffragettes, not the Emily Pankhursts, who got force fed and tortured, you know. So there's a play there somewhere that we're investigating.*

Where we're placed is interesting. Near Yorkshire Dance, right in the posh part of town. Cultural quarter, apparently, BBC, the music college and the rest of it. Across the road is the bus station, and the bus station in every city is a real sort of magnet for social misfits isn't it? You've got that on one side of the road, and on the other is a new art gallery. I went in there and they had photographs, massive black and white photographs by some famous photographer and this really London woman came up to me and gave me the price list, although I just wanted to look at the pictures. The top price was six grand and I thought: this is so ironic that there, right next door to me – Mr Angry Red – is this pretentious bloody London art gallery, opposite the bus station which is full of smack heads.

Conclusion

Red Ladder might be accused of complacency or even a sense of entitlement to the public support that it had enjoyed for almost four decades, but that would be to underestimate the company's ability to reinvent itself periodically in the face of such challenges. Despite needing to consolidate its operations, after a period of re-adjustment it returned to the theatrical ambition and risk-taking of its earlier years with *Big Society!* and a revival of Anthony Clavane's and Nick Stimson's celebration of football culture *Promised Land* (as part of the Olympic celebrations in 2012), both musicals with large casts and notably celebratory, festive moods as well as a wryly ironic view of the contemporary political situation that is distinctly Red Ladder's. Dixon's plans for the coming year show no less ambition either, as he continues Red Ladder's long-standing tradition of commissioning new works from young as well as established playwrights (including Trevor Griffiths). Indeed, there seems little chance that 'Mr Angry Red' will be quietened by Red Ladder's recent setbacks, and the theatrical culture of the region will only be enriched as a result.

Acknowledgements

Thanks to Alex Monk and Sam Berrill for assistance in preparing the original transcript of the Rod Dixon interview.

References

Billington, M., 2012. '*Big Society!* Review', *The Guardian*, 22 January.

Craig, S., 1980. *Dreams and Deconstructions: Alternative Theatre in Britain*. Derbyshire: Amber Lane.

Davies, A., 1987. *Other Theatres: The Development of Alternative and Experimental Theatre in Britain*. London: Macmillan Education.

Itzin, C., 1980. *Stages in the Revolution: Political Theatre in Britain Since 1968*. London: Methuen.

McGrath, J., 1981. *A Good Night Out: Popular Theatre – Audience, Class and Form*. London: Methuen.

———, 2002. *Naked Thoughts That Roam Around: Reflections on Theatre 1958–2001*. London: Nick Hern Books.

Pal, S., 2008. *Look Back at Anger: Agit Prop Theatre in Britain*. Berlin: VDM Verlag.

Whalley, B., 2012. *Big Society! A Music Hall Comedy*, programme notes.

Notes

1   Cartoon Archetypal Slogan Theatre, an agit-prop company founded in 1967.
2   McGrath, J., 2002. *Naked Thoughts That Roam Around: Reflections on Theatre 1958–2001*. London: Nick Hern Books.
3   Red Ladder's first artistic director, appointed by the company's Board of Directors in 1985.
4   Sammy Metwasi was with Red Ladder as Artist in residence from June to August 2007.

Chapter 7

Intercultural to Cross-Cultural Theatre: Tara Arts and the Development of British Asian Theatre

Victor Ukaegbu

Introduction

Tara Arts is Britain's longest-running Asian theatre company. The company is an example of how specific sociopolitical incidents help to define the artistic philosophies of small-scale theatres and their overall impacts on the British theatre landscape. Jatinder Verma founded Tara Arts as a contribution to the upsurge in Asian youth movements and their vociferous outcry following the racist killing of 17-year old Sikh teenager and aircraft engineering student, Gurdeep Singh Chaggar on July 4th 1976. According to the company, its history of 'making cross-cultural theatre began on 25th August 1977, with Nobel Prize-winning author Rabindranath Tagore's anti-war play, *Sacrifice*' (Tara Arts, 'History': online). The choice of play was more than a cultural riposte to the racial tensions of the period:

> [the] production marked both a response to Gurdeep Singh Chaggar's death and a critique of injustices within Asian communities. Tara Arts' mission was clear: to make imaginative connections across cultures, through presentations of classics and new theatre work.
>
> (Tara Arts, 'History': online)

From the very beginning the company focused on Asian stories not because they were merely responding to what Kobena Mercer refers to as the 'burden of representation' (1994: 91) or to the then 'obsession with positive/negative image debate as part of a stereotyping theory' (McMillan 2006: 54). Tara is interested, as Verma points out, in 'different ways of looking at norms, at familiar stories' (cited in Schlote 2006: 314). The company goes beyond simply resisting misrepresentations and tackling *us-them* polarisations but more crucially, to interrogate collective Asian historical experiences and the contradictions surrounding multiculturalism in Britain. The cross-cultural dialogue espoused in the company's first production soon became an ideological and artistic pivot for countering reductionism, homogenisation and stereotyping. Today Tara is not only

> positioned between East and West, ... [it] has pioneered cross-cultural theatre for over three decades, producing global theatre for local audiences ... tours vibrant adaptations of European and Asian classics and new work, ... and develops emerging artists and new audiences.
>
> (The Big Give: online)

Tara's development, aesthetically and as a company and business, is linked to a combination of significant sociopolitical factors and personal decisions. Among the latter is the ideological rejection of narrow nationalism in the company's definition of Asian race and cultural identities as characterised 'not by essence or purity, but recognition of a necessary heterogeneity and diversity: by a conception of "identity" that lives with and through as process, the idea of difference, of hybridity' (Hall 1993: 401). This ideological stance, linked with political events such as rising cultural nationalisms in black and Asian groups in Britain at the time, led the company towards a transnationalism that transcends the limitations of interculturalism and which, crucially recognises the diversity of cultural and historical experiences that make up black British theatres (McMillan 2006). Tara Arts, like Talawa and Tamasha theatres (founded in 1986 and 1989, respectively) is arguably the theatrical beacon for the second generations of black (African and Caribbean) and Asian immigrants that reject tags of second-class citizens and the other but claim and assert their British citizenship in various politicised actions from fashion statements to disrupting spatial relations and cultural homogeneity from the late 1970s (cf. McMillan 2006). Tara Arts' theatre recognises and celebrates the diversities in South-East Asian communities as an essential component of a cross-cultural dialogue with other sections of British society and in the words of Hingorani (2010) for mapping a 'Binglish' diaspora that has helped shape British Asian social identities.

A Prodigious Performance Repertory

In over four decades of its existence, Tara has built up a sizable repertory of nearly one hundred performances following the aesthetic principles established with the first production of Tagore's *Sacrifice*. According to Hingorani (2010), the company's early plays (*circa* 1977–84) can be divided into three distinct thematic and contextual categories designed

(i) to recover histories of the subcontinent from a subaltern perspective and make connections between those colonial histories and the contemporary British site; *Inkalaab 1919* (1980), *Yes Memsahib* (1979)
(ii) to perform the hidden histories of Asians in Britain long before post-war immigration; *Lion's Raj* (1982)
(iii) to look at the contemporary 'second generation' British Asian experience in Britain; *Diwaali* (1977), *Fuse* (1978) and *Chilli in Your Eyes* (1984)

(Hingorani 2010: 19–20)

Thematically, these early plays signalled the diverse Asian historical, mythic and cultural topographies and tropes that would define Tara Arts. For example, in *Sacrifice* (Bengali) the priest Raghupati perceives the king's banning of blood sacrifices as a threat to his power and cultural tradition. He instructs his daughter Jaising to kill the king but trapped between duty and loyalty to her father and her personal conviction in the king's command, Jaising commits suicide. *Inkalaab* (Punjabi, India) comes from different cultural and historical strains. Its metaphoric deconstruction of racism against British Asians is framed by the deaths of the family of a demobilised soldier from the 8th Punjab Regiment killed by British soldiers in a demonstration against the Raj administration. The company's practice of adapting western classics such as Shakespeare's *The Tempest* (1993), which was adapted for children using only three performers and Japanese Bunraku puppets, *Troilus and Cressida* (1993), *Cyrano* (1995) and *A Midsummer Night's Dream* (1997) continued for most of the 1990s and early 2000s. These 'classics' were interspersed with such original pieces as *Crazy Horse* (1997), *The Exodus* (1998), *Genesis* (1999), *Genesis Stories* (2000), *Revelations* (2000) and *Adventures of Dum* (2000). *A Taste of Mangoes* (2003), a play about Anglo-Indian relations, was based on a nineteenth-century painting by an unknown Indian artist depicting the visit of Sir David Ochterlony, the first representative of the East Indian Company to the court of Mughal Emperor Shah Alam. The emphases in these plays, on social geographies and cross-cultural encounters is more than an overarching metaphor of the consequences, logicality and inevitability of British/Asian relations in India subcontinent and in Britain. These plays, in the words of Buonanno, Sams and Schlotte, 'highlight the dialectic between the local and the global' as well as 'producing a revisionist glocal historiography for British audiences and alternative pretext for the depictions of modern diasporic conditions' (2011: p. 3; and cf. 1–3).

Crazy Horse was a co-production between Tara and Paines Plough about a filial relationship between son and father. In the play Jas and his father Jutla are emotionally adrift following the death in childbirth of their mother and wife 22 years ago. They are jolted into the present by the discovery of a dead body in a Porsche sent to their garage in the dead of night for repairs. *The Exodus* dramatises the flight of East Africa Asians to Britain and the cultural diversities among the many strands of British Asian immigration. Although the western adaptations attracted criticisms about the quality of Tara's productions (Hingorani 2010) and questions about abandoning its Asian constituency, the company has never ignored its cultural base. It continues a tradition of collaborations with artists from various race and artistic backgrounds, maintains a broad artistic base, goes on international tours and makes works for schools and youth audiences. The emphasis on collaborations has seen the company work with directors such as Muraly Menon (*Marriage of Convenience*, 1991), Phillipe Cherbonnier (*Heer and Romeo*, 1992), Arti Prashar (*The Tempest*, 1993), and Mukul Ahmed (*People's Romeo*, 2010), designer Magdalen Rubalcava and musician V. Chandran (*Tartuffe*, 1990), and hundreds of performers including Ayub Din Khan, Vincent Ebrahim, Yogesh Bhatt, Yasmin Sidwha, Shelley King, Cuckoo Parameswaran, Sanjeev Bhasker, Shehnaz Khan, Kumiko Mendl and Yasmin Alibhai Brown. The sheer numbers of collaborations and the diverse backgrounds of collaborators demonstrate the extents Tara has gone to reinforce a cross-cultural credential that is occasionally overshadowed whenever critics and Jatinder Verma himself read specific performances narrowly for their intercultural and multicultural features. These collaborations have contributed in no small measure to enriching the work undertaken by small- and mid-scale British theatre companies and transforming people's understanding of them.

Crucially, Tara's adaptations of European classics have 'successfully carried' the company 'from the margins of British theatre to the centre' (Hingorani 2010: 69). The company have received some criticism for such work; for example, Martin Esslin questions whether the 'transposition of a classical text into a new mileau brought new insights' (Hingorani 2010: 69) to such texts. While there may be some justification for such criticisms, these are outweighed by the ability of such productions to speak across cultural divisions and by the growing recognition of Tara's aesthetic contributions to British theatre and performance discourse and praxis in general. Secondly, the strategy of combining familiar cultural ideas ensures that Tara's work speaks to Diaspora Asian communities and their host societies simultaneously. Although the company returned to Asian pieces in response to criticisms about abandoning its cultural roots (Hingorani 2010) the adaptations and collaborations with artists from many backgrounds have continued to characterise the company's work to date. Its 2012 production *Home: scape* is definitive of this approach. The piece is a physical, online multimedia performance in which artists from Britain, Hungary, the Netherlands and the Czech Republic share stories of home from the perspectives of those living in cosmopolitan London, Prague and Budapest.

Despite continuing the practice of adapting western classics the company's focus on Asian stories has continued throughout the 2000s. Many of the productions – such as *Slavery* (2006) and *Motherland* (2007) – implicate specific South-East Asian social norms in the problems and challenges experienced by its diaspora communities. In *Slavery* (2006) the ancient practice of slavery is used as a metaphor to remind and warn of the trans-historical connections between past, present and future problems experienced by diaspora Asians. In *Motherland* (2007) Tara collaborated with Sampad South Asian Arts to fuse dance, music and poetry into a compelling story of conflict, love and revenge in a world shaped by slavery and forced migrations. The soul-searching story, like *Slavery* before it, called for serious examination of the power old traditional social conventions hold over the present. In *The Black Album* (2009), a co-production with the National Theatre, Asian youngster Shahid leaves the restrictions of home in Kent for university in North London. There he confronts the disturbing, uneasy personal battle of balancing his social liberalism against the religious fundamentalism of his friends opposed to the sensual delights of a hedonistic relationship he began with his western lecturer. Shahid battles through questions of individual and group identity and freedom in an attempt to reconcile his own personal contradictions. *The Black Album* is Hanif Kureishi's witty stage adaptation of his 1995 novel of the same title. The play is a social commentary on 1980s Britain: it tries to make sense of many subjects that confront Britain and British Asians from religious and political radicalism to rock music, racial violence, tensions between cultural identity and multiculturalism, sociocultural disjunctions and dysfunctions, the stultifying effects of orthodoxy, and, on the individual level, the fatwa against Salman Rushdie.

Aesthetic Topography

The choice of *Sacrifice* was significant for many reasons in helping to define what would be Tara's enduring artistic and ideological philosophies. Rabindranath Tagore's text demonstrates the playwright's cross-cultural credentials, his opposition to armed conflict and the capacity of great literature to transcend narrow nationalisms. The cross-cultural aesthetic suggested in the text's anti-war theme and the racial tensions in 1970s Britain helped ground Tara Arts' artistic vision. However, it was Jatinder Verma's reading of Tagore's works as transnational, cross-cultural dialogues determinedly speaking across cultural and geographic boundaries that philosophically and ideologically drove the company towards becoming a small- to mid-scale theatre. The emphasis on Asian stories and voices led to a production methodology characterised by the use of Asian and later mixed casts, the integration of Asian dance, music and costumes. This 'vision' was something that Verma began publically to elaborate on and articulate vigorously by the 2000s:

> This dialogue between past and present, between ethnicity and nationhood, between a sense of belonging and of alienation, has been central to Tara's work over the past 30 years. In our productions of Indian, French, Greek, Russian, English and contemporary Asian plays, we have sought dialogue by claiming ownership of the world's stories.
>
> Sometimes, this ownership proves contentious. As our production of *The Tempest* transfers to London's West End, I recall how … an outraged academic asked why my company was producing Shakespeare at all – and if we were, why could we not 'do it straight'? Another wondered whether we were going to 'Bollywood-ise' it, complete with cod-Indian accents… The story of Prospero and his slave Caliban is a classic story of Them and Us, a prophetic story about colonialism. [...] One of the most moving lines comes when Prospero acknowledges Caliban as 'the thing of darkness I acknowledge mine own'.
>
> (*The Guardian*, 10 January 2008)

Tara Arts started as an intercultural (see Notes 1 and 3) outfit but is now arguably more cross-cultural than anything else. Verma himself described the company's founding performances as intercultural; he began to use the term cross-cultural in the early 1990s to explain Tara's celebration of British Asian cultural pluralism and diversity. Recognising local and regional distinctiveness is not the peculiarity of any one of these closely related forms; postcolonial, intercultural, multicultural, intracultural (Bharucha 2000), transcultural and cross-cultural performances. It is an essential ingredient of all. Despite their normative and performative peculiarities all stated forms are designed ultimately as 'encounters between and across specific communities and regions within the nation-state' (Lo and Gilbert 2002: 38). Interestingly, Verma (1996) had much earlier employed the same terms, used later in 2002 by Lo and Gilbert for intercultural and transcultural theatres, to describe cross-cultural performances as presentations based 'upon the encounters between different cultural sensibilities' and designed 'invariably to re-imagine the world, with the conventions of the English or European stage largely ignored, or seriously questioned' (1996: 194). Verma uses 'intercultural', 'multicultural' and 'transcultural' to describe Tara's work in his early writings, his preference from the mid-1990s for the overarching term 'cross-cultural' is arguably an attempt to avoid the very tendency (in intercultural, multicultural and transcultural theatres) to marginalise that Tara set out to contest from its founding (see Notes 1, 2 and 4).

The cross-cultural sentiment expressed by Verma depicts Tara's aesthetic journey from intercultural theatre and why the company's performances defy neat categorisation. Aesthetically Tara's work is simultaneously multicultural, postcolonial (syncretic and non-syncretic) and intercultural (transcultural, intracultural, extracultural). As a 'hybrid derived from an intentional encounter between cultures and performing traditions' (Lo and Gilbert 2002: 36), Tara is also multicultural in its use of materials from different cultures, especially in deploying:

> racially mixed cast[s] that do not actively draw attention to cultural differences among performers or to the tensions between the text and the production content. One of the most common strategies [...] is to use [...] 'blind casting' – usually in productions of canonical plays staged for a mainstream audience – to signal commitment to cultural pluralism.
>
> (Lo and Gilbert 2002: 33)

Although overwhelmingly Asian externally, the company's storytelling format reveals a sophisticated combination of Asian and non-Asian performance conventions that is explicitly aimed at a very mixed audience. This aesthetic topography has come to reflect what Steve Doughty and Mathew Bayley describe as a 'global masala' (cited in Lucas 2007: 241); that is, a performance that addresses the cultural and social specificities of the various sub-sections of a mixed British South Asian audience.

Tara performances 'promote cultural diversity, access to cultural expression, and participation in the symbolic space of the national narrative' (Lo and Gilbert 2002: 34) and 'the management of cultural/ethnic difference' (ibid.: 36) but they do more and go much further. They 'explore and critique alternative forms of citizenship and identity across and beyond national boundaries' (ibid.: 36) and emphasise the heterogeneity of British Asian communities. Their themes and mixed casts de-stabilise race and cultural borders and insularism, these features transcend and de-stabilise the partisanship of 'migrant theatre'. The use of 'a combination of ethno-specific languages to denote cultural in-between-ness' and the 'exploration of cultural hybridity reflective in aesthetic form as well as narrative content' (ibid.: 34) birthed 'Binglish', the company's most enduring, often cited aesthetic legacy. The aesthetic syncretism resulting from the combination of Asian and western conventions and the company's broad Asian identity in dance, music, movement, characters, costumes and storyline evolved through what Stuart Hall describes as 'complex historical process of appropriation, compromise, subversion, masking, invention and revival' (1993: 401).

The appropriation of material from diverse cultures, at aesthetic and ideological levels, builds bridges across cultures and makes the company's work accessible to a much wider audience. Tara's aesthetic and ideological journey from intercultural to cross-cultural theatre confirms, in my view, the extent to which art practices can be used to achieve, in the words of Helen Davis, 'democratic socialism through a solidarity that unites different groups and individuals while valuing diversity' (Davis 2004: 2).

Performance Language and Dramaturgy

Starting with what Amkpa (2004) describes as postcolonial desire for audibility and visibility, Tara has moved from postcolonial and intercultural performances to multicultural and cross-cultural theatre with performances such as its 1989 *Ala Afsur/The Government Inspector* and 1990 *Tartuffe* being distinctively transcultural (cf. Buonanno et al. 2011). Since Rabindranath Tagore's postcolonially framed *Sacrifice* (first published in 1917) and other pieces staged for their social and historical relevance, the company has moved 'away from a text-based realism towards a performance methodology in which 'movement and music [...] are not ancillary to the spoken word but form an integral part of the "text" of performance' (Verma cited in Hingorani 2010: 45–46).

The linguistic thread of this aesthetic development led in 1984 to the creation and use of 'Binglish' and 'Binglishing', the former, a theatrical language and philosophy that integrates Western European conventions and much older classical Asian theatre writings such as the Indian folk forms *Natyasastra* and *Bhavai, circa* 200 BC (Hingorani 2010). Binglish is rooted, or in Verma's own words 'routed', in a postcolonial hybridity and syncretic construct that exemplifies thematically and contextually what the company is about. Buonanno et al. (2011) provide very succinct and effective definitions for 'Binglish' and 'Binglishing' and how they are used in this chapter:

> Verma has described as '"Binglishing" the stage', that is, creating a theatre tradition that is black and English, exploring a distinct theatre practice that 'puts together fragments of diverse cultures', places cultural hybridity at the centre of the stage, and 'seems to point Asian theatre in two directions at once: towards the memory of ancestral lands in India and Pakistan and towards the reflection and refraction of contemporary England'
>
> (2011: 3)

As a distinctive aesthetic language and production model, Binglish and Binglishing allow Tara Arts to celebrate the broad, pluralistic, multicultural and multilingual South Asian sociocultural landscape within a continuously evolving British theatre topology.

Arguably Binglish and Binglishing started as a response to interculturalism or what Phil Wood, Charles Landry and Jude Bloomfield (2006) would describe as 'seeing the world through an intercultural lens' (p. 21). It soon became synonymous with the rejection of 'a crude understanding of ethnic difference', especially one that overlooked 'the internal diversity of such communities limited by a perspective that recognises the views of the white population as the cultural norm and the views of ethnic minorities (or in some places ethnic majorities) as inevitably different or aberrant' (Wood et al. 2006: 22). Its success as a performative vocabulary has become part of South East Asian cultural street language. Verma contends that alongside other cultural practices and languages from Tamil, Nigeria, Somalia and Ghana, Binglish has 'form[ed] part of the linguistic map of Britain' and as such 'cannot be expected to be absent from modern British theatre' (Verma 1996: 198). Binglish has not only created a template for accommodating 'a range of Asian languages, accents and dialects alongside English' but has also 'had the further function of performing the plurality of the signifier "Asian"' (Hingorani 2010: 47). Furthermore, both have shown that 'the syncretic and hybridised nature of postcolonial experience refutes the privileged position of a standard code in the [English] language and any monocentric view of human experience' (Ashcroft et al. 1989: 41).

For South Asian audiences in particular, Binglish owes its success as a distinctive language to cultural and ideological factors. Although the dialogues spoken are in a mixture of South Asian languages and accents 'and not in the "correct" British English often erroneously assumed to be the only language worth staging – they understand it through literal, metaphorical, and political frames of reference which are specific to their own culture and experience' (Gilbert and Tompkins 1996: 169–170). Binglish has also been described by Verma himself as 'a theatrical language for modulating with the centre' (cited in Cook 1991: 6) and resisting marginalisation and othering. Functioning as an alternative local language for British diaspora South Asians, Binglish 'localises and attracts value away from a British "norm" eventually displacing the hegemonic centrality of the idea of "norm" itself' (Ashcroft et al. 1989: 37). The sociocultural and aesthetic disruptions proposed here by Verma have been a key feature of Tara's attack on 'monolithic perceptions' (ibid.: 37) of a British theatre language 'norm' and the artistic, as well as ideological underpinnings in the company's move towards cross-cultural theatre.

Among the features of Binglishing are the use of detailed, stylised bodily movements/ physicality, actors' voices, visual and imagistic spectacles, stylised costumes, elaborate non-naturalistic make-up, and emotions integrated with music and song. This syncretic aesthetic particularises and reflects without generalising the heterogeneity of South Asian British experiences. Hingorani (2010) lists other features of Binglish theatre as minimal props, open stage, continual on stage presence of all performers, absence of section breaks, direct address, invocatory preludes, a narrator, and a dramatic convention in which actors and audiences make no pretence about the event as theatrical encounter. Tara's Binglishing, syncretism, and celebration of cultural diversity, alongside their quest for transcultural dialogue is a

> rejection of the dominant convention of the modern English stage – the spoken word. Gesture became speech, as much as a phrase of music a sentence – or the passage of time.

It is in this sense that the word, in Tara's productions, took on the texture also of dance and music.

(Verma 1998: 129)

The results are not only the privileging of Asian stories and presenting materials through an Asian gaze; subtle dramaturgical shifts from a singular to multifocal gaze makes productions accessible to a wide multicultural audience. As Verma puts it:

I have a kind of vexed relationship between the centre and the margin... I'm also working with people who are on the margin. And so the dialogue is not, if you like, a configuration of outsiders who are commenting on the dominant. It's insiders who are looking at the dominant from another perspective... Now that's a different thing altogether, and I think that for me in a way the Schechners and the Brooks more overtly represent, if you want to put it that way, more of a kind of multicultural exercise rather than a cross – cultural one, because they are not actually engaged with the migrant perspective at all.

(Schlote 2006: 316–17)

The following interview was conducted specifically for this volume and further elucidates the distinctiveness of the Tara ethos and aesthetic.

The Interview

The Inspiration behind Tara Arts

Ukaegbu: *Jatinder, your entry into theatre is fully documented; have you and Tara moved aesthetically and ideologically from that uncomfortable and politically charged starting point? If not, why if so, how far have you and the company moved away from your founding principles?*

Verma: *We started Tara Arts in 1977 following the racist killing in 1976 in Southall of a young Indian boy, Gurdeep Singh Chaggar. This callous killing led me to a personal questioning of the self and the collective, to personal debates for meaning and search for space in British society. These led to our first production in 1977 and set the parameters for what Tara's artistic charter and ideological character would be; we have not changed from that but have grown with what we started with. Our first play was* Sacrifice, *written by the first Indian-born Nobel Prize winner for literature, Rabindranath Tagore – poet, playwright, philosopher, educationist and social activist who was awarded his Nobel Prize in 1913.*

  In the play the writer explored the idea of belief, an idea that refuses to die. The piece was adapted with the director choosing to infuse the adaptation with Indian black-speak, making the story a dialogue with the present, not necessarily with the past. We have been on the same dialogue ever since, using the same aesthetic imprints but growing and responding as the dialogue has charted new contours and routes.

Ukaegbu: *Since the founding of Tara Arts you have been involved, perhaps more than any other practitioner, in some of the most enduring aesthetic developments in small-scale British theatres. Drawing from your prodigious performance-making experiences, how would you describe the aesthetics of small-scale British theatres today?*

Verma: *Performance aesthetics are never fixed; they are always oscillating and responding to a number of sociocultural factors, some of them inside and others outside what you may call the parameters of theatre. Essentially, British theatre aesthetics are linked to a sense of nationalism; in other words, the aesthetics of small-scale theatres in Britain are invariably associated with a continuing dialogue between the fringe and the centre. Despite the astonishing changes we have seen in theatre-making in the last 40 years and more, there are still many challenges in the politics of funding and scale, diversification of content and modes of presentation. These challenges, like this dialogue, are still ongoing. The specifics of some small-scale theatres such as personnel, types and sizes of venues, and politics have changed in their search for new audiences or maintaining their patronages. Tara, on the other hand, has remained faithful to its founding principles whilst expanding its aesthetic brief and artistic constituencies.*

Ukaegbu: *Constancy and consistency, artistic, cultural or political, are not necessarily the norm or goal of theatre. To what would you ascribe Tara's enduring aesthetic and artistic legacies? Is it because you have remained at the helm throughout the company's existence?*

Verma: *Not necessarily, but for what you refer to as consistency or constant, I would say we have evolved logically within our artistic and aesthetic policies, working essentially towards a cross-cultural and transcultural framework that embraces theatrical ideas from several cultures whilst rejecting none. I'd like to think that whoever takes over from me would build on the legacy we already have, not because of me but from a shared sense of what Tara is about.*

Ukaegbu: *That's an interesting concept, let's pursue this* cross-cultural transculturalism *a while. In one of your writings, you stated that you came to Britain and British theatre in 1968, a time when the very idea of 'standard' English created a cultural schism between white and non-white Britain and questioned the authenticity and place of dialect English and the creolisation that occurred in former colonial territories. Given your earlier comment about society impacting theatre, how did cross-culturalism and transculturalism and their opposition to sociopolitical schism impact the artistic direction and aesthetics of Tara Arts?*

Verma: *Since then, [referring to 1968] the notions of Britishness and 'standard' English have changed radically. The dialogue between the fringe and the centre has made it possible for several disruptions of 'what is British', to the point that* Britishness *is itself a constantly oscillating concept.*

Ukaegbu: *I'm not sure I understand. How did your reading of Britishness as an oscillating idea define Tara's development as a theatre and as a company?*

Verma: *You see, black and Asian peoples and theatres may have started in the British context as othered outsiders or marginals but beyond that point, they are existential as well as artistic points. By definition Asians and Asian theatre are black and othered because their cultural identities and aesthetic sensibilities are on the margins or at least started on the margins of dominant discourse. The questions for me have always been very clear: what can the fact that black British theatre is small-scale contribute to the body of British culture? This could be ideological and stylistic. Does Tara theatre need to draw from Europe or look outside to its roots beyond Britain? The answers to these questions, and by the way we have answered them aesthetically, have shaped Tara Arts' direction and style. The company has drawn from 'outside' to enrich itself 'inside', without losing its unique position on the fringe. The Tara story accepts and embraces rather than resisting and contesting the existential facts of its origins and style. As a company we have transformed our 'smallness' into an artistic essence.*

Tara's Artistic Ideology and Legacy

Ukaegbu: *In 30 years, Tara's productions have covered a wide spectrum of forms and styles from classic Asian and European to modern texts. In the process you have embraced a huge array of aesthetic and artistic influences from all over the world. In your interview with Christiane Schlote (Schlote 2006) you claimed that your journey or position in theatre 'is a contrary one' yet in 'What the migrant Saw', your piece for* The Guardian *(10 January 2008) you stated: 'In an era when intelligent men considered people of another colour less than human, the story resonated with our own lives in Britain. I have been looking, ever since, for answers to the relationship between Them and Us, and between father and son, that has made modern Britain. When we formed Tara, we became accidental exponents of "Asian theatre": at that time, we were the first and only example of it. But why was such a distinction needed?" My question is: how did Tara, an idea and theatre that started from a postcolonial desire (cf. Amkpa 2004) to contest negative stereotypes and to dialogue with the centre, arrive at the cross-cultural, transcultural junction you articulated in the interview with Christiane Schlote?*

Verma: *This derives from the circumstances of my birth and [life] experience: my history and birth in Africa, to my parents of Indian origins and from living in the United Kingdom. Unlike when I came to the United Kingdom, migration is now no longer an academic concept, it is a reality with cultural ramifications that will continue beyond any of us. Britain will never become a black nation; consequently this elicits a dialogue between the centre and the margins, between the old and new and between its various sections. This is what we set out to do. Today Tara is prepared to dialogue with the mainstream on its own terms, remaking and transforming existing classics in the creation of a black theatre aesthetic sensibility and artistic imprint. Small scale goes beyond the pragmatic; fundamental to this sensibility is the absolute recognition that small scale is not at the expense of the term itself. Small scale is a different window, another 'gaze' with its own historical and aesthetic perspectives. Dialogue and scale are the life blood of theatre; through the particular you see the global, a fact that theatre-makers have to keep in mind in this highly mediatised age.*

Ukaegbu: *Are there conflicts in what you do as a small-scale theatre and what mainstream British theatre does or defines you by?*

Verma: *No, I see no conflicts; there are instead rich opportunities. Regarding the latter, small-scale theatres are trapped in arguments about philosophy of scale especially with funders; this is fundamentally wrong. For the artistic and aesthetic health of British and in fact any theatre, it is vitally important to have small-scale outfits. Such small- to mid-scale operations are ideal platforms for few people to work artistically and/or ideologically in order to challenge and de-stabilise institutional and cultural inertia and the debilitating 'for grantedness' that reinforces mainstream cultural hegemony in the arts and in the setting of aesthetic parameters. Rather than conflict and othering, I think that's what you're implying by mainstream defining us, I see inevitable connections; theatres like Tara do different types of work that feed into the mainstream.*

Small scale is the voice from the margins. In some sense the centre has taken on the margins in terms of types and numbers of small-scale theatres and non-white performers. Starting from very few there are now many more black actors, writers, designers, directors etc., coming into the mainstream. There is a flow of stories from the margins [and while] these are being heard it is only now that they are beginning to be heard on the national stages. Far from the silences and the cold indifferences of the past, the margin is speaking openly to the centre. The result is a margin-centre dialogue that guarantees a to and fro of aesthetic ideas and practices. This makes the centre a cacophony of small voices that contribute to what the centre thinks of itself, makes of itself and embraces to itself.

Ukaegbu: *That is a non-political but very perceptive reading of centre-margin relations. Using that as a base, what will you say are the contributions of Tara and similar outfits in the making of British theatre aesthetic?*

Verma: *All small-scale theatres develop from and feed society through looking at new ways of making theatre; they are the breeding grounds for innovation, invention and experimentation. British theatre would be sterile without them. A good number of features and ideas that start life on the fringe – here I mean small scale, not political fringe – are fed into mainstream theatre, where they are received and re-configured as the norm. In this respect and because we're using the present to work for the future, we view small scale as part of an aesthetic of making, of definition, of identity and of process. These features, which will continue to define Tara and the work we do, are something you will find in nearly all small-scale theatres.*

The Challenges Ahead: A New Funding Climate

Ukaegbu: *Do you still see a space for new small-scale theatres and the work they do in the current harsh economic climate?*

Verma: *Absolutely, and without a shadow of doubt. Yes, there is still a great room for small-scale theatres. After all, mainstream theatre is like the great River Nile yet what makes the river great are its numerous tributaries. One way of understanding the importance and aesthetic significance of small-scale theatre is to attempt to answer the question: 'Since I cannot help being black in Britain, what is my discourse with other Britons?' The answer could mean surprising connections or disturbing disconnections. When it comes to how audiences receive stories and the packaging of such stories, small-scale theatre will always be a site for experimentations on form, style and dramaturgy. Small-scale theatres have always charted choppy waters and it is their very nature to demand dialogue all the time, with the past, the present and the future irrespective of the economic and political climates. The current climate may force changes on some aspects of small-scale theatres but they will endure and survive in the long term.*

Ukaegbu: *What are the new challenges for Tara Arts in particular?*

Verma: *The challenges we face currently are simultaneously daunting and exciting: we have a small 50-seat theatre space that requires physical work and alterations and our plan is to turn it into a producing theatre with a 'small-scale' sensibility, making work that is experimental and public facing. The changes we're planning are artistic and spatial. In other words, our aim is to institutionalise small scale as a theatrical sensibility in terms of the structure and aesthetics of both the nature of work and the place it is produced and presented. Right now, this is our main challenge; the result will be our future and a legacy beyond Tara Arts itself.*

Ukaegbu: *Going back to your previous comments, you seem to envision new ideas on the back of challenges. How will you go about realising your current visions?*

Verma: *One of the visions of Tara Arts is to transform the floor of the performance space from wood/concrete to mud floor in a conceptual effort to incorporate African spatial construct into a typical British space in a typical British building. This is an extension of the continuing story of experimenting on the stories and arts of different peoples and cultures that defines small-scale theatre work.*

   To achieve this it is important to re-read the discourses on size and position and to understand that small scale is not small worldview. We are talking about a multi-layered shift: firstly, artistic and strategic and secondly, social and ideological but without the baggage of mainstream and othering. In other words, another challenge is searching for this theatre of the future whilst working with the huge possibilities that there are in a refocused small theatre for a global audience. In the face of challenges there are also exciting possibilities: We may be small or medium in scale, but I will not exchange a big or mainstream theatre for all that it stands for. I will go for a duplication of small-scale theatres and the aesthetics and ideologies they bring to the continually changing debate and dialogue in theatre and society. I will rather keep our stature and style of work than lose both for mainstream status.

Ukaegbu: *So, what would you say is your greatest challenge to date and how has this challenge impacted Tara Arts' work?*

Verma: *The greatest challenge to small-scale theatre is funding; any small cut in grants by arts and government funding agencies affects the arts where cuts cannot be absorbed because all the workers are frontline. This may result in 'cuts' in the work itself. Few, if any, small-scale theatres attract commercial funds, but the current cuts proposed by the government will not kill them; many small-scale theatres will reinvent their presentation and reception strategies as well as reconfigure their relationships with funding agencies. I see a new form of localism emerging with small-scale theatres cashing in on big funders with an interest in tailoring their products to particular markets and establishing a strong presence in local communities. The way we respond to things like budgetary cuts, falling audience figures and other restrictions is part of the make-up and evolutionary strategies of British theatre, and something small-scale theatres are very good at.*

Ukaegbu: *Tara has also grown in the diversity of its work, in terms of context and content, in aesthetic approaches, audiences and types of work. Can you comment on one of the many directions you've charted, say about your education outreach?*

Verma: *This has been going on informally and is developing in the direction of collaborations on work, spaces and experimental workshops. Tara collaborates with other outfits on the basis of artistic sensibilities rather than as a matter of policy. Policy and formal collaborations may exclude some, while sensibility makes for inclusion and inclusivity, a practice DV8 and Frantic Assembly have popularised.*

Ukaegbu: *In a sentence, what is the future of small-scale British theatres?*

Verma: *Small scale has to be prepared to tilt the axis of the world towards the East. It will probably show us the first glimpse of what the absence of centre-margin and what effective cross-cultural theatre will mean.*

Conclusion

Tagore's Nobel Laureate citation reads: 'Because of his profoundly sensitive, fresh and beautiful verse, by which, with consummate skill, he has made his poetic thought, expressed in his own English words, a part of the literature of the West' (Tagore: online).

In this, Jatinder Verma recognised the potential for language to be a creative space for negotiating cultural pluralisms as well as for evolving Tara's own distinctive aesthetic vocabulary. With Binglish, Tara has created a modern day creole that celebrates the diverse cultural expressions and experiences in a highly diverse British Asian diaspora. With the combination of Binglish and a panoply of Asian aesthetic practices – dance, music, costumes and themes – Tara Arts started out speaking to a multilingual, multi-social South Asian diaspora audience. Today it straddles small-scale and mid-scale theatre spaces, a clever move towards the establishment of cross-cultural discourse on the British stage. Nevertheless, the company has remained true to its founding principles. Its production conventions transcend migrant-immigrant-migration marginalisation discourse, while its performances problematise the politics of multiculturalism as well as achieving the double objective of mirroring the internal dynamics of British Asian diaspora as well as interrogating cultural homogenisation and stereotypes about this community.

As an outfit whose aesthetic imprint evolved from postcolonial and intercultural dialectics, Tara's cross-cultural policy started earlier but became established in the early 2000s as the company re-emphasised performances that sought 'to transcend culture-specific codification in order to reach a more universal condition' (Lo and Gilbert 2002: 37). The company's performances, as entertaining as they are, are designed to function as ideological and pedagogic instruments for breaking the cycle of misrepresentation and 'chains of ignorance' that one of the characters in Caryl Phillips's *The Prince of Africa* blames for preventing 'people from communicating with each other and from understanding that "[their] past, present and future are inextricably inter-woven"' (Phillips cited in Ledent 2006: 198). Cross-culturalism and Binglishing may be two aesthetic ideals shared by small-scale Asian theatres, however both are harder to realise on a grand scale on the British stage as the experiences of Tara Arts suggest. Tara Arts, however, has been more successful in both regards than most companies of the small- and mid-scale theatre persuasions.

References

Amkpa, A., 2004. *Theatre and Postcolonial Desires*. London: Routledge.

Ashcroft, B., Griffiths, G. and Tiffin, H., 1989. *The Empire Writes Back: Theory and Practice in Post-colonial Literatures*. London and New York: Routledge.

Ashcroft, B., Griffiths, G. and Tiffin, H. (eds), 2004. *The Post-colonial Studies Reader*. London: Routledge.

Bharucha, R., 2000. *The Politics of Cultural Practice: Thinking through Theatre in an Age of Globalisation*. London: Athlone Press.

Buonanno, G., Sams, V. and Schlote, C., 2011. 'Glocal routes in British Asian drama: Between adaptation and tradaptation'. *Postcolonial Text*, 6: 2, pp. 1–18.

Cochrane, C., 2011. *Twentieth Century British Theatre Industry, Art and Empire*. Cambridge: Cambridge University Press.

Cook, W., 1991. Review of *Little Clay Cart* adapted by Jatinder Verma and Ranjit Bolt, 'Indian Summer'. *City Limits*, 21–28 November, p. 6.

Davis, H., 2004. *Understanding Stuart Hall*. London: Sage.

Davis, G. V. and Fuchs, A. (eds), 2006. *Staging New Britain: Aspects of Black and South Asian British Theatre Practice*. Oxford: P.I.E. Peter Lang.

Frenz, H., 1969. *Nobel Lectures, Literature 1901–1967*. Amsterdam: Elsevier Publishing Company.

Gilbert, H. and Tompkins, J., 1996. *Postcolonial Drama: Theory, Practice, Politics*. London: Routledge.

Hall, S., 1993. 'Cultural identity and diaspora', in P. Williams and L. Chrisman (eds). *Colonial Discourses and Post-Colonial Theory: A Reader*. London: Harvester & Wheatsheaf, pp. 392–403.

Hingorani, D., 2010. *British Asian Theatre: Dramaturgy, Process and Performance*. New York: Palgrave Macmillan.

Ledent, B., 2006. 'Caryl Phillips's drama: A blueprint for a new Britishness', in G. V. Davis and A. Fuchs (eds). *Staging New Britain: Aspects of Black and South Asian British Theatre Practice*. Oxford: P.I.E. Peter Lang, pp. 189–201.

Lo, J. and Gilbert, H., 2002. 'Toward a topography of cross-cultural theatre praxis', in R. Schechner (ed.). *The Drama Review: TDR*, pp. 31–53.

Lucas, V. K., 2007. 'Performing British identity: *Fix Up* and *Fragile Land*', in J. Kuortti and J. Nyman (eds). *Reconstructing Hybridity: Post-Colonial Studies in Transition*. Amsterdam & New York: Rodopi, pp. 241–55.

McMillan, M., 2006. 'Rebaptizing the world in our terms: Black theatre and live arts in Britain', in G. V. Davis and A. Fuchs (eds). *Staging New Britain: Aspects of Black and South Asian British Theatre Practice*. Oxford: P.I.E. Peter Lang, pp. 47–64.

Mercer, K., 1994. *Welcome to the Jungle: New Positions in Black Cultural Studies*. London: Routledge.

Schlote, C., 2006. '"Finding our own voice": An interview with Jatinder Verma'. *Staging New Britain: Aspects of Black and South Asian British Theatre Practice*. Oxford: P.I.E. Peter Lang, pp. 309–20.

Tagore, R., 1917. *Sacrifice: And Other Plays*. New York: Macmillan.

Verma, J., 1996. 'The challenge of Binglish: Analysing multi-cultural productions', in P. Campbell (ed.). *Analysing Performance: A Critical Reader*. Manchester: Manchester University Press, pp. 193–203.

———, 1998. 'Binglishing the stage: A generation of Asian theatre in Britain', in R. Boon and J. Plastow (eds). *Theatre Matters: Politics and Culture on the World Stage*. Cambridge: Cambridge University Press, pp. 126–34.

———, 2008. 'What the Migrant Saw'. *The Guardian*, Thursday 10 January.

Wood, P., Landry, C. and Bloomfield, J., 2006. 'Cultural diversity in Britain: A toolkit for cross-cultural co-operation'. Joseph Rowntree Foundation. http://www.jrf.org.uk (accessed 3 August 2012).

Websites

Nobelprize.org. http://www.nobelprize.org/nobel_prizes/literature/laureates/1913/ (accessed 13 August 2012).

Early Life of Rabindranath Tagore. http://en.wikipedia.org/wiki/Rabindranath Tagore (accessed 30 November 2011).

Company History. http://www.tara-arts.com/about_tara/mission_statement (accessed 21 March 2012).

About Tara Arts. http://www.tara-arts.com/about_tara/history (accessed 21 March 2012).

The Big Idea. http://new.thebiggive.org.uk/charity/view/1570/projectshttp://new.thebiggive.org.uk/charity/view/1570/projects (accessed 15 October 2012).

Notes

1 Lo and Gilbert (2002) describe cross-cultural theatre in 'Towards a Topography of Cross-Cultural Theatre Praxis' as inevitably entailing 'a process of encounter and negotiation between different cultural sensibilities'. They describe 'intercultural' performances as those that explore 'the interstice between cultures' and that draw audiences' 'attention to the hyphenated third space separating and connecting different peoples' (2002: 44); in other words, a model that 'rests on a notion of differentiated hybridity that works in multiple and sometimes opposing ways' (p. 45). Their normative classifications identify three broad categories of cross-cultural performances: multicultural, postcolonial and intercultural, the latter including transcultural, intracultural and extracultural, all of which can be used to describe specific Tara performances.

   While Lo and Gilbert provide a more detailed aesthetic blueprint for performances in their three categories of cross-cultural performances, their reliance on Verma's (1996) much earlier definition for cross-cultural work justifies the latter's use of the term for the diverse range of performances staged by Tara Arts.

2 At various stages in the company's first and second decades of existence Verma described Tara's work as multicultural, defining it as 'those productions featuring a racially-mixed cast which, by not seeking to draw attention to the racial mix of the producing team, are not generally attempting to confront the dominant text-based conventions of British theatre' (1996: 194). See also, Verma's 'Binglishing the Stage: A generation of Asian theatre', in Richard Boon and Jane Plastow (eds). *Theatre Matters: Performance and Culture on the World Stage.* Cambridge: Cambridge University Press, 1998, pp. 126–34.

   After this period he began to use the terms transcultural and cross-cultural more consistently and almost synonymously as most of Tara's productions tended to dialogue between what he describes as 'different cultural sensibilities', a phrase later repeated by Lo and Gilbert (2002).

3 For information on Verma's view on intercultural theatre see

   (a) 'Jatinder Verma discusses Intercultural Theatre', *Asian Voices*, 15 December 2010;

   (b) Godiwala, D. (ed), 2006. *Alternatives within the Mainstream: British Black and Asian Theatres.* Newcastle: Cambridge Scholars Press, pp. 101–16, 174–97, 381–87.

   (c) Verma's 'Binglishing the Stage: a generation of Asian theatre', in Richard Boon and Jane Plastow (eds). *Theatre Matters: Performance and Culture on the World Stage.* Cambridge: Cambridge University Press, 1998, pp. 126–34.

4. For Verma's reading of transcultural and cross-cultural performances see Schlote, 2006.

Chapter 8

Kind Acts: Lone Twin Theatre

Eirini Kartsaki

We're going to tell you a story – it's a story we made up. It begins with two dogs following three people.

(Alice Bell Script 2008: 1–2)

1.

Lone Twin Theatre is a small-scale British theatre company formed in 2005 by Gary Winters and Gregg Whelan. Since its formation, the company has produced three performance works: *Alice Bell*, *Daniel Hit By A Train* and *The Festival*, which constitute *The Catastrophe Trilogy*. The trilogy uses experiences of catastrophe to narrate stories of love, failure and loss. Yet, the 'catastrophic', they tell us, is always contoured with hope (Williams 2009: n.p.). Winters and Whelan are the artistic directors, who work with David Williams, the dramaturge of the company and the following performers: Antoine Fraval, Molly Haslund, Nina Tecklenburg, Paul Gazzola, Cynthia Whelan and Guy Dartnell (the cast of the performances rotates; Guy Dartnell joined the company for *Daniel Hit By A Train* and replaced Cynthia Whelan in *Alice Bell*). Winters and Whelan have been making work themselves as Lone Twin for last 14 years. However, this chapter will be dealing with the work of Lone Twin Theatre, work that can be situated on the cusp of live art, theatre and performance writing. Although I will refer to all of the three pieces named above, my principal focus is *Daniel Hit By A Train* in a discussion that centrally attends to aesthetics, working processes, the use of repetition and the spectator's experience of performance.

2.

The Catastrophe Trilogy narrates stories of hope, where 'something of life is affirmed even in the dying' (Williams 2009: n.p.). The catastrophe takes place on different levels: the catastrophic, whether epic or intimate, domestic or social 'is always contoured with hope and the possibility of change' (Williams 2009: n.p.). The hopefulness of the piece is created through its structure, as I will discuss later; however, there is something else at stake here: 'What is it that drives someone into the fire, the path of the train, the sinking ship, the toxic pit, the sea, canal, pond, lake and river? What is it at play in this instinctive self-forgetting?' (Williams and Lavery 2011: 305). In the preface of the recent publication *Good Luck Everybody: Lone Twin: Journeys, Performances, Conversations* (2011), Alan Read, in a conversation with Joe Kelleher, gives that quality a name: kindness. The company communicates within the work a sense of affirmation, optimism and enthusiasm; this 'kindness', Read continues, could be thought of in terms of an 'instinctive sympathetic identification with the vulnerabilities and attractions of others', according to Adam Phillips and Barbary Taylor (Williams and Lavery 2011: 11). Lone Twin Theatre's kind acts of theatre allow us to recognise our vulnerabilities but also the vulnerabilities of others. They seem to narrate stories of companionship and lonesomeness, where one is alone but also with others, where one becomes oneself in the act of this instinctive self-forgetting.

3.

Lone Twin Theatre's frames of reference are rooted in music, film and contemporary fiction (Williams 2009) and their approach to devising is characterised by a sense of modesty. José A. Sánchez argues that theirs is 'a modesty with which they assume the creative function and the lack of pretension with which they go from the great discourse to the small discourse, from the circus to the theatre', which also manifests in the works of Buster Keaton, Erik Satie or Piero Mannzoni (Sánchez 2004: 39). Aesthetically, this modesty is exemplified through the use of minimal objects on stage: a drum, a flowerpot, five ukuleles. The use of modesty evokes a necessity to repeat elements of the performance and each show has its own logic, its own lexicon. As Whelan puts it:

> Since you can't put everything in, you look for words or phrases that might do a few jobs, if you were only allowed to have ten objects in this space where we're sitting now, each object would have to function in lots of different ways, otherwise we'd have to get rid of it and get a more durable thing in and also then the room becomes populated with very identifiable things. So, I think it always seems necessary to repeat things because I don't know why one wouldn't, in a way. I don't know why you wouldn't.
>
> (Kartsaki Interview with Gregg Whelan 2011)

Repetition is at work and serves a number of purposes: *Alice Bell*, the story of a girl that chose to sacrifice her life to save the lives of others, uses repetition as part of the narrative as well as the structure and imagery:

> Look again. Look again at me, look again at these people, see them differently, see me differently, look through their eyes, see what your singing does, see what your dancing does, see what your jumping up and down does, *feel* what your hate does. [...]

I leave behind the man I changed my name for and my daughter. Good luck the man I changed my name for, good luck my daughter.

I leave you here on ... I will let you go and you will change your heart. You will change your heart. You will change your heart. (REPEAT)

(Alice Bell Script 2008: 3)

Repetition is used here in an invitational, open-ended structure, which allows the spectator to engage with the narrative in a number of ways: 'Look again. Look at me, look again at these people, see them differently' (*Alice Bell* Script 2008: 3), the performer says in an attempt to invite the audience to look again and again on each character of the story, to experience each fragment again and again. The structured repetitions of the sequence cited above generate an intense feeling of hope: the work of hope, Ernst Bloch argues in *The Principle of Hope*, 'requires people who throw themselves actively into what is becoming, to which they themselves belong' (Williams and Lavery 2011: 305). According to another thinker, Henri Bergson, hope is such an intense pleasure because it gestures towards the idea of the future (1960: 9–10). The sense of the catastrophic is underpinned by ideas of kindness and hopefulness; *The Catastrophe Trilogy* invites us to give in to a world of cyclical events and made up stories, where 'this is all there is – people, and chairs and musical instruments' (*Alice Bell* Script 2008: 1–2). It is through these repetitions – both the staged ones and the ones that take place as a result of the invitation – that the story emerges. Its invitational structure and the perpetual process of becoming, which 'presupposes both that there is something fixed and something that is in flux' (Eriksen 2000: 14), render the work 'unfinishable' (Williams 2009: n.p.). This ties in with the particular quality of the work, as it does not impose a certain understanding of it, but rather offers to the spectator the opportunity to engage with it and allow for things to occur.

4.

The present writing is using Lone Twin Theatre's particular preoccupation with fragmentary structure to discuss the work itself. The different fragments of thought refer to different aspects of the work; the numbers in fragments do not imply a hierarchy of ideas, but rather a playfulness, also evoked by the work itself, which allows the reader/ spectator to engage with the ideas, rhythms and structures in a non-prescribed and, echoing the quality of the performances noted above, invitational manner. The reader is therefore invited to work through meanings and create a constellation of ideas, in the same way that the spectator might experience the work: 'The structure of this work will be, strictly speaking, *rhapsodic*, i.e. (etymologically) sewn' (Barthes 1986: 281). The 'rhapsodic' element might be applied both in the experience of performance as well as the current writing.

5.

A significant issue arises when discussing work such as Lone Twin Theatre's: the work becomes something else through writing about the performance, a writing that attempts to somehow recover the event. That is because the visual language and aesthetics of Lone Twin Theatre function in such ways that enable a diverse number of experiences; a great sense of contingency is therefore at stake: things do not just mean, meaning is contingent. I refer here to meaning deriving not only from some kind of narrative that *makes sense* as such, but rather to a logic at work: 'the work is elliptical and open-ended; although it insists on making available its modes and mechanisms, it never tells the spectators what to think. It is up to us to fashion connections, to make our own readings, to own it' (Williams and Lavery 2011: 21). A sense of potentiality emerges through the narrative. The fragments of stories create constellations, which form different configurations, through which meaning arises. This is true for the *Trilogy* as a whole; however, the structure of *Daniel Hit By A Train* is of particular interest in terms of the narrative that emerges from it.

Daniel Hit By A Train stages 53 true stories. In each one a person loses their life in an attempt to save the life of another. The piece draws on 'The Watts Memorial of Heroic Deeds', a nineteenth-century memorial in Postman's Park in the City of London. The audience sits on both sides of the stage, as it happens throughout *The Catastrophe Trilogy*; a bright red rectangular carpet floor constitutes the performance scenery. The performers in everyday clothes enter and exit from a sketchy plastic outline of a door opening. The whole piece is punctuated by the beats of a big drum attached to the waist of one of the performers. The performance consists of a series of deaths, a countdown of the 53 stories it narrates. Fifty-three plaques recording acts of impulsive bravery become the focus of the improvisations; the lens through which the company is looking for forms, languages and rhythms (Williams 2009). The performance concerns the telling of a story, yet, as Williams argues, 'the telling itself can be an event in itself – the fashioning, staging and communicating of a world here now' (Williams and Lavery 2011: 279).

PAUL
Who saw the train?
BEAT
Who saw the train?
BEAT
Who here saw the train?
BEAT

GROUP STEP BACK
ANTOINE WALKS FORWARD TO DOOR END – GROUP LOOK UP

ANTOINE
I did, I saw the train.
My name is Daniel.

I was working on the tracks with my friend, my friend didn't see the train.
I pushed him out of the way and the train hit me.
This is me, hit by a train.

ANTOINE IS HIT BY TRAIN – HE WALKS BACKWARDS
(*Daniel Hit By A Train* Vienna Script 2008: 3)

The repetitive structure of the performance text invites us to create our own meaning: the story we are being told is a *writerly* one, following Roland Barthes' distinction between *writerly* and *readerly*: 'the goal of literary work [Ö] is to make the reader no longer a consumer, but a producer of the text' (1974: 10). The spectator is actively engaged in the creation of meaning, in the process of putting the fragments together. The narrative created is therefore personalised, subjective and unique in each particular case. This 'text' is a 'plural' one, a galaxy of signifiers, rather than as a 'structure of signifieds' (Barthes 1970: 4) In *Daniel Hit By A Train* meaning can be written and rewritten in the act of performing and each performance is a different one. The spectator 'writes' and 'rewrites' the meaning of the text and therefore every reading of the performance appears as new.

PAUL
(SNIFF) Smell that? – Something's burning
Regard the fire, regard the smoke – what is burning?
BEAT
What is burning?
BEAT
What is burning?
BEAT
What in here is burning?

GUY ENTERS – TAKES ONE STEP INTO SPACE – FACING PAUL

GUY
I am, I am burning – I am on fire (GESTURE)
My name is Thomas – I am the plumber
There was an explosion at the factory, I tried to save my friend I ran into the fire
This is me, burning

GUY CHECKS HIS MOUTH AND EAR AND MOUTH – DROPS HAND

PAUL
BEAT
Thomas, the plumber, burning

(*Daniel Hit By A Train* Vienna Script 2008: 3)

The story here is offered in constellations of fragments and the non-linear narrative is constructed through cyclical events and relations; that is a narrative 'which creates suspensions and returns in our experience, problematises our tendency to rationalise time' (Heathfield 2006: 192). The 53 stories, punctuated by the beat of a drum, have a similar structure. They are written in such a way so that one evokes the memory of another. Each time we are told about Thomas, the burning plumber, we are also reminded of the priest in the river, of Mary, going down with the ship, or of Daniel, hit by a train. Performance invites us to return to it again and again and re-experience the cyclical events and relations that emerge from the narrative.

In *Rhythmanalysis*, Henri Lefebvre refers to the rhythm that constellations might create: he quotes Julio Cortázar's *Les Gagnants*:

'When we look at a constellation, we are certain that a rhythm comes from the stars, a rhythm that we suppose because we think that there is "something" "up there" that coordinates these elements, which is more substantial than each star taken separately' (Lefebvre 2004: 24).

Although each story in *Daniel Hit By A Train* is a story in itself, something else happens when we experience the repetitive structure and its shape as a whole: we become familiar with the rhythm, anticipating each next time and gaining satisfaction from its repetitive nature, once each next time takes place. This excitement, which derives from the re-experience of the scene as a source of pleasure, is also bound with a fearful desire for the ending of the scene. In his account of repetition in Beckett's *Watt*, Steven Connor describes this sentiment: 'always mixed with a longing for the series to stop, there must also be a kind of fear that it *will* stop' (1988: 32). The narrative structure of the piece, built in repetition, generates a satisfaction concerning the sense of progression and the holding on to the sequence, as well as a simultaneous longing for closure and relief, as identified above.

Performance therefore becomes something else through this kind of writing. I write and re-write my experience of it, in a Barthesian *writerly* sense, as each experience constitutes a new performance. The repetitive structures and cyclical events that *Daniel Hit By A Train* makes use of influence the way in which the performance is narrated through writing. I therefore write in an attempt to re-experience the performance's rhythms and configurations of fragments, or to reconfigure the fragments again and again. This is consequently a personal account of this work, in which 'all sorts of braidings of different kinds of meeting occur, or might occur, within those event structures' (Williams and Lavery 2011: 46).

6.

It starts with an attempt to sing a song, to make a rhythm. It starts with two dogs following three people. It starts with Alice Bell: 'Put your arms around me. How does it feel to be that close to me?' (*Alice Bell* Script 2008: 2). *Alice Bell*, which has toured extensively throughout Europe since its Brussels premiere in 2006, is a story of love, transformation, betrayal and forgiveness. It is a story that invites us to question how it is 'to live with others, loving something of their difference, their elsewhere' (Williams 2009: n.p.). At one point early on the devising process, Williams writes:

> We look closely at some of Alice Munro's remarkable stories. In part as structural and textural case studies and possible triggers for our own fictions: resonant 'shapes' and 'feels'. In part for their graceful anatomising of everyday lives, their repressed yearnings, confusions, compromises and mysteries. In *Lives of Girls and Women*, Munro writes: 'People's lives were dull, simple, amazing and unfathomable – deep caves paved with kitchen linoleum'. Elsewhere in an interview, Munro suggests: 'The complexity of things – the things within things – just seems to be endless. I mean nothing is easy, nothing is simple'.
>
> (Williams 2009)

This is the fictional story of Alice Bell, who has to run away from home to save her life and who returns sometime after to fall in love and re-invent her identity, in order to be able to stay. When the truth is revealed, Alice has to sacrifice her life in order to save the lives of others. Her story, as Munro would have it, is simple, amazing and unfathomable, the everyday of life becoming the heart of the narrative.

Both *Daniel Hit By A Train* and *Alice Bell* are using stories of love, loss and catastrophe to create narratives, which gracefully dissect the everyday and reveal its yearnings, confusions, compromises and mysteries. *The Festival*, the third of *The Catastrophe Trilogy* continues the exploration of narrative and the catastrophic (at the level of the quotidian). It narrates the story of the 42-year-old Jennifer who, following her family's tradition, visits Crescent Head in New South Wales to see the migration of humpback whales in the company of her mother, after her father's death. In Crescent Head, Jennifer meets Oliver and they promise to meet again a year after their initial encounter in the same place. On the anniversary of this first meeting, and although Jennifer seems to long for the love of Oliver, she returns to Crescent Head to end their relationship.

During the creative process, Williams notes, four words appear on the flip chart: 'NO DEATH, NO INSTRUMENTS' (2011: 321). In this one, again, the action is in a state of becoming: 'events in their unfolding in which people are exposed, vulnerable, present, trying to deal with it' (Williams and Lavery 2011: 322). As Carl Lavery suggests, *The Festival* 'de-dramatises tragedy, thematically and formally, by basing its tragic vision not on an exceptional individual undergoing purification through violence', like perhaps in the two previous works, 'but on what Maeterlinck terms, in a beautiful phrase, "someone approaching or retreating from his own truth"' (Williams and Lavery 2011: 334). This movement towards or away from one's own truth seems to be manifesting itself in the many repetition and returns to specific events of structures, as shown above.

Aesthetically, the *Trilogy* is making use of a 'populated yet empty' approach which Whelan describes as follows:

> Gary and I might talk about it as being empty; the idea really is to be able to see people totally, see somebody in front of you, and listen to them, without anything else going on; the stage is empty but the space is populated.
>
> (Kartsaki interview with Gregg Whelan 2011)

The action takes place in the centre, so the audience has the opportunity to be looking at people looking at other people:

> We want to foreground the idea that these shows are shows with just people saying things, people in front of people, it's the simplest way we could think of it. It's not people in front of a castle, or it's not people in front of a wall, it's not people in front of, you know, anything, it's just people in front of people, and that's endlessly what you see in those shows.
>
> (Kartsaki interview with Gregg Whelan 2011)

Throughout *The Catastrophe Trilogy* the audience is seated on both sides of the stage, looking at the performers on stage who enter and exit, carrying with them, from time to time, objects or musical instruments. This particular 'populated yet empty' aesthetic allows for the stories to unravel again and again creating a multitude of possibilities to do with the making of the narrative and its meanings.

7.

The idea of Britishness in the context of Lone Twin Theatre that will be further explored in the interview section of this chapter becomes an important question, which might be thought of on different levels. The company has been presenting work in the United Kingdom and abroad and, although based in the United Kingdom, its cast is not distinctly British. The intercultural influences therefore become part of the work itself, and the different voices shape the making process.

I meet three members of Lone Twin Theatre (Nina Tecklenburg, Guy Dartnell and Molly Haslund) at the café of Lilian Baylis studio, where they are rehearsing *The Catastrophe Trilogy*, to discuss Britishness and aesthetics. The idea of a British live art aesthetic seems to be central to our discussion: Dartnell and Tecklenburg argue that Lone Twin Theatre's work could not be seen as typically British; yet, it has a live art aesthetic, which they identify as something of a British 'product'. Tecklenburg suggests that for her live art could be seen as 'mostly solo or duo performances, small-scale performances, people standing in front of microphones, using animal masks. It can be very decomposed and fragmented with some sort of heart-felt genuineness about it' (Kartsaki Interview with Nina Tecklenburg, Guy Dartnell and Molly Haslund 2011).

Live art, of course, cannot be defined fully. According to Lois Keidan, 'it is not a description of an art form or discipline, but a cultural strategy to include experimental processes and experiential practices that might otherwise be excluded from established curatorial, cultural and critical frameworks', (2009: n.p.). It explores the idea of liveness in ways that differ from traditional theatrical forms and has generated 'an explosion of conventional aesthetics' (Sofaer in Keidan 2009: n.p.). Dartnell's suggestion of a continuum of theatre and live art is useful here: 'I would say that Lone Twin Theatre is the theatrical end of live art. If you compared it to Improbable Theatre you would say Improbable Theatre is the live art end of theatre. [Ö] Lone Twin Theatre is very narrative based; so that makes it odd from a live art point of view' (Kartsaki Interview with Nina Tecklenburg, Guy Dartnell and Molly Haslund 2011). Although the binary set-up here is an interesting way of thinking about the particular aesthetic that certain companies have adopted, it might also appear as problematic. Lone Twin Theatre is interested in merging live art and theatre aesthetics in a celebration of narrative, where the stories and the characters borrow from film and contemporary fiction and encompass singing and dancing in imaginative and audacious ways.

David Williams, whom I meet at the National Theatre to discuss the work of Lone Twin Theatre, suggests that traditionally the conception of British theatre 'relates to a very particular set of relationships to writers, purportedly a very evolved set of actor training regimes in relation to existing text and to particular means of production' (Kartsaki Interview with David Williams 2011). British theatre has been over the years very insular and perhaps suspicious of some aspects of European theatre practice, he notes (Kartsaki Interview with David Williams 2011). Of course this has evolved through time and the landscape of contemporary British theatre has changed dramatically. However, some companies have attempted to distinguish themselves from British theatre and to create a distinct identity, one of them being Complicité, which, as Peacock points out, attempted to distance itself from 'British theatre' by adopting a foreign name despite making their work in the United Kingdom (Peacock 2007: 18). Williams also refers to Peter Brooke, who, although having worked with the National Theatre and the Royal Shakespeare Company, 'moved to the more progressive theatrical climate of France to pursue his work' (Peacock 2007: 18).

At the end of the twentieth century, British companies such as Forced Entertainment have delved into a lucid exploration of text and the live stage, 'influenced by the enigmas of Robert Wilson's lyrical images, Pina Bausch's dancers' frenzied yet perfectly measured movement performances, the intellectual curiosity of William Forsythe and inspired more directly by the remarkable Wooster Group' (Phelan in Etchells 1999: 10). The work of the above European and American practitioners has been significant in the development of a contemporary aesthetic, which can be situated on a continuum of theatre and live art, which might be seen as a British 'product'. Companies based in Britain, such as Forced Entertainment, Punch Drunk and Pacitti Company, are showing an interest in duration, text, improvisation and writing. These companies have developed unique working methods as a response to the need for a different aesthetic, which is permissive and allows for endless variables, opening a dialogue with the limitations of more established forms in terms of space, time, plot and characters. Avant-garde theatre, performance art and live art practices have been working towards the direction of providing an artistic medium, which is open minded and challenges the relationship between director, dramaturge and performer, and introducing new ways of making and thinking about collaborative processes.

Lone Twin Theatre's work has developed as a result of a long tradition of work, which experiments with theatrical language, such as work by Peter Brooke, Odin Theatre and others, drawing on contemporary fiction, film and music but also moving beyond those influences to create a different language; a language to do with the ways in which bodies are placed on stage, next to other bodies. An interesting quality emerges in terms of the performance mode and the way the story becomes accessible to the audience. The company could be seen as European rather than singularly British in so far as a lot of the collaborators are not British, which has a particular effect on the use of language. As Williams points out, '[we] have always been interested in people making language strange or making language unfamiliar' (Kartsaki Interview with David Williams 2011). The stylised form of acting and the deadpan delivery, or the 'speaking of sentences as sculptural "objects"' (Williams and Lavery 2011: 284) propose a different dramaturgical approach that is interested in new forms and shapes, enabling the material used to 'reverberate in ways that are more than the sum of its parts' (Williams 2009). The company has been creating work with a particular aesthetic, which embraces theatricality, experiments with text and its delivery and asks the spectators to do more than they expect to, being attentive to the reverberations of the material, bringing something of themselves into the making of the story. Things, as Joe Kelleher suggests, 'will do what they are capable of doing, no more, no less. The rest is imagination' (2009: n.p.).

8.

Lone Twin Theatre's work narrates a story that reveals kindness and modesty, a story that invites us to fill in the gaps and fissures. The work invites us to look at each other across the stage and discover the cracks in the texture of the story. This is an invitation; to follow the rhythm of the constellation and reconfigure its meaning. The telling of a story, offered as a galaxy of signifiers, is constructed through cyclical events and relations and invites us to 'throw ourselves actively into what is becoming' (Bloch in Williams and Lavery 2011: 305), to linger, to approach or retreat from our own truth (Maeterlinck in Williams and Lavery 2011: 334).

> Put your arms around me. How does it feel to be this close to me? [...] I leave you here on ... I will let you go and you will change your heart. You will change your heart. You will change your heart... (REPEAT)
>
> (*Alice Bell* Script 2008: 3)

Interview

I meet Gregg Whelan (June 2011), the artistic director of Lone Twin Theatre, in Thornham Marina, Emsworth, where Lone Twin prepared their Boat Project for the Cultural Olympiad, 2012.

9.

Whelan discusses the idea of Britishness and its use in their work as Lone Twin and Lone Twin Theatre and the ways in which the work might be located within the European rather than British scene.

Kartsaki: *Lone Twin Theatre has been touring extensively both in the United Kingdom and abroad since the 2006 premiere of* Alice Bell *in Brussels. The company consists of five performers that come from all over Europe and Australia. As this publication is concerned with the idea of Britishness in small-scale theatre production, could you discuss whether you consider Lone Twin Theatre as a British small-scale theatre company?*

Whelan: *The work is in a sense empirically British, as the company is based in Britain, and Gary Winters and myself are the artistic directors. However, I think it has a kind of purposeful Britishness as well; we have made so much work internationally, that we have become very aware of 'being British'. There are certain jokes we tell about each other that are funnier in America, for example, than they are here [in the United Kingdom]. We are, to some degree, aware of our identity in the making process, especially if the work is going to tour in America, Europe or Australia.*

Kartsaki: *Lone Twin Theatre has an international cast. However, Lone Twin consists of yourself and Garry Winters. Do you consider Lone Twin's work more British than Lone Twin Theatre's?*

Whelan: *When Gary and I started thinking about making work as Lone Twin Theatre, we very purposefully wanted to populate this group. At the time, we were working in Europe, so by pragmatic circumstances, we created a European group, but we also very much liked the fact that we were creating a European group. We liked the different voices, not necessarily in terms of different accents; but rather in terms of where people come from; this was an opportunity to work with different contexts, places and voices.*

Kartsaki: *Would you locate Lone Twin Theatre within the British scene?*

Whelan: *I do not have an overview of British theatre, other than perhaps Forced Entertainment; I know there are companies, such as Spy Monkey and Told By An Idiot, etc., yet, I do not have a relationship with their work. Gary [Winters] is a*

	little bit different. So, I cannot locate myself within British theatre; I do not feel I'm part of British theatre in that sense.
Kartsaki:	*It might then be more useful then to think of a European rather than solely British scene?*
Whelan:	*Yes, I would locate all our work within the European scene in terms of touring places, key partners, venues and commissions. All of the above can be found within the recent publication (2011)* Good Luck Everybody: Lone Twin: Journeys, Performances, Conversations *by Performance Research.*

10.

Whelan takes me on a tour around the marina and explains the ideas behind the Boat Project. I donate a little pencil to be included into the construction of the boat, which will be part of the Cultural Olympiad, 2012. We then sit down again and discuss the influence of international audiences and the reception of the work within and outside the United Kingdom. Whelan suggests that a British identity functions as a frame within the work, which allows for an international understanding of Britishness to take place, but because of the international influences on the company, the idea of a British aesthetic is more difficult to define.

Kartsaki:	*How has the work been influenced by the fact that your audiences might not be solely British?*
Whelan:	*Within the work, there has been a real interest in an international understanding of Britishness. Our first Lone Twin piece* On Everest *addresses the idea of the Empire and colonialism in a playful manner. The mountain has been called after Sir George Everest who was surveying the Himalaya during the nineteenth century. We are interested in the idea that Everest was authored through a sense of British endeavour, but it is itself clearly not British. The idea of British explorers and British endeavour to chart and map the world, the high comedy of that becomes important. When we made work that addressed the above, we were very aware of that dynamic but we found that dynamic to be essentially comic.*
Kartsaki:	*I am interested in the notion of a British aesthetic, is there such a thing in your work?*
Whelan:	*Do you want there to be a British aesthetic?*
Kartsaki:	*From my point of view, your work aesthetically resonates more with the work of Goat Island or Tanztheatre to some extent, rather than Improbable or Forced Entertainment.*
Whelan:	*It is much more complicated talking about Britishness in Lone Twin Theatre than in our own work [Lone Twin]. When we started making* Alice Bell, *we knew that it would premiere in Brussels, at the Kunstenfestivaldesarts and so Gary [Winters]*

and I made that piece thinking about that particular audience, which, in that instance was international.

Kartsaki: David Williams talks about the notion of amateur in his account of the Lone Twin Theatre work. Is that something that influences the work?

Whelan: I think the idea of the amateur is what happens when Gary [Winters] and I make work. It's not necessarily an aesthetic. It is a thing that occurs quite naturally in what we are doing because, to some degree, we are amateurs. We are not quite the right people to be doing a number of things we do. We're the right people to be talking to an audience, because that is what we do, but we are amateur cyclists, we are amateur dancers or we're amateur singers.

Kartsaki: Do you get better at it with time?

Whelan: What you get better at is being fine with it. I haven't got any better at singing; I've just got better at being fine with it.

Kartsaki: How was Alice Bell received during its premiere in the Kunstenfestivaldesarts, Brussels, 2006?

Whelan: The reception of the piece was positive and the performers did a really great job, taking into account the fact that the piece was only finished the evening before. Gary and myself had previously performed To The Dogs in the same festival in 2004; so, the experience of watching a Lone Twin Theatre piece was very different. Yet, we felt very positive about it, for what was a very strange and quite fragile piece of work.

Kartsaki: Do British audiences respond to the work differently?

Whelan: It's never really perhaps a good idea to talk in generalisation, but then in general, people laugh more at those three shows in mainland Europe. When we show Daniel Hit By A Train in the United Kingdom, audiences respond to it in a very serious way and nobody laughs, apart from during specific sections of the performance.

11.

A family who arrives to contribute wooden donations to the Boat Project interrupts us. When we resume our conversation, Whelan suggests that laughter seems to become an interesting parameter for the work, in terms of particular cultural contexts and one that might reveal something about the making process. Lone Twin Theatre's work asks the audience to become part of it, to join the conversation. As noted previously, The Catastrophe Trilogy resembles an open-ended invitation, to which the spectator is asked to bring something of his life.

Kartsaki: So, is laughter one parameter or objective of the work?

Whelan: Gary [Winters] and I have thought about laughter a lot, as we do endlessly want to make people laugh. It is one of the objectives. We want to entertain people. Laughter is like a conversation; when people laugh in a group, they participate in that conversation; they join the collective. It is like everyone says YES, or everybody says NO, or MAYBE, together. I do not think laughter is a banal thing; it is evidence of a thought process happening.

Kartsaki: Laughter is one thing that might show how people respond to performance work; however, I rarely laugh out loud in performances, although I might be enjoying myself very much. I am therefore thinking of the subtleness of certain moments in The Catastrophe Trilogy and the narrative that you are slowly building; there is a certain sense of excitement that goes with that in the way I experience the work. Is there a way to relate to the audience in that sense? In other words, besides laughter, how do you think about the audience when constructing the work?

Whelan: I suppose we begin from thinking that people will find sad what we find sad, and people will find happy what we find happy, and people will enjoy the texture of the nuance in the same way that we do. But then of course that might not happen; yet the whole thing might have a quality that the audience can look at in a different way. I imagine that everyone is going to understand what I understand and everyone is going to see what I see and everyone's going to see it as I see it, and of course that is a fallacy, but that is how we make something.

Kartsaki: As a spectator, I feel that there is something about the experience of the work that needs to be worked out; there is the sense of constructing a vocabulary or a different language.

Whelan: That's right. You have got to think. There is a lot of work to be done from the spectator's point of view. You have to bring something to it if you are going to enjoy it I think. You have got to bring to it a bit of your life.

Kartsaki: Perhaps give in to it as well?

Whelan: Yes, perhaps, but like anything else, you have got to place it. It is not our job to place it inside your life. I can just place it in front of you and I can sort of try to make it easy or easier. But if you want to take it into your life, then it will be fine. I am sure you will have a good time.

Kartsaki: It is an invitation.

Whelan: Yes, the work does not display itself; you see somebody trying to communicate. What is interesting to us is the act of trying, as opposed to being able to do something. If someone walks on stage and throws knives skilfully, you know that he is able to do that; however, then if someone gets up and fails to throw the knives and the knives hit the floor or the ceiling, then you are really engaged, because you see that he is trying.

12.

A group of locals arrive at that point to have a look at the process of building the boat. I take that opportunity to thank Whelan for the conversation and for showing me around Thornham Marina.

Kartsaki:	As a final point, I would like to ask whether there are any future plans for Lone Twin Theatre. Will you be making more work?
Whelan:	I imagine we will yes, at some point.
Kartsaki:	With the same cast?
Whelan:	Yes, I imagine that something like that could happen. We have no sense of that at the moment at all. The Boat Project keeps us very busy. We are also thinking about other duo work we could do. We made Nine Years about five years ago, so it has been five years since myself and Gary [Winters] made something together; I think we are interested in doing that again.
Kartsaki:	Do you think that the next thing that you will do on stage will look like what you've done already, or do you think you might take a completely different direction?
Whelan:	I don't know really. I suppose that if the next thing we make is something that myself and Gary [Winters] are in, then it would perhaps be radically different to other things we have done together; it is all out there already and we have done it, and we don't seem to need to continue any of that.

References

Barthes, R., 1970. *S/Z: Essais.* Paris: Éditions du seuil.

———, 1974. *S/Z* (trans. Richard Miller). New York: Hill & Wang.

———, 1986. *The Rustle of Language* (trans. Richard Howard). New York: Hill & Wang.

Bergson, H., 1960. *Time and Free Will: An Essay on the Immediate Data of Consciousness* (trans. F. L. Pogson). New York: Harper & Brothers.

Eriksen, N. N., 2000. *Kierkegaard's Category of Repetition: A Reconstruction*, Kierkegaard Studies, Monograph Series 5. Berlin and New York: Walter de Gruyter.

Etchells, T., 1999. *Certain Fragments: Contemporary Performance and Forced Entertainment*, London: Routledge.

Heathfield, A., 2004. 'In memory of little things', *La Ribot II*. France: Merz, Centre National de la Danse.

———, 2006. 'Writing of the event', in J. Christie, R. Gough and Peter Watt (eds). *A Performance Cosmology: Testimony from the Future, Evidence of the Past.* London: Routledge, pp. 179–82.

Kartsaki, E., 2011. Interview with Nina Tecklenburg, Guy Dartnell and Molly Haslund, London.

Kartsaki, E., 2011. Interview with David Williams, London.

Kartsaki, E., 2011. Interview with Gregg Whelan, London.

Keidan, L., 2009. *What is Live Art.* http://www.thisisliveart.co.uk/about_us/what_is_live_art. html (accessed 1 June 2012).

Kelleher, J., 2009. 'The breaking and renewing of promises'. http://www.thisisperformancematters. co.uk/words-and-images.post70.html (accessed 27 July 2011).

Lefebvre, H., 2004. *Rhythmanalysis: Space, Time and Everyday Life.* New York: Continuum.

Lone Twin Theatre, 2008. *Alice Bell* script.

Lone Twin Theatre, 2008. *Daniel Hit By A Train*, script for Vienna performances.

Peacock, D. K., 2007. *Changing Performance: Culture and Performance in the British Theatre Since 1945*. Bern: Peter Lang AG.

Sánchez, J. A., 2004. *La Ribot II*. France: Merz, Centre National de la Danse.

Williams, D., 2009. 'Sky-writings'. http://sky-writings.blogspot.com/2008/07/alice-and-daniel.html (accessed 2 January 2009).

Williams, D. and Lavery, C. (eds), 2011. *Good Luck Everybody: Lone Twin: Journeys, Performances, Conversations*. United Kingdom: Performance Research Books.

Chapter 9

Political Theatre 'without Finger-Wagging': On the Paper Birds and Integrative Aesthetics

Patrick Duggan

We need a type of theatre which not only releases the feeling, insights and impulses within the particular historical field of human relations in which the action takes place, but employs and encounters those thoughts and feelings which help transform the field itself.

(Brecht 1964: 190)

Acting styles reflect, enforce and critique models of behaviour. New styles, often created collaboratively by actors and playwrights, can suddenly make visible the outdatedness of certain notions of performance, not only in the theatre but also in daily life.

(Gibson Cima 1993: 1)

Foundations

The Paper Birds is the 'youngest' theatre company represented in this volume. The all-female collective have been making performance work professionally since 2003, developing a collaborative, physical theatre style that is both aesthetically and technically accomplished but also rigorously researched and politically nuanced [1]. It is a style that continues to grow in complexity and virtuosity. While discernibly their own, the company's aesthetic practice is identifiably built on the shoulders of companies they were exposed to as students at Bretton Hall on the BA Acting programme (2000–03) [2] and during their time on the MA Theatre Collectives at Chichester University (2008–09).

In our interview, Jemma McDonnell, the company's artistic director, highlighted the importance of the company's training at Bretton, in particular exposure to the work of a wide variety of practitioners coupled with an encouragement to explore, question and experiment:

McDonnell: What was wonderful about the training we received at Bretton Hall was the period of theoretical introduction/examination of companies and practitioners followed by the opportunity to practically explore and respond to the styles, methodologies and working approaches that most appealed to us. I remember reading a lot about The Wooster Group, Forced Entertainment, Complicité, Robert Wilson, Pina Bausch, DV8 and where possible travelling down to London to see the work when it was touring. These artists/ companies proved to be very influential in the work we were making; as undergraduates we imitated them, as graduates we were inspired by them and as a young company we admired the practicalities of their success as well-established companies [3].

At both aesthetic and political levels, the list that is drawn here speaks to a history of experimental performance practice, physical and dance theatres, 'postmodern' performance, overt theatricality – performance which 'present[s] spades as spades' (Ridout in Castellucci et al. 2007: 104) – and a rich visual depth. Theirs is a practice that owes much to the praxis model of the university training they have undergone. Braiding theoretical understanding, practical application and subject research the company have developed a performance mode that, to reprieve Gibson Cima, is most certainly engaged in reflecting, critiquing and questioning the status quo of performance 'not only in the theatre but also in daily life' (1993: 1). Although the political complexity [4] of the company's work has developed in the almost 10 years they have been making work, it is from these roots that they emerged:

> *McDonnell:* When we started we were really interested in experimenting. One of the joys of being a collective that is formed at university (but also one of its pitfalls) is that you are incredibly influenced by everything you have just been learning and watching. I would certainly say the first couple of shows were directly influenced and shaped in this way; borrowing and adapting the working processes of our predecessors and seeing where this led us. It came to a point a year or so in, where we needed to ask 'who are we, what grounds us, what makes our collective what it is and what makes our work interesting?'

It is not by accident that many of the companies McDonnell cites above might be thought of as physical theatre companies. While the polyvalent nature of that term is well documented (cf. Murray and Keefe 2007: 13–20) the concern with visual complexity and what Murray and Keefe term 'heightened physical theatricality' (Murray and Keefe 2007: 21) remains a constant feature of the company's work. Ideologically and aesthetically, The Paper Birds' work shares common ground with a multiplicity of other physical theatre companies as it seeks to 'break down barriers between dance, theatre and personal politics' (Newson cited in Murray and Keefe 2007: 14) as well as striving to make work that is 'most alive, integrating text, music, image and action to create … a common physical and imaginative language' (Complicité website cited in Murray and Keefe 2007: 15). While these descriptions are reflective of a great many physical theatre practices (including those of Volcano discussed in Somers' chapter in this volume), they are nevertheless a useful frame for viewing and historicising The Paper Birds' work:

> *McDonnell:* Our work has always been very visual. We've always had live music and we're really interested in physicality and the body, but I suppose one of the most fundamental changes to our approach to making theatre came when we began to prioritise the content rather than the style and form of the work.

When we first formed we had always referred to ourselves as an all-female collective but I don't think we knew what that meant to us at the beginning. *In a Month of Fallen Sundays* [the company's second show, 2004] was based on the Magdalene Asylums and in retrospect I think we side-stepped making any kind of political or feminist statements within the work. By the time we made *In a Thousand Pieces* (2008) there was a shift in our approach to making theatre. I remember that I approached Elle and Kylie and said 'we have spent the last five years developing and defining our own theatrical style, now let's put it to some use; let's make a show that is as aesthetically interesting and as theatrical as our previous shows, but one that also has a voice'. The work retained a strong physical aesthetic but we were beginning to prioritise the *point* of the work.

The company makes work that is undeniably 'issue based'; productions thus far have tackled topics ranging from sex trafficking to the disenfranchisement of the other to Britain's binge drinking culture. The company website states that The Paper Birds 'create and share devised work that is important; work that is culturally, socially and politically observational and conversationally urgent' (The Paper Birds 2011: online). These aims might suggest a political and didactic theatre that would be more at home in the late 1970s or early 1980s than the early part of the twenty-first century; but theirs is not didactic theatre in the way that some of Foco Novo's 'socialist phase' (see Chapter 1 in this volume) or Red Ladder's early works might have been seen to be [5]. The work of The Paper Birds is contemporary, poetic, physical and moving while remaining deeply engaged in a process analogous to an educational model in so far as it is designed at aesthetic and political levels to stimulate discussion around a given topic. As McDonnell put it in our discussion 'we don't make the work for ourselves, we make it to share and to start discussions and debates and to engage other people'. For this company, political theatre is most certainly not dead and, as McDonnell asserted in our interview, the company is not interested in making 'safe' work *about* a topic but is concerned to explore those areas of the world that speak to them and have wider sociocultural and political implications, now and in the future.

More often than not, that will be work, which 'emerge[s] from a female perspective and often this female voice will prioritise stories of women' (The Paper Birds 2011: online):

Forging relationships and initiating new partnerships and collaborations, The Paper Birds aim to utilise a dynamic performance vocabulary that speaks to its audience visually, physically, and musically. From this The Paper Birds hope to touch and engage their audiences both intellectually and emotionally and ensure that the work remains to be diverse and relevant in the theatrical climate.

(The Paper Birds 2011: online)

The company's website thus sets out an ambitious mini-manifesto for their work and this is rigorously upheld in all that they write, say and produce on stage; but perhaps the clearest and most constant elements of their work is their focus on political efficacy and the prioritising of 'stories of women'.

Questions of aesthetics, politics and the wider 'function' of theatre are central within the company's concerns. As such, the rest of this chapter seeks to open up these areas to consider what The Paper Birds' work might tell us about small-scale British theatre at the beginning of the second decade of the twenty-first century.

A contemporary Political Theatre

Political theatre is even more important than it ever was, if by political theatre you mean plays which deal with the real world, not with a manufactured or fantasy world. We are in a terrible dip at the moment, a kind of abyss, because the assumption is that politics are all over. That's what the propaganda says. But I don't believe the propaganda. I believe that politics, our political consciousness and out political intelligence are not all over, because if they are, we are really doomed.

(Pinter cited in Luckhurst 2006: 369)

Susan Bennett suggests that theatre practices can only be fully understood through an engagement with mutually informative, co-dependent 'inner and outer frames' (1997: 1–2, 106–24). The outer frame considers the impact of the cultural context(s) within which the theatre event is made on the theatre event itself. That is, the wider world brought to bear on the production through the audience's histories, politics and cultures. The inner frame asks us to look closely at the theatre event itself: director, performers, venue, publicity, narrative, dramaturgy, scenography, etc. Thus, the theatre event is established as a collaborative creative and meaning making process between audience and production. In so doing, I suggest we are returned to a cultural materialist position in which the theatre must be considered as part of a process of making and understanding the world, not simply reflecting it. This is of paramount importance for thinkers such as Raymond Williams who contends that innovations in art practices are not simply reflections of the shifting aesthetic and ideological sensibilities of the practitioners but also point towards shifts in wider sociopolitical thinking (cf. Williams 1966 and 1987). Just as Guy Gibson Cima sees innovation in acting as possibly identifying 'outdatedness' in social and aesthetic performance practices, a cultural materialist reading of theatre, after Williams, suggests that shifts in conventions and developments in aesthetic practice can illuminate, articulate and facilitate changes in the way a society experiences the world and the way it thinks itself through. Performance practices are then deeply, sociopolitically active at a fundamental level. The extent to which that discourse is made explicit is up to individual companies and productions but small-scale British theatre has a long history of political engagement through both aesthetic innovation and detailed ideological interrogation.

In 2008 The Paper Birds created and toured *In a Thousand Pieces*. Through a 'patchwork of [verbatim] accounts, misunderstanding, movement, text and live original music' the piece told 'the physically and visually moving tale of a young Eastern European girl and her journey to England' and 'the violent, isolated and brutal world home to thousands of women forced into the British sex trade' (The Paper Birds 2011: online). The piece was nominated for and won a number of prestigious awards including a shortlisting for the 2008 Amnesty International Freedom of Expression Award. The Amnesty award is for 'an outstanding Fringe production carrying a human rights message' (Amnesty International 2012: online) and while *In a Thousand Pieces* did not ultimately win it, the piece marked a turning point for the company's work. As McDonnell said in our interview:

> After making *In a Thousand Pieces* there was no going back for us. We love the shows that we made prior to 2008, but this was a big turning point for the company as we realised how engaged we were in making political work.
>
> We're certainly not there to launch a polemic against our audience. In fact, because we are not experts on the subjects that we tend to base our shows on, we normally start with our own experiences, prejudices and understanding or misunderstanding of the given subject. I think it's very easy to make political theatre but I think it's very hard to make it well. You have to include and engage your audiences and we now have some really interesting theatrical tools to try to do this. It's not good enough to just stand up and say the facts; people can read these in any newspaper on any given day.

Beyond the wider political impetus signalled by McDonnell's comments, the point that the company make use of, indeed often start with their own experiences is important. It signals a particular form of political activism that begins with a local, personal desire for greater understanding of and agency in the world. Not only does this add weight to the claim that their work is political theatre but it also positions them firmly within feminist theories and discourse. As Murray and Keefe point out, while the notion that 'the personal is political' became something of 'a mantra of 1970s feminism' which 'at its most extreme' might 'be accused of strategic naivety, or of rendering the political almost meaningless', it has been (and still is) a productive and fruitful framing in relation to (physical) theatre practices (2007: 30). Indeed, Judith Butler has powerfully argued that in the idea of the personal as political there is a latent supposition that 'the life-world of gender relations' and, I would argue, a great many other sociopolitical relations and contexts, 'is constituted ... through the concrete and historically mediated *acts* of individuals' (Butler 1990 274; emphasis is original). She proposes that:

> my pain or my silence or my anger or my perception is finally not mine alone ... it delimits me in a shared cultural situation which in turn enables and empowers me in certain unanticipated ways. The personal is thus implicitly political inasmuch as it is conditioned by shared social structures.
>
> (Butler 1990: 273–74)

Thus, in starting with and then building from their own experiences, The Paper Birds is making work which is explicitly engaged in the discourse of the personal as political and through this it explores wider, 'shared' social contexts, situations, structures and issues. Nevertheless, while undoubtedly politically engaged their work is not 'overwhelmed' by an explicit desire to be Political.

Duggan: *It seems to me that the politics of any story might be seen as the scaffolding on which you build your performances, and the performances in turn become a theatrical mechanism with which to more deeply to interrogate those politics?*

McDonnell: *Completely. You need to have a subject that you find to be urgent and you want to speak about it but it's our job as artists to do that well! I'm never apologetic for being theatrical in the way we approach our political interrogations, we really enjoy the challenge of making political theatre. But making it exciting, accessible and engaging as a piece of theatre is just as important as your political or ideological intentions.*

Duggan: *It has been suggested that 'big P' political theatre is dead, how do you respond to this idea?*

McDonnell: *I think our approach is completely different. You have to read and respond to the current climate, the theatrical landscape and to your audiences in the here and now. In a Thousand Pieces was brutal, there were no holds barred and it was really uncomfortable to the point that people walked out or would not/could not watch certain scenes. We didn't try to soften it around the edges and it was aggressive in that sense. But I think that the theatricality of the show, the leaps from performance to non-performance and the confessional nature of us sharing our process made the show more accessible. You can't be aggressive all the time, you have to choose your moments and make them really work. I also don't think that people feel like they're coming to see Political work when they're coming to see us.*

We had a really interesting discussion with Sue Parrish and Rod Dixon recently. We ran a symposium named 'Feminist Futures' at The Carriageworks Theatre in Leeds (March 2011) and we discussed with them our approach to selling our work. We don't overtly publicise our work as being feminist or political theatre because audiences tend to think that this is all they are getting and they have preconceptions of what this is.

Some political theatre of the 1970s and 1980s seemed to be the first and foremost about the politics – with the theatre taking a close second place. This is not a criticism, I believe that this form of political theatre was doing what was necessary at the time and those artists have paved the way for companies such as ourselves. But as we are now making political work for our generation my feeling is that if it's not a great piece of theatre, then regardless of what it's trying to say, it's irrelevant – theatre is not only our vehicle, it is our craft. Political theatre can and should be captivating.

The desire for a 'captivating' political theatre that speaks to contemporary sociocultural concerns has resulted in a performance aesthetic that owes much to understandings of postmodern and physical theatre practices, alongside nuanced dramaturgy and a good story.

News media 'hot topics' such as binge drinking, human trafficking and the alienation of disenfranchised peoples have provided solid ground on which to build their performances, as well as ensuring the work is keying into what might be thought of as dominant social concerns. In staging works that draw on verbatim transcripts alongside the company's own histories and stories framed by wider sociopolitical concerns, the work is not only building on the personal as political but also seeks to stage the reverse: to make clear that the political is also personal. In so doing, it is not making propaganda as theatre, nor even is it agitprop; rather this is a contemporary political theatre that through theatricality attends to 'real' questions about the 'real' world and as such can be considered political theatre that broadly adheres to Harold Pinter's definition set out at the beginning of this section. The Paper Birds' work discernibly participates in thinking through and making our 'world'. It is a theatre that in Raymond Williams' terms is speaking from (or about) a residual structure of feeling to the dominant one and pointing towards emergent, future possibilities both aesthetically and ideo-politically (cf. Williams 1966 and 1987; Brannigan 1998). This tripartite cultural process offers a framework for understanding the complex, continuously shifting territory of cultural development and discourse. While I am not suggesting that this is an explicit goal of The Paper Birds' work, it strikes me as an apposite and useful model through which to consider their aesthetic approach and political ethos. Their aesthetic has developed from a dialogic process that tightly mirrors the residual-dominant-emergent mode: the residual traces of the companies they have been influenced by are in constant conversation with their dominant practices/processes, and this in turn suggests avenues of development and the emergence of a new aesthetic. Of course, this aesthetic practice does not exist in a contextual vacuum; it responds to and actively engages in affecting the world in which it is made. Company literature, their performances and talking to them makes it apparent that their political ethos is about learning from and questioning recent political histories while pressing for brighter futures via rigorous interrogation of pressing contemporary problems.

Duggan: *In Paul Rae's* Theatre & Human Rights *(2009) he claims that theatre is a quest for differences, and for interrogating differences. What kind of differences are you interested in exposing and how are you putting those into discussion with each other theatrically? And to what end?*

McDonnell: *The pieces always have to start with something that matters to us in some way – if it grips us, personally intrigues, excites, scares us or leaves us outraged or perplexed, it's probably worth pursuing. I think recently we've often been concerned with difference – exploring someone or something that is fundamentally different to ourselves, our beliefs, or the lives that we lead.*

Sometimes this concern manifests itself in a desire to look outward around human rights, ethics and the other. But it can be just as interesting to look inwards and interrogate something closer to home. With Thirsty *we didn't begin with any ideological desires to discuss alcohol, the sociopolitical dynamics and questions at play in the show grew from very personal stories and questions we were asking of ourselves.*

Duggan: Do you think with Thirsty *and binge drinking you are addressing particularly British concerns and thus making a particularly British piece of theatre?*

McDonnell: We're interested in researching drinking cultures worldwide, but we are focusing on examining the UK's relationship with alcohol. The general attitude here towards alcohol is one of acceptance; there are scare-mongering stories in the press about 'binge Britain', but in the main, drinking is part of what we do and is deeply embedded within our society. Thirsty *is asking very specifically why our nation has such a love affair with alcohol and if this excessive or 'binge' drinking culture is a symptom of something else, some other deeply rooted problems within our society, and if so, what?*

    I suppose the show will be very British as not only is it concerned with drinking patterns and habits here, but we also use a great deal of verbatim material within our shows and we gather most of our research from the British public. But, we're certainly not the only nation who drink in this way, but the responses that we've had from non-UK residents is overwhelming as they repeatedly tell us: 'I've never seen anything like it, your love of alcohol; everything, all your social time revolves around it' and I'm really interested in that.

Duggan: There is a very public performance of drunkenness in Britain (echoed in the 'Brits abroad' reputation) that tends to reinforce the image of Britain as a drinking culture.

McDonnell: The work is being made by a British company, in Britain for a mainly British audience, so it seems to speak to those concerns. The process is by no means objective; who the work is being made by and for is fundamental to the way the work develops. So, with Others, *for example, it was very much about admitting that myself and Kylie are white British women looking at three other women from outside our immediate cultural and social spheres. I think that's really important and if you're making a show about binge drinking culture in the United Kingdom then, again, you've got to start with looking at that culture specifically; where it's set, where we do this drinking, how we learn/are taught to drink.*

Beyond the specific thematic/subject concerns of the productions being discussed here, McDonnell is highlighting a working process that is rooted in a detailed examination of and responding to the particulars of the social, cultural and political context within which the work is being made. While this is nothing unique – theatre practices around the globe have been engaged in such a process for millennia – it explicitly positions The Paper Birds as a contemporary company precisely concerned with questions of what we might think of as 'Britishness'. This interest is not merely at the level of social commentary, it extends to problematising, challenging and deconstructing personal and collective preconceptions. In admitting their own personal biases and stereotypes as central in their artistic practice 'the personal' becomes crucial to the wider theatrical investigation. Personal histories and perspectives are thus not only political at the local, individual level but become foregrounded as part of (made by and making) wider, shared social structures and discourses (*vide* Butler, cited above).

A Modern Feminist Theatre

It has been convincingly, if somewhat reluctantly and disappointedly, argued that we have moved past feminism to occupy a 'postfeminist' epoch in which 'feminism' and 'feminist' have become terms with negative associations that in turn have produced a resistance in their use in everyday, academic and performance contexts (cf. Aston and Harris 2006a: *passim*). Western, late capitalism has, Janelle Reinelt contends, seen 'young women' move towards an ideological position of individualism and a move away from identity politics, characterised by a growing distaste for being labelled as feminists and decreasing sense of the need 'to organise' (Reinelt 2006: 19). In arriving at this moment we may have lost some of the political efficacy that feminist performances of the second wave embodied so powerfully.

> What also seems to us to have 'got lost' in the postmodern, postfeminist utopian moment is the understanding that differences (ethnic, sexual, class, sexuality, age, religion, national, etc.) cannot be 'dealt with' instantly in a single performative gesture or through a series of 'stylised acts'. Neither can they be 'dealt with' by simply listing them, embracing them, celebrating them or remarking their proliferation. As is evident in both the micro-personal and macro-political spheres, encountering, engaging with, negotiating and living with and alongside differences, is extraordinarily demanding. It is also risky: there is the risk of failure, of antagonism, of misunderstanding, of pain; a risk that the sense of 'self' (however this is understood) might have to move, might *be* moved.
>
> (Aston and Harris 2006b: 12)

These are concerns that The Paper Birds have found themselves grappling with both explicitly within their work and implicitly at an ideological level. While they very clearly and with celebration declaim their all-female status, the process of 'becoming' – or identifying themselves as – a feminist theatre company was not an easy one.

Duggan: *Earlier, you mentioned the symposium 'Feminist Futures' and your company literature talks about your being a feminist collective, influenced by feminist discourses. Could you elaborate on that and perhaps talk a little about how it affects you at practical, aesthetic and conceptual or ideological levels?*

McDonnell: *We started as an all-female company and the work was not [overtly] politically driven. We didn't know what it meant to be feminist, we were scared to go there – as if 'feminism' was a foreign and dangerous place that we daren't explore for fear of getting it wrong. And then we made* In a Thousand Pieces *and I wondered what up until that point we had been nervous about. I think that it's the connotations associated with the word; it makes people uncomfortable, it's still a dirty word and why is this?*

At 'Feminist Futures' Rod Dixon [Red Ladder] asked people to raise their hand if they considered themselves to be a feminist. One of the young women in the audience was honest enough to share that she didn't consider herself to be feminist because she associated feminism with women hating men. That's really problematic because it's a very outdated concept of what feminism is, but it's clearly still in circulation. We actively engage in trying to host conferences and workshops that address modern feminist discourses, but mostly I hope that the work itself challenges and makes people reconsider what feminism and indeed feminist theatre is, and can be.

Feminism is not so black and white. The more that I interact with the world, the more I come to understand how that interaction is felt through a complex matrix of conditionings; people experience things through not only their gender, but their religion, their sexuality, their upbringing and that experience is individual and very unique. Everybody's positioning in the world is so different for such a number of reasons, not just because they're male or female, there's so much to take into account so it is essential when making work that in some way we respond to, address or at least acknowledge these complexities.

In addition, we've always set out to prioritise the stories of women on stage and it makes total sense to simply start with who's making the work; The Paper Birds are Jemma, Kylie and Elle, so we start with that and often the stories we want to tell or share are those of women.

Here, McDonnell is tightly mirroring feminist discourses around the complexity and fluidity of gender, interpersonal relationships and wider engagements in the world. While the company might be making work in 'a time when Western feminism has no high-profile political movement, and when debates about feminism, in both the public and academic spheres, circulate in a climate of "postfeminism"' (Aston and Harris 2006b: 2), theirs is certainly an active and dynamic theatre that draws on the histories of feminist theory and physical theatre. In embodying both physical theatre practices and feminist approaches to cultural discourse and production, The Paper Birds attempts to counter the 'postfeminist' argument which, according to Aston and Harris, suggests that 'younger generations of women do not 'need' and/or prefer to disown and/or cannot identify with feminism and therefore, presumably, with 'the established feminist tradition in the theatre' (Aston and Harris 2006b: 2).

While feminist theory and approaches to theatre making are not limited to physical theatre practices, both emerged and found purchase – publically, academically and artistically – within broadly the same historical moment and have been argued to be mutually enriching vectors of sociopolitical engagement with the world (cf. Murray and Keefe 2007).

If most feminist theories demand that we challenge traditional representations of our bodies, and acknowledge that they are sites which articulate our histories, our struggles and our living in a – patriarchal – world, then this becomes territory rich with possibilities for theatre makers concerned with the languages and vocabularies of physicality and movement.

(Murray and Keefe 2007: 29)

The mix of verbatim and physical theatre practices underpinned by a political and ideological desire to privilege the stories and voices of women suggests that The Paper Birds is very much engaged in creating a modern, accessible feminist theatre. Certainly this was a central concern in our interview:

McDonnell: *Women are grossly under-represented in the theatre and it's really important that we address that. We're very proud to have a company that is founded and run by women. It also allows us to make choices about the kind of work that we're staging, and the stories that we want to tell; so, yes, some of the work does engage with feminist ideology, but also on the most basic level; we put women on stage and we are in control of the way we represent them.*

Sometimes people say, 'oh is it an all-female cast again', and I think, 'well yes' because not only do we want to create roles for women on the stage, but also we're not trying to make work where, for example, we employ a male actor to be the sex trafficker/rapist in a piece like In a Thousand Pieces. *That's not what we're trying to do.*

Duggan: *That would be reinforcing a power dynamic rather than interrogating or problematising it, making it difficult for an audience. So it's not as interesting theatrically. In casting a man as a rapist you create a situation where your audience can associate the male rapist as male other in order to distance the act, whereas with a female cast you're having to make those representations very theatrical in order for them to work, and that brings the questions that you're asking to the fore for the audience.*

McDonnell: *Precisely, and whilst we have had men in our previous work and are likely to in the future this was not an instance where we thought it would be necessary or indeed useful.*

'Britishness': Contemplating Theatre's Futures

In deliberately colliding different aesthetic practices with key contemporary issues the work of The Paper Birds might be seen to produce a productive space – theatrical, imaginative, political, social – that functions as more than simply a barometer of contemporary attitudes and social 'temperatures'. Joshua Abrams has suggested that 'art allows us to draw neat lines around the key political, moral, economic, and structural issues of the day and to interrogate past, present and future … to grapple with these issues and to try to find a productive way forward' (2010: 16). We currently inhabit a historical moment when Britain is still trying to 'deal with' the fallout of the global financial crisis that began in 2008 [6] and when questions of globalisation, migration and immigration, multi- and inter-culturalism, terrorism and fear, class and otherness are at the forefront of news- and popular-media discourse/representation and thus by extension, of Britain's national consciousness. Within this mix, questions of national identity and what contemporary Britain might 'be' have become a constant seam of political and journalistic debate [7]. As is evident, The Paper Birds' political and theatrical concerns are diverse and ambitious and while, like many of the theatre companies discussed in this volume, their work speaks from the local to the global, the British context of their work (in terms, for example, of location, audience, performers, et cetera) is paramount within this discussion.

In the final part of our interview, we turned from the broader focus of politics, aesthetics and feminism to particular questions of 'Britishness' and the place and future of theatre in contemporary Britain:

Duggan: Others *explicitly foregrounded the stories of three disenfranchised women, but it seems to me that other bits of your work are dealing with notions of diaspora and disenfranchisement of communities and individuals. So, I'm wondering where that sits within our multi- or intercultural community in Britain and how your work is placed within our very diverse, very complex, very difficult-to-define society.*

McDonnell: *The first thing that you have to do is put your hand up and say that we're aware of who's making the piece; again, you can't make a show that explores otherness or sex trafficking or any of the topics that we explore, if we don't begin by acknowledging that we haven't experienced these things first hand. We also have to be aware that as artists we are sometimes very far removed from the economic and social aspects that affect our 'subjects'.*

But we're interested in exploring people and difference. Audre Lorde made an interesting observation about the way that oppressed people respond to each other and how amongst them there is a perception that there is only a certain amount of freedom and everyone's grappling over it. She goes on to suggest that white, middle-class, educated women need to be cautious about speaking on behalf of 'all women' regarding female oppression. I think, in this way that it's important to be fully aware of who you are and where you are located [socially, culturally, politically, economically] if you're going to try to speak on behalf of other people or about their situation, otherwise this becomes a form of oppression in itself.

Naturally the work we make is a reflection of the society we live in, and if that society is multicultural and includes diasporic peoples then we are likely to present this within the work but it wasn't a definite intention that we reached as a company (although it's certainly there, especially in Others *and* In a Thousand Pieces*).*

I would like to think that the way our work sits within this diverse, difficult-to-define Britain, is that a range of audiences can engage with the work. We don't intend for our pieces to be solely accessed by white, middle-class people. We aim for the work to speak to a range of audience regardless of age, race, cultural and economic background.

The multicultural composition of Britain and the complexity, diversity and dynamic that that brings to cultural outputs and particularly theatre has been the focus of much of the work within this volume. Indeed, the sociopolitical, cultural and aesthetic differences and influences that are traced throughout the book and across the recent history covered therein speaks precisely to what might be thought of as 'Britishness'. If we accept that theatre might act as a mechanism for a culture to think itself through, *vide* Williams, then it is a short intellectual leap to contend that it might also function as a prism through which aspects of nationhood and national identity might be viewed. Indeed, Homi Bhabha, in *Nation and Narration*, has suggested that the way a nation conceives of itself, projects itself in the world and thus is perceived, is tied to the cultural narratives it tells itself and creates for itself both in content and form (1990: 3). The theatre, then, opens up a creative space for 'exploring the paradoxes, ambiguities and complexities around issues of tradition, identity, authenticity and belonging associated with the nation' (Holdsworth 2010: 7). While The Paper Birds is not making 'state-of-the-nation' plays, it is obliquely attending to questions about the composition and ideological purview(s) of 'our' nation.

Duggan: *What do you see as the future of British theatre?*
McDonnell: *That's really difficult.*

It shocks me when I go to see a large-scale theatre because it is so far removed from what we do. It is self-sufficient as an industry; it has guaranteed bums on seats and ticket prices to ensure that profit is made. The future of a large-scale theatre therefore is already laid out; it will keep going forever as it is such a part of the cultural identity of London in particular and is so crucial in relation to tourism, it's got a life of its own. For that reason, it seems to me that it will always remain safe and try not to push many boundaries. But it will employ exciting technological advances, no doubt as it has the budget and resources to do that.

I'd like to hope that there is still something exciting happening with emerging artists and companies making work that's classed as fringe or alternative or small-scale. I would like to believe that some of those companies will be able to make it to mid-scale or even large-scale venues and share that kind of work with larger audiences. I don't know if it's possible or if funding opportunities would support that, but there is a rumble of it at the moment. Venues like the West Yorkshire Playhouse are starting to make this kind of shift in their programming with festivals such as the Transform festival. It was the first time I knew WYP to programme small-scale work, and maybe it has evolved because of the funding cuts and an attitude of 'let's not let all this work, interesting work, and companies fall away'. So, I really hope that part of British theatre's future includes venues developing support networks that allow smaller companies to flourish.

Duggan: *We have a long history in Britain of small-scale theatre, touring theatre, but given the kind of political and funding climate that we find ourselves in [2011/12], do you think there is an opportunity for those smaller-scale companies, who are large in ambition, to find bigger houses with bigger audiences without it damaging the aesthetic or changing the underlying political and ideological concerns of the work?*

> *If so, maybe we can be excited about the future of British theatre in light of the funding cuts because we might think and try harder to make and expose audiences to dynamic, exciting and difficult work.*

McDonnell: *Well I hope so, but I've watched companies who have made the leap to bigger venues and their work has changed. That worries me; I wonder how much pressure they feel to fill those seats and what needs to happen in order to do that. Once you have that larger stage, can you really stick to what you set out to do? Are you brave enough to do that?*

Duggan: *Bigger stages might swallow certain aesthetic choices, so those choices have to shift and even if your ideological and political positions don't change, an aesthetic shift will impact the way in which you interrogate those positions. Part of the exciting history that we have in British theatre is the fact that the smaller-scale companies have been more subversive, they've been more invisible, for want of a better word, and they have been able to vibrate at the borders of subversion and expose tensions and social problems in really productive and exciting ways.*

McDonnell: *I just wonder if companies, when they're about to make that leap, really consider how they will now reconcile having a bigger stage and bigger audience with the things that they were achieving before, an intimacy, an aesthetic and approach to theatre that they had mastered and with which they were doing exciting things. How you transfer that and what needs to change is very difficult to know. Even when we play slightly larger audiences, I feel completely different about the work, something gets lost.*

Duggan: *What do you think the place or the function of small-scale theatre is in British theatre now?*

McDonnell: *To continue to be brave and to make the work that we really want to make. To take risks and to tour and share that work. It's really hard to talk about the function of small-scale theatre outside of that.*

I like to go and see small-scale work because that's often where I'll find something that really excites me. There is more freedom and more creativity; there's less money so you really have to be creative in what you're doing and how you're going to do it, and that's where I find the work to be exciting. People really push themselves in order to make the kind of work that they want to make.

Duggan: *In light of that, do you think there is an aesthetic or a philosophy for small-scale theatre in Britain today?*

McDonnell: *I've been wondering about that too. It's connected to the fact that with small-scale theatre the work is being made by people who are very committed to what they're doing. I think maybe with big companies or in larger productions where you're employing other people you can lose the sense of the person or the thing that was driving the work. You keep that passion and sense of the work's centre with small-scale theatre because you know everybody who's involved in it. There is a real sense of being completely committed to what it is that they're doing and often people are* directly involved in more than one way, I think that's really important to small-scale work.

Duggan: Smaller-scale companies are fighting for every bit of space and every bit of funding they can get, so the work becomes fundamentally about those people and about their desire to make that work. Whereas, perhaps, when you go to the West End it's not necessarily just about making the work because economic conditions become so central to the process.

McDonnell: Yes, it becomes a very distancing process. If a playwright has written a script that they are extremely passionate about and has a clear focus; the script is then handed on to somebody else to produce it, to someone else who's going to cast it, a director who reworks it into their own vision, etc. The piece becomes so distant from the original and from the intention of the playwright or devising team that began the project. The very core of it becomes lost in layers and layers of people and time and a massive, expensive venue. With small scale it's so much closer to what the original intention was; that need to make the work remains within arm's reach of whoever started it and audiences can feel that in the work.

Duggan: So, in that dynamic the intention of the work is palpably felt in the room rather than it being something that is analysed from a distance?

McDonnell: Or kind of lost somewhere along the way, maybe. It's not fair to say that about all work, but I feel like this about a lot of performances I see. For the same reason, I don't go to big [music] gigs; I don't go because I like to be in the room with someone and not at the back where you could have been playing a CD or watching a close up of the singer on a large screen at the side of the stage – I know the atmosphere might be great but when you go to a very intimate gig and you are really seeing and hearing that person, they're connecting with their audience and that's when I get the most enjoyment out of theatre as well.

For Nadine Holdsworth, after Benedict Anderson, national identity is 'the meeting point between the individual and the collective conception of nation, but crucially both are variable. An individual changes his or her opinions, attitudes and levels of identification, and the nation is similarly an ongoing process' (Holdsworth 2010: 21). Thus any notion of 'Britishness' will be a negotiation; a slippery construct in part facilitated through exposure to cultural objects such as the theatre. Beyond the broad point that all theatre discussed in this volume is in some way attending to that construction, The Paper Birds' work is precisely staging that meeting point. In *Others* variously disenfranchised individuals are put into conversation with each other to worry at preconceived, nationally recognised stereotypes; in *Thirsty*, Britain's long established binge-drinking habit (cf. Withington 2011), its place as an engrained national pastime and part of our cultural construction is critiqued through plethora voices, both from those engaged in and those opposed to the culture of alcohol consumption in the United Kingdom; and with *In a Thousand Pieces*, the company ask how individual national identity is disrupted and threatened by the clash of perceived notions of nation and the material conditions of inhabiting that nation. While discernible narratives that hold on to something of an Aristotelian structure and the British history of the 'well-made play' are evident in the company's work, they tell their stories in fragmented, physical compositions that owe much to – and continue the work of – what Claire Warden (2012) has defined as the British avant-garde. In that tradition

> The plays are not plotless, but rather full of multiple, at times conflicting, plot fragments… Genre became a complex notion and the audience members were suddenly plunged into a complicated world where the relationship between cause and effect, logic and action was questioned.
>
> (Warden 2012: 23–24)

In so doing, The Paper Birds speaks to the multiple histories and practices that are embodied in (small-scale) British theatre. But more than this, they rework and appropriate those histories and practices into their own theatrical voice which re-aestheticises a new form of political theatre and points towards a rich, sociopolitically active future for British theatre.

Duggan: *What ideological positions or structures do you think drive Britishness and how does your theatre respond to or challenge these?*

McDonnell: *I think Britishness is a lot about achieving. Rod [Dixon] said something very interesting about how when you first get introduced to someone new, the first thing we ask is 'what do you do?'. This is triggered by a desire to understand what people bring to their society, what do they add, and where do we sit in relation to them. I think this is very true of our contemporary moment. It's endemic even from school when we are given those document wallets to put all our achievements in. But at that age, you don't really have anything. You've got some swimming badges or something like that, but a focus on achievement is set up from a very early age. It's not good enough to have just done it, there needs to be a certificate; you need some proof, you need a list of things that show what you can do and how well you can do them! That spirals off into life where it becomes about a culture to earn and achieve. I've never been particularly interested in it. In terms of our work, we've certainly never been driven to do this in order to make money. We're interested in getting audiences and we're interested in making connections with theatres and funders that want to see the work grow, not because they might be able to make a lot of money out of it but because they think that there's something important there, something for us to share.*

Duggan: *I like the idea that achievement might be one of the key elements of Britishness and potentially then of concern for British theatre. I think achievement is a very powerful word and you've highlighted some of the negative ways in which that might be part of our society but it seems to me that it's also an incredibly powerful and positive thing in certain ways; I wonder what achievement is for you/The Paper Birds?*

McDonnell: *Finding big and diverse audiences to see the work. Although it's nice to be small scale and to have that intimacy with people, we don't make the work for ourselves, we make it to share and to start discussions and debates and to engage other people. So, for me, the biggest achievement that we can have is to keep doing that and not fall into the trap of being a company that produces the same kind of work and attracts the same kind of audiences year after year. If we had the same people come to see the work repeatedly and that's all we ever achieved, it would feel like we weren't doing our job properly.*

Duggan: *It seems, then, that part of the goal of making work for you is to have a sense of its impact in the world and that you want that impact to facilitate debate in interesting and productively problematic ways.*

McDonnell: *Absolutely. Most reactions to the work we present are characterised by our ability to present cases, arguments and politics without wagging a finger or making the audience feel like they are attending a lecture. This reaction enables social change on a much larger scale than if the audience member were to feel ashamed of their politics or ideology.*

References

Abrams, J., 2010. 'This Scepter'd Isle: State of the nation in Recent British theatre'. *PAJ: A Journal of Performance and Art*, 32: 2, pp. 8–16.

Amnesty International, 2012. 'Record number of entries for Amnesty theatre award'. http://www.amnesty.org.uk/news_details.asp?NewsID=20255 (accessed 30 October 2012).

Aston, E. and Harris, G. (eds), 2006a. *Feminist Futures? Theatre, Performance, Theory*. Basingstoke: Palgrave Macmillan.

———, 2006b. 'Feminist futures and the possibilities of 'We'?', in E. Aston and G. Harris (eds). *Feminist Futures? Theatre, Performance, Theory*. Basingstoke: Palgrave Macmillan, pp. 1–16.

Bhabha, H., 1990. *Nation and Narration*. London: Routledge.

Brannigan, J., 1998. *New Historicism and Cultural Materialism*. Basingstoke: Palgrave Macmillan.

Brecht, B., 1964. *Brecht on Theatre* (trans. John Willett). London: Methuen.

Butler, J., 1990. 'Performative acts and gender constitution: An essay in phenomenology and feminist theory', in S.-E. Case (ed.). *Performing Feminisms: Feminist Critical Theory and Theatre*. Baltimore, MD: The Johns Hopkins University Press, pp. 270–82.

Castellucci, C. et al., 2007. *The Theatre of Societas Raffaello Sanzio*. London: Routledge.

Gibson Cima, G., 1993. *Performing Women: Female Characters, Male Playwrights and the Modern Stage*. Ithica, NY: Cornell University Press.

Holdsworth, N., 2010. *Theatre & Nation*. Basingstoke: Palgrave Macmillan.

Luckhurst, M., 2006. 'Torture in the plays of Harold Pinter', in M. Luckhurst (ed.). *A Companion to Modern British and Irish Drama*. Oxford: Blackwell Publishing.

Murray, S. and Keefe, J., 2007. *Physical Theatres: A Critical Introduction*. London: Routledge.

Paper Birds, 2011. 'The Paper Birds Theatre Company'. http://www.thepaperbirds.com/ (accessed July 2011).

Reinelt, J., 2006. 'Navigating postfeminism: Writing out of the box', in E. Aston and G. Harris (eds). *Feminist Futures? Theatre, Performance, Theory*. Basingstoke: Palgrave Macmillan, pp. 1–16.

Williams, R., 1966. *Modern Tragedy*. London: Chatto and Windus.

———, 1987. *Drama From Ibsen to Brecht*. London: The Hogarth Press.

Withington, P., 2011. 'Intoxicants and society in early modern England'. *The Historical Journal*, 54: 3, pp. 631–57.

Notes

1 The core members of the company are Jemma McDonnell (artistic director) and Kylie Walsh (co-founder and outreach director) and Elle Moreton was also one of the founding members of the company. They have a long-standing collaboration with composer and sometime on-stage presence Shane Durrant.

2 Although the University of Leeds historically awarded the degrees gained at Bretton Hall, the two formally merged in August 2001, with Bretton Hall becoming the School of Performance and Cultural Industries. The Bretton campus has now closed and the School of PCI is housed at the main university campus in Leeds. The BA Acting degree was 'taught out' with its final cohort graduating in 2007.

3 All interview material cited is from an interview conducted between the author and Jemma McDonnell at the Barbican Centre, London, April 2011.

4 I will attend in more detail to the specifics of the company's 'politics' later in the chapter; however, it is worth noting here that the all-female composition of the company and a desire to create work which is resonant with contemporary sociopolitical concerns is central to their practice.

5 The Paper Birds has worked closely with Rod Dixon/Red Ladder on a number of projects and in research and development activities.

6 As I finish this chapter in October 2012 the so-called 'credit crunch' is still very much part of national and international press cycles and at the centre of political discourse in Britain.

7 Especially in relation to economic, policing and judicial connections with the European Union and particularly since May 2010 when the Tory-led coalition government came to power.

Chapter 10

'Angels and Modern Myth': Grid Iron and the New Scottish Theatre

Trish Reid

Thinking about the place of small-scale theatre companies in British theatre from a Scottish perspective raises a number of particular questions. Funding mechanisms in Scotland differ in a number of significant ways from elsewhere in the United Kingdom, for instance, and the Scottish sector is considerably smaller which necessarily affects conceptions of scale. How exactly do we define smallness within the context of the cultural sectors of small nations? Perhaps more significantly, however, the very idea of Britain has come under renewed and sustained pressure north of the border since the establishment of the Scottish Parliament in 1999. Subsequently, this pressure has intensified with the election of the UK coalition government in 2010, the majority Scottish National Party (SNP) government in 2011, and the announcement in autumn 2012 of a referendum on Scottish independence to be held in 2014. The future of the Union, and hence Britain as a political entity, is uncertain. For theatre artists living and working in Scotland, this has meant that the imperative to interrogate, reassess and re-imagine the idea of Scotland and its relationship to Britain has become more powerful. As David Pattie has observed:

> … post devolution, Scottish culture operates in different territory. The threats and promises of the devolution debate – a debate, which Andrew Marr's *The Battle for Scotland* makes clear, lasted for most of the twentieth century – are no longer enough; we need new maps to help us negotiate the terrain ahead.
>
> (Pattie 2008: 143)

Scottish artists, like their peers throughout the United Kingdom, have also been developing work against the backdrop of, and partly in response to, equally seismic shifts in the international landscape that include the reconfiguration of Europe after the end of the Cold War, the unprecedented demographic shifts caused by globalisation, the rise of new media, the war on terror and the economic crash of 2008. All of these raise questions about the limits of political authority, the security of borders and the criminally unequal distribution of the world's wealth. We live in interesting times. The Scottish theatre sector has been able to respond with remarkable flexibility and imagination to these shifting national and international trends. Consequently, a significant number of chapters, articles and books have appeared drawing attention what is now generally acknowledged to be a renaissance in Scottish theatre. (see Holdsworth 2008; Muller and Wallace 2011; Reid 2011; Scullion 2007; Sierz et al. 2011) These accounts have largely, if not exclusively, focused on a smallish group of contemporary Scottish playwrights who have achieved international success including Gregory Burke, David Harrower, Anthony Neilson and especially David Greig. While this renewed interest in Scottish theatre is to be welcomed, it is noticeable that relatively little has been written about Scottish performance companies and their place in the newly energised Scottish theatre scene. This chapter is intended to redress this balance, however slightly, by considering the output and impact of Grid Iron, a multi-award winning Edinburgh-based company that since its inception in 1995 has built an international reputation by engaging creatively with audiences in a diverse range of Scottish and international settings.

Grid Iron has been well placed to contribute to and benefit from the resurgence of Scottish theatre culture. Originally conceived as a new writing company by co-artistic directors, producer Judith Doherty and writer and director Ben Harrison, Grid Iron has become strongly associated with site-related work. This chapter aims to provide an overview of the work of the company with particular reference to the ways in which its site-specific focus has allowed it to engage creatively and influentially with the shifting dynamics of the contemporary Scottish theatre scene and with identity politics in Scotland in the aftermath of devolution. As Fiona Wilkie notes in her essay on site-specific performance, 'Mapping the Terrain', the decision to move away from traditional theatre space is often motivated by a desire to foreground 'ideas of place and community' (Wilkie 2002: 144). Since ideas of place and community have taken centre stage in Scottish politics and culture in recent years, site-related practice might seem a convenient and potentially rich field through which Scottish theatre artists might engage with the shifting dynamics of contemporary Scottish identity politics. This is not to imply that the increased interest in site-specificity – for both theatre artists and audiences – that has marked the last several decades in British theatre has been limited to Scotland. What does seem clear however, especially in the range of work produced and co-produced by the National Theatre of Scotland (NTS) since 2006, is that site-specific practice has been key in enabling the new national company to fulfil its remit of engaging creatively with local theatre companies, artists and communities in a diverse range of Scottish settings. Not only was the NTS's inaugural project *Home* (2006) largely site-specific, but it also commissioned a major work from Grid Iron in its first year. The resulting production, *Roam,* was performed by an international cast at BAA Edinburgh International Airport in April 2006. It won Best Ensemble, Best Technical Presentation and Best Theatre Production at the Critics Awards for Theatre in Scotland that year.

Although Grid Iron has produced around 20 productions since its incorporation in 1995, this chapter focuses on three of its major works, *The Bloody Chamber* (1997), *Decky Does a Bronco* (2000) and *Roam* (2006), each of which engaged with the possibilities of site-related performance rather differently. Before describing these productions and their effects, it seems useful to locate Grid Iron's practice within the wider preoccupation with identity, memory and 'space' that has marked this strand of contemporary British theatre practice. A consideration of the Welsh company Brith Gof is useful in this regard because it has been key in developing the vocabulary of site-specific performance both in theory and practice. In a number of seminal productions including *Gododdin* (1998), *Pax* (1991) and *Haearn* (1992) Brith Gof consolidated a model of site-specific practice in which the site itself functioned as an active metaphor within the performance. Premiered in a disused Rover car plant in Cardiff's Docklands, *Gododdin*, for example, utilised cutting edge performance technologies and practices to stage a retelling of *Y Gododdin*, a medieval Welsh elegiac poem commemorating a sixth-century battle in which a large Anglo-Saxon army defeated a small band of heroic Celtic warriors. The production's primary focus was not the distant past, however. As Jen Harvie emphasises, '*Gododdin*'s more immediate and urgent stimuli were the industrial and social conditions in South Wales in the mid- to late 1980s' where rapid de-industrialisation had resulted in mass unemployment (Harvie 2005: 49). As the backdrop for a tale of heroic defeat, then, the abandoned Rover factory called into play both memories of former productivity and also the realities of a harsher present. Moreover, what Harvie describes as the 'show's physical labour' – which was particularly large scale and intense – in combination with Cliff McLucas's scenography, conjured the site's former use as an industrial space further activating the space as metaphor (Harvie 2005: 49). During this phase of their work Brith Gof became particularly associated with the utilisation of site for the interrogation of cultural identities and socio-economic relations. Equally importantly, McLucas and to a larger extent his co-artistic director Mike Pearson became influential in setting out the organising principles and theoretical paradigms through which site-specific performance has been understood (see Pearson 2010; Pearson and Shanks 2001; McLucas 2000).

Subsequently, as Fiona Wilke has shown, a range of new articulations of site-specificity emerged in the 1990s in the work of Brith Gof and others. These included the 'large scale grand event, the small scale fleeting encounter and the many performance models in between', each representing not only 'formal and aesthetic but also political choices' (Wilkie 2008: 96). Within the context of this developing field Grid Iron has tended not to work on a monumental scale, nor has it systematically adopted a directly political agenda. It has instead created a number of promenade performances in which audiences are led or enticed through cleverly chosen interiors – and sometimes exteriors – and encouraged to explore their own response to the environment and its effect on their reading of the performance. Such practices work to throw spectators into awareness of themselves as interpreting subjects, and often lead to particularly vivid experiences. Its breakthrough production, *The Bloody Chamber* (1997), for instance, involved staging an adaptation of Angela Carter's retelling of the Bluebeard myth, in Mary King's Close, one of many seventeenth-century streets built over during the modernisation of Edinburgh's Old Town. Now an established tourist attraction, the subterranean street was carefully chosen by Harrison and Doherty. Not only does it have a general reputation for being haunted, it is widely believed that when plague struck in 1645, the city elders had the residents walled up inside. Harrison's production, which featured live piano and cello, made extensive use of the corners and crannies of the underground street taking its audience on a torch-lit journey through the rooms where victims of the plague were said to have been left to die – much like Bluebeard's former wives in the dungeons of his castle. The small audience was led by a lantern-bearing woman – in Keith Lodwick's adaptation an older version of the young bride narrating her own tale – through a dark labyrinth of passages to the threshold of the room in which the heroine makes her grisly discovery. When the young bride finally entered the 'bloody chamber', no attempt was made to represent the horrors she discovers there. The crucial elements of the picture were supplied not by the physical resources of the production, but in the imaginative or metaphorical space that had been produced in the relationship between the performance and the space it occupied. In this regard *The Bloody Chamber* provides an evocative example of the relationship that Cliff McLucas terms 'the host and the ghost', in which the site or 'host' can be seen through the performance or 'ghost' creating a kind of layering effect, or a palimpsest, a term commonly used in contemporary discussions of site-specific performance (McLucas 2000: 128). The show toured successfully in 1998 to among other places the London Dungeon and the concrete chambers under Belfast's Lagan Weir, but never quite recaptured the atmosphere supplied by Edinburgh's gothic past. In the event, the production established the company's reputation, winning a prestigious Herald Angel Award. Unearthing performance spaces in Scotland's capital was to become a habit. In the summer of 1998 their next show, *Gargantua,* was performed in the vaults beneath the Central Library on George VI Bridge, a venue christened the Underbelly by the company.

The idea of a 'ghost that haunts the site' is 'recurrent in site-specific performance' as Cathy Turner has noted, but the question of 'whether the site haunts the work or vice versa often seems intriguingly unclear' (Turner 2004: 374). Grid Iron's next significant piece of work, its production of Douglas Maxwell's *Decky Does a Bronco* (2000), provides a more complex example of the potentials of this relationship. Staged outdoors in a purpose built swing park *Decky* tells the tale, narrated by the grown-up David, of a group of nine-year-old boys in Girvan on Scotland's west coast in the summer of 1983. Capturing the excitement and danger of school holidays, at a time when these were spent relatively free of adult supervision, the adult cast's death-defying displays of playground gymnastics centred around the 'bronco' of the title, the ultimate swing trick that the boys use to vie for status. As the smallest and least confident of the group, Decky's inability to perform this trick leads to constant teasing and ultimately to the play's grim dénouement. In Harrison's production adult actors played the boys and their grown up selves, these older selves constantly circling their younger ones. In combination with the outdoor setting, this doubling created a kind of palimpsest of memory and nostalgia. Adult performers were employed not as a gimmick, but to suggest that vivid experiences in childhood are inevitably carried into adulthood. At the Edinburgh Fringe in August 2000, *Decky Does a Bronco* was performed in the Scotland Yard Playground in the New Town. Here as elsewhere, the sounds of real children playing in the distance added atmosphere and poignancy. In addition, and in common with other performances in genuinely public spaces, the site carried the threat of possible disruption, however accidental. Occasionally such interventions proved entirely fortuitous, as Susannah Clapp acknowledged in her review for *The Observer*:

> … as the hero reflected on the persistence of things after childhood tragedy, a real – proper-size – child burst out of the bushes surrounding the stage and gamboled towards it, carefree and callous – as if to prove his point.

(Clapp 2000: 8)

Decky Does a Bronco won a Scotsman Fringe First award for innovation in theatre and outstanding new production and a Stage award for Best Ensemble. The production was toured extensively in Britain and Ireland and successfully revived by Grid Iron in 2010. In 2012 the Wales Millennium Centre, in collaboration with Theatr na n'Óg, toured a Welsh language version of the play retitled *Ma Bili'n Bwrw'r Bronco*.

Grid Iron continued to produce award-winning work and to explore the relationship between performance and found or transformed space in the years between *Decky Does a Bronco* and *Roam*, in the process consolidating its reputation as an important contributor to the developing landscape of Scottish theatre. *Those Eyes, That Mouth* (2003), for instance, a site-specific promenade piece performed by one actor and one musician over four floors in an abandoned Town House won several awards. Lyn Gardner captured some of the shows atmosphere when she described how it took its audience 'into yellow wallpaper territory' as they followed an artist 'imprisoned by the tricks that her own mind plays upon her' from room to room, bearing witness as she confronted 'her demons and a love spoiled by jealousy' (Gardner 2004: 17). 2005 saw Grid Iron expand its international reach with a new work commissioned as part of Cork's European Capital of Culture celebrations. *The Devil's Larder*, adapted by Harrison from the novel by Jim Grace, premiered at the Old City Morgue as part of a larger project, entitled *Relocation*, which brought together four of Europe's established site-specific companies, Teatr Buiro Podrozy (Poland), Jo Bithume (France), Corcadorca (Ireland) and Grid Iron. By the middle of the first decade of the new millennium the company was therefore very well placed to contribute to and benefit from the expansion in opportunity provided by the newly established National Theatre of Scotland.

The NTS, which began producing work in early 2006, attracted immediate praise for its buildingless model: an exceptionally flexible co-producing remit enabled it to make work across a remarkable variety of scales in an equally wide variety of contexts from the outset. Nadine Holdsworth has emphasised, for instance, how far the NTS's institutionally collaborative practice allows it to stage a 'rich programme of events that encapsulate the multiple communities that constitute the Scottish nation in a way that is outward looking, forward thinking and internationally significant' (Holdsworth 2010: 37). Fiona Wilkie has also suggested that at its inception, the NTS found in site-specificity 'a convenient marker of a set of ideas with which' it wanted 'to be associated' including 'experiment, accessibility' and 'a shift away from the primacy of the metropolitan theatre building' (Wilkie 2008: 88). By 2005 Grid Iron was Scotland's pre-eminent site-specific performance company. Its practices, alongside those of other companies such as Suspect Culture, Theatre Cryptic and Vanishing Point and playwrights such as David Harrower, David Greig and Anthony Neilson, had been key in establishing contemporary Scottish theatre's reputation as eclectic, internationally engaged and formally inventive. It was from this lively sector that the NTS was born, and it is therefore unsurprising that the new company commissioned a major work from Grid Iron in its first year.

In an age of heightened airport security, it seems remarkable in retrospect that BAA Edinburgh International Airport ever agreed to host *Roam*. Performed as the final flights of the day left the runway, Harrison's show utilised four airport check-in desks, several TV monitors, a baggage carousel and a section of the departure lounge. Audience members, who were bussed in from Edinburgh city centre, were told to bring passports to guarantee admission. *Roam* worked in a range of modes, some comic, some serious, to expose the institutional conditions in which the site habitually worked, drawing attention to borders within borders and the hierarchies that allow some people free passage where others are denied it. On boarding the bus, for instance, audience members were welcomed by a young woman standing by a box of confiscated knives holding up a tomato and asking them to identify it. Thus discourses of identity – in this instance citizenship tests, which invariably require applicants to answer questions about the country's society, history and culture – were problematised from the outset. In the airport itself, two immigration officers – positioned next to a sign requesting the removal of all beards – quizzed a Palestinian traveller who claimed to be Scottish on the exact nature of his national identity. All international airports work under specific ideological constraints, of course, which do not always relate to passenger safety or national security. In its self-conscious appropriation of this highly controlled space, *Roam* emphasised the constructed nature of identity and its relationship to place, while in the process engaging with contentious questions about international terrorism and political refugees in the post-9/11 world. Harrison, who was writer and director on this project, clearly intended his audience to identify imaginatively with the degradation suffered by many – particularly those from the Arab world – in their attempt to negotiate international borders. As the narrative of piece developed, TV monitors announced that a civil war had prompted an exodus from Scotland to the safe havens of Sarajevo, Beirut and Kigali, cities synonymous with the war torn histories of Bosnia, Lebanon and Rwanda. As desperate refugees began to arrive the audience were obliged to line up under 'them' and 'us' signs. *Roam* moved its audience around in a way that echoed the institutional practices of the airport itself. Crucially, it positioned its audience extremely carefully and consequently bodily positioning in relation to space, or 'place', became vital to the show's sense making.

In *Roam*, more clearly than in the other major projects discussed above, Grid Iron's choice of site recalls what the anthropologist Marc Augé has termed 'non-place'. For Augé such places are constitutive of super-modernity and are thus emblematic of the contemporary moment, and of the process usually referred to as globalisation. His definition of non-place relies on a distinction in anthropological terms between substantive and transitive sites: 'If a place can be defined as relational, historical and concerned with identity, then a space which cannot be defined as relational, or historical, or concerned with identity will be a non-place' (Augé 2010: 63).

Non-place implies two separate but related meanings: 'spaces formed in relation to certain ends (transport, transit, commerce, leisure) and the relations that individuals have with these spaces' (Augé 2010: 76). The airport, like the luxury hotel room, is an archetypal non-place. In *Roam* Grid Iron attempted to explore its significance from perspectives that called into question, or at least were not constrained by, fixed regional or national boundaries. That is not to say, of course, that *Roam* failed to acknowledge the extent to which advances in communications and exchanges between cultures are conditioned by economic or political factors. On the contrary, *Roam* worked precisely to uncover these inequities and was informed throughout by an awareness of the tensions between the local and the global, tensions that provide the backdrop to all current discussions about the future of Scotland and, by extension, of Britain and the idea of Britishness.

As I hope the above account illustrates, small-scale companies such as Grid Iron have played a significant role in the development of contemporary Scottish theatre. They have enriched its vocabulary and, perhaps more than any other part of the sector, embodied its newfound confidence. All is not rosy in the Scottish garden, however. In June 2012 controversial changes to funding were announced by Creative Scotland, which involved 49 of its flexibly-funded organisations – including Grid Iron – moving over to a system based on project funding. Such an arrangement would inevitably threaten the continued health of a company on Grid Iron's scale, severely limiting their ability to maintain a core team or engage in effective forward planning, for instance. The Scottish arts sector – the proposed changes are not confined to theatre – has staged a mighty fight back, however, which led to the resignation of Creative Scotland's chief executive, Andrew Dixon, in December 2012. Grid Iron is currently working on a new site-specific show for Edinburgh 2013. Details will be forthcoming.

Interview Ben Harrison and Trish Reid, 10 November 2012

Reid: *I wanted to start with an observation. Your company is known substantially, if not exclusively, for work that is site-specific or at least not created in traditional theatre spaces. I wondered if you could talk a little about what first attracted you to this kind of work and what opportunities you feel are still offered by the opportunity to work outside the traditional proscenium arch theatre.*

Harrison: *The first site-specific piece I did, and I wasn't in any way conscious of labelling it as such, was by chance really. It was a piece that I did in 1994 while I was still a student at Edinburgh about the notorious murderers Burke and Hare. An academic at Edinburgh had written this play and it was performed at the university's Bedlam Theatre, which is in an old gothic church that happens to be very close to Greyfriars Kirkyard. Coincidentally, the second half of the play took place in a graveyard so we thought let's use what's here. The second half became a promenade led by a fiddle player that featured lots of running around tombstones and ghost appearing and so on. But I stress we did this in a very untutored way. After the first half all the actors simply leaped off the stage into the auditorium and kind of manhandled the audience out of their seats in a very coarse way. Nevertheless, there was something about having that second half in the 'real' world that was key for me. In particular I remember one moment where the ghost of Mary Patterson had a speech in which she accused her murderers. She was saying 'may your body be corrupted by lust' and just at the moment she uttered the word 'lust' Edinburgh Castle turned red – and the audience gasped. It was an eye opener for me because it showed the audience was looking at the whole frame, not just the action, not just the immediate setting of the gravestone but everything. The whole landscape had become theatricalised. Of course it just so happened that the lighting technicians at the Tattoo were testing their settings at that moment – an instant of good fortune really – but nevertheless it brought home for me the potential benefits of disturbing the traditional frame. More variables come into play whether accidental or otherwise. For me working in 'real' spaces also opened up greater possibilities for collaboration or rather changed the grounds on which collaborations were negotiated. There are always elements of site-specific work that are installation based so you are immediately into a more fine-art-based collaboration with your designer, which I find very exciting. Also the promenade aspect, the moving together through a space, was very important for me. I felt and still feel that the sense of a shared journey makes the experience more visceral for audiences and performers alike. They are somehow more alive in it. I think when you are sitting watching a stage you are reminded of other habits you engage in while sitting, like watching TV, or sitting in a classroom, which are arguably more passive. Promenade, partly because it engages you kinetically, is for my money the most profound form of site-based work. It's about mobility and it provides the opportunity to explore what theatre is or might be.*

Reid: *And mobility is a very current concern, or motif even, in the wider cultural context.*

Harrison: *Yes, the movement of people across borders, through different identities, that's certainly been a preoccupation for some years and was certainly a major focus in* Roam.

Reid: *In your work, and that of others of your generation, I detect a shift in focus from the work of earlier influential site-specific companies or productions. One associates the work of Brith Gof, for instance, or Bill Bryden's The Ship (1990), with post-industrial spaces and consequently with discourses of class and gender, especially in relation to workplace. Can you comment?*

Harrison: *Generally, yes, I agree there has been a shift but it does depend on the individual project. For instance, I did a project in 2009 as part of the NTS's Transform/Learn in the old Dunlop factory in Dunfermline, where they used to make inner tubing for tyres. The site was chosen, and seemed relevant, because the factory had only closed eight years before so a lot of the parents of the kids we were working with had once been employed there. The piece, which was partly about what their parents told them about the space, was called* You Tell Us What Was, We Tell You What Is. *It was at that time, like so many of these sites, on the verge of being converted into posh flats. To go back to your question though, it hasn't been a conscious choice to avoid such sites. I imagine had Grid Iron been born in Glasgow things might have been very different. Edinburgh is not, and never has been, an industrial city, so we have necessarily worked in different sort of spaces. We opened up Mary King's Close, for instance, for* The Bloody Chamber *(1997) and established the Underbelly with* Gargantua *in 1998. We named that space underbelly partly because of the subject matter of the piece, but also because it was in the vaults of an old bank, a very Edinburgh kind of space. Edinburgh is a mercantile city, a city of bankers and lawyers, and I've found that very useful to kick against, culturally. It has this explosion of arts and culture in the summer, but there is a certain sense in the city, perhaps less so now than before, that well, yes, that might be the sort of thing we do in August but the rest of the time we return to propriety, remain essentially puritanical and Presbyterian.*

Reid: *Edinburgh is also a city of ghosts and ghost stories, and of extraordinary architecture.*

Harrison: *Yes it is – buildings built over buildings and hauntings. In fact, our breakthrough piece,* The Bloody Chamber, *which was our first fully site-specific work, was staged in Mary King's Close, in the Old Town. Nothing had ever been done there before. There was a tour available every couple of months, which was not publicly advertised but if you knew the guy from the council who had the key you could arrange to go in, which of course we did. It's now a big tourist attraction advertised on the side of buses but at that time many people didn't even know it existed. But that was a real archaeologist's project. This history of the Close, at least according to many, was that the inhabitants had been walled in. They were plague victims and were left to die there while the city continued to build on top of them. So I think from the show in the Kirkyard through Mary King's Close to the Underbelly those early shows are all occupying a kind of Gothic imaginary space, although* Gargantua *was much more exuberant in tone, all three were digging into the underbelly of the city as it were.*

Reid: *Can you talk a little more about your relationship with Edinburgh?*

Harrison: *I first came here to live as an undergraduate although the first company I was involved with as a teenager toured to the Fringe. In fact I came here three years in a row and I fell in love with the city naively assuming that it had a festival atmosphere all year round. It is remarkable, that explosion of culture in August. I also came here on holiday with my folks when I was about 16 and that was more or less the first time I'd been to the theatre on my own. I went to the Traverse and sat next to Tilda Swinton in the bar, I remember that felt very glamorous. But more seriously, the old Traverse did have a particular pull for me. So I did an undergraduate degree in English literature and lots of plays at the Bedlam. Then I went to Amsterdam for a year, then toyed with the idea of going into academia so did a post graduate at Warwick, and then trained as a theatre director at Central School of Speech and Drama (CSSD) having throughout this whole period constantly been trying to get into drama school as an actor. But the year at CSSD was the most intense. The intensity of a full on practical course after handing in a couple of essays a term for four years was palpable. We did one site-specific project during that year but the course was really about honing my skills, particularly my collaborative skills. It was the first time I had worked with designers, for instance, in a considered way.*

Reid: *And the decision to bring your company to Scotland?*

Harrison: *Well Judith (Doherty), my business partner, and I had already had the idea while we were studying in Edinburgh. She was in the year below me and by the time she graduated I was already in Warwick and heading to CSSD. I really wanted to train as a director. In a sense, and particularly in that period, the director was seen as the only amateur. It seemed more than a little ironic that the person with most power was the only one who hadn't trained. So I was very keen to train and very glad I did. For me it drew a clear line between my time in amateur/student theatre and my subsequent professional life. Anyway, Judith set up Grid Iron with another director the first year and I joined in 1996. I redirected the first show for the Traverse 2 and the Arches, but it was only after that was done that we sat down and really talked about what we wanted to do. I had studied* The Bloody Chamber *as a student and a friend of mine from CSSD had done a design for it and adapted it for the stage in Bristol. At exactly this time Judith had heard rumours about Mary King's Close and people being walled up there and this obviously chimed with the Bluebeard myth. It was one of those magic moments where it all came together. Our approach remained fairly naive though. For instance we wanted to hide the technical crew, to make sure only the performers were visible to the audience, because the idea of the piece is that it's set in an abandoned castle. So we had the lighting designer three floors up but no idea how to cue the show. Eventually we just put a microphone in the room and cued the show on audio. And when we've required an invisible crew that's pretty much how we've done it ever since. It's always trial and error.*

Reid: *Is the problem solving aspect something you've become attached to?*

Harrison: *Yes. Each piece is like a puzzle and each new site is a different puzzle. The biggest puzzle of all, of course, was Edinburgh Airport, which is a very complex site.*

Reid: *The project you made there,* Roam *(2006) is very strongly associated now with the extraordinary success of the NTS's first year. Can you say something about how the project came about?*

Harrison: Sure. We were in trouble, financially, with another project so we went to Vicky (Featherstone) whom I'd known for some time, to ask for help. She said, well that's all very interesting, but tell me about the project you really want to do, money being no object. As it happened I'd been thinking about doing a project in an airport for ten years. It took ten years from the initial idea to actually making Roam. It was inspired by the Michel Serres book Angels and Modern Myth, which is a philosophical tract but also a very beautiful picture book about conversations between a doctor who is resident in Charles De Gaulle Airport and an airline employee who travels all over the world. They meet when the employee is back in France and talk about modern air travellers being angels, in the sense that they carry messages around the globe. So that was the starting point for it, but by the time we made the piece I had worked a lot in the middle east so it also became partly about Arab identity and about immigration control. The finished piece touched, I hope, on many aspects of the airport experience. We had refugee children coming in and an over fifty's group going out on their holiday. We had ordinary children just messing about and a Roma musician. It was a collage piece but still with this philosophical text in the middle of it. I think what attracted Vicky to the idea was its scale. Also I had been thinking about it for so long I was able to articulate it convincingly. When I look back on it now I think it is remarkable that we were allowed to do it. I don't think it would be possible now. It was just before the liquid bomb plot and I'm not sure Vicky, or Laurie now, would write a cheque for quarter of a million, which is what she did. She just said, I love this idea, let's do it. The NTS was properly funded but had the added advantage of having few ties. No building. That's key, I think. Also the co-producing model allowed them to plug quickly into a vibrant theatre culture that was already there. Paradoxically, although Roam was one of our most successful shows it was also one of the ones in which I had to surrender the most aesthetic control because you can't really control an airport. You can intervene but you can't control it. We did things like subverting signage. So rather than EU and Non-EU in Arrivals it was US and THEM, but using the same typography. We also replaced slogans in the baggage reclaim areas with things like 'We Miss You' or 'We Travel Too Much' rather than duty-free adverts. So there was a certain amount of subversion. What I really wanted to do was change all of the advertising in the airport, everything the audience looked at I wanted to change, which of course we couldn't possibly do. There are a lot of invisible borders in an airport. The area behind to check-in desk, for instance, is a security zone and in order to allow an actor behind there they had to suspend the law. Also the laws around allowing access without travel documents were suspended for three weeks. The biggest thing though was the final scene, based in the baggage carousel area, which we had chosen because it was a rather austere grey environment and a very cool space. By the time we got to use it the whole area had been rebranded by Forth FM, a local radio station, in orange *with cut-outs of the DJs. There was nothing we could do about that. So yes, we did okay with* Roam *under the circumstances.*

Reid: *Are there any other pieces that you feel are central to your development as a company?*

Harrison: *I'd say another key show for us was* Decky Does a Bronco *(2000). Up until that point we'd tended to make pieces in aesthetically controllable, closed spaces, spaces where you could shine a light on a crumbling brick wall and create something magical and atmospheric. But* Decky *was performed in wide-open spaces, initially in a series of west coast public parks before coming to the Fringe. As we were researching the sites we made a series of videos of the parks. I particularly remember visiting a swing park in Portree on Skye and there were kids playing around. We showed them our cameras and the first thing they asked us was 'Are you the modern artists?' As we were leaving one of the girls said, 'Just remember it's our swing park'. This was after we'd explained to them what we were planning to do. And that remark really resonated with Jude and me because we'd been thinking of ways we could secure the park and of course you don't secure a park because it belongs to the children who use it. So the piece then became partly about collaborating with groups of local kids. We had an acrobatic trainer attached to the project but actually the most difficult trick on the swings was taught to us by a nine-year-old boy. So the project grew out of each local space in that way and in the end the local kids were quite loyal audiences. They'd come in during the more acrobatic sections and sometimes fade away during the longer speeches. And towards the end of the play when it shades into something very, very sad, quite often as the characters are realising what has happened you can hear local kids playing quite innocently in the distance. That definitely gave the piece added poignancy and power, that counterpoint. That was an important piece for us.*

Reid: *That was definitely a piece that utilised nostalgia in so far as most of us have memories from our own childhoods in relation to swing parks. Although the nostalgia was not entirely sentimental since Douglas Maxwell's play evokes the brutality as well as the freedom of childhood.*

Harrison: *Yes absolutely, all of those ideas impinged. It became clear to us, for instance, that we should perform in the round because kids play in the round. Also there was something about starting at a time of when it was bright and it gradually becoming darker that added to the experience. The swing park itself becomes a more liminal and potentially dangerous place when the sun goes down.*

Reid: *Did you amend the starting time when you toured the show?*

Harrison: *Yes. I remember starting at odd times depending on the sunset. Often people booked the show because they had seen it and they specifically wanted to recreate that effect among other things. Also that show was very economical to tour partly because of the very portable set. We had our own swings and could set up anywhere, in principle. So that although the piece obviously worked better in parks it could* be performed anywhere, on any bit of grass. Often people didn't realise it was a set at all. Douglas's text was also remarkable in that it was largely free of irony. Many of the characters were children in any case, but even the adults had to speak with real directness and open-heartedness. That was part of its appeal for audiences I think, it had a kind of emotional honesty and candour that is quite unusual in contemporary theatre and really caught the imagination.

Reid: In retrospect much of your work, including Decky and Roam, seems very prescient, very much of its time, Scottish theatre having become increasingly outward looking and issues of identity and memory having become additionally live in the years around devolution.

Harrison: Yes I think that's true. Questions of how we might engage with the past or with 'others' have been especially pressing in Scotland in the years we have been working here. It's only very recently that I've become interested explicitly in the independence debate, but I can see that Roam was definitely about national identity. There was a sequence where a performer from the Basque country talked about her sense of national identity in relation to Spain, for instance, and how she used to go on political demonstrations in the playground when she was about four. We also had a Hungarian actor who talked about growing up as a member of the Soviet Pioneers and actually quite liking it. For him it wasn't necessarily a negative thing. And then we had Andy Clarke who is an actor from the Dundee area talking about growing up in the city and how Dundee United was an important part of that. We actually developed scene with or Wullie sitting on his bucket, which was very funny, but we were definitely riffing on notions of identity and place. One of the main narrative devices of the piece was the idea that Scotland was having a civil war and the only safe places to get to were Beirut, Kigali and Sarajevo. So those were the destinations on the screens. And we had news footage about Edinburgh Castle being on fire and so on. We wanted to turn the tables really, to ask people to imagine what it would be like to be on the other side of such news stories. One of the most disturbing and disappointing aspect of recent debates on the movement of peoples and immigration has been the failure of empathy, the reluctance to properly imagine what would motivate people to abandon their homes in search of a better life.

Reid: The comparison between the Scots and the Basques is an interesting one because, I think, Scotland is so clearly a nation, a stateless nation perhaps but a nation nonetheless. Did you experience that sense of difference when you first arrived here to study?

Harrison: Yes. It always felt more like being on the continent to me. I always felt more like I was in Europe. I guess it's partly to do with the close relationship with France, but regardless of whether we go for independence or not I have the sense Scotland will remain a small country with an internationalist outlook. My own interest in the Arab world, which was apparent in Roam for instance, has been enabled, I think, *by being based in Scotland where international engagement is par for the course, feels entirely natural.*

Reid: *We've talked a little about the efficacy of site-specific theatre in dealing with issues of identity and place and of course this isn't a phenomenon that's been limited to Scotland.*

Harrison: *No, that's right. There has been a definite interest in this kind of work for the last 20 years or so, across the United Kingdom and beyond, since the 1980s really. In fact it's becoming a rather crowded field, one on which it's increasingly difficult to remain distinctive. I remember when I started teaching it, in the late 1990s, I'd ask a group of students, 'Do you know what site-specific is or means?' and absolutely no one would answer, whereas now, they're all doing modules in it. They've done three projects each. So it is popular yes, but as it happens I've done a lot of work in theatres in the last couple of years. Just to reconnect and to figure out what a studio can do and what a proscenium can do. Although when we did* Spring Awakening *(2010) at the Traverse 2, I did spend a lot of time just figuring out what we could do with the space, with the doors that were already there, for example, so there is a kind of site-based mentality that I carry with me. I think it's a useful toolkit to have even when you are working in conventional spaces, because it allows you to really see the space.*

Reid: *Are there any projects you've worked on that have been less than successful, in your own view.*

Harrison: *We did a show called* Monumental *(1999), years ago at the Glasgow Citizens. In retrospect, what we did was take a well-made play best suited to a studio theatre and we tried to stretch it across the canvas of backstage, and the foyer, where the statues are and outside into the alley. But that was an artificial thing. She really hadn't written that, she'd written a play for a studio theatre, so it really didn't work at all. But some things work better than others. I've just done my first opera – in a stables in Aberdeen. I really know very little about opera, I mean I don't even read music, so I was treating it as an experiment but it worked beautifully, mostly because the hosts were so welcoming. There is always this thing about the host and the guest in site-specific work. The theatre company is always the guest and the owners of the site the hosts. Sometimes inevitably it is a tense relationship but this was just wonderful. They provided everything we asked for, were very accommodating, they really wanted us to be there and that just lifts the whole thing. In the end it was fantastically successful and pretty much effortless, well it certainly felt effortless considering we only had two weeks. It was so cold there you could actually see the singer's breath, so the whole thing felt very immediate. There is a lot of growth in that area now, in music and site and dance and site.*

Reid: *So what's next for you?*

Harrison: *It isn't a site-specific piece nor is it a Grid Iron piece; I do quite a bit of independent work as a director. I'm flying to Beirut on Thursday to do a project with my partner who is an aerial choreographer. The piece is called* Bed Sheets. *There is a phenomenon in Lebanon, although I think this is a global problem, where several hundred thousand people – mostly women – working as domestic servants are imprisoned in their workplaces. They are systematically deprived of their basic human rights, many having their passports removed for instance. There are cases of women who haven't left the house for ten years. As a protest a number have hanged themselves from knotted bed sheets, which of course look like aerial silk. So we are using the silk as a metaphor for that. We will have three weeks there.*

Reid: *The future of Grid Iron has been called into question by the controversial and highly unpopular approach to funding adopted by Creative Scotland in their review in May this year. You have been quite vocal in your resistance to their methods.*

Harrison: *Indeed. I feel they have displayed such a profound ignorance of the sector in Scotland, partly because they have been brought in from other parts of the United Kingdom. They just don't understand the ecology of it, an ecology that was actually quite robust. It quite simple really – the NTS at the top, established companies like us in the middle, emerging artists down below, and the buildings, of course, doing their stuff. I feel, and doubtless other would disagree, that there are lots of opportunities for young artists to come through. I have mentored lots of them.*

Reid: *One of the things the NTS model enables it to do is to reach down beyond the next layer to the grass roots.*

Harrison: *Yes and I think they've been brilliant at that. They are running an auteur's scheme at the moment, for example, and through that they are giving significant support to really very young artists. The point is that in Scottish theatre we are all dependent on each other, and for two people to come in from outside – outside the theatre sector even – and say, 'no we want to curate all this', it's just laughable.*

Reid: *There has been a good deal of negative publicity about it. Do you get the sense they are on the back foot?*

Harrison: *They are in denial, I think, although they have made some concessions. They have extended our fixed-term funding for six months, for example, and Vanishing Point has applied and seem to be okay. But it's not really about money, it's about the way the sector has been talked to and treated. It's on these grounds that artists have been lobbying Fiona Hyslop the Scottish culture secretary. There is even anecdotal evidence of people being threatened – artists being told they have made 'powerful enemies' by speaking out. It's outrageous really. It's an arts funding organisation not the bloody Mafia. David Greig has been really instrumental in gathering support in terms of protest. There are over four hundred signatures on the open letter now, including leading visual artists, writers and musicians. Initially, though, a lot of people were nervous of signing it because of the potential impact* on their current or future funding. Within Grid Iron, we were certainly cautious and willing to give Creative Scotland the benefit of the doubt but we snapped quite quickly. Most worryingly, they deliberately put people in decision-making positions that had no experience of the sector. We were put together with someone from literature, for example, and this approach was repeated elsewhere. I think they believe they are being iconoclastic but actually it is just vandalism. There is a deliberate strategy to blow the whole thing up, and then just see what happens. Meanwhile they are spending £30,000 on their Creative Scotland Awards party, for which they are charging £100 a ticket.

Reid: It's most disappointing and alarming because, from the perspective of a cultural commentator, it has been increasingly easy to argue that the last 20 years or so have been the most successful in Scottish theatre history bar none. This has been and continues to be our moment.

Harrison: Yes there is no need to throw everything up in the air and see what comes down. It's actually working quite well. I mean how much more success do they want?

References

Augé, M., 2010. *Non-Places: An Introduction to Supermodernity*. London: Verso.

Clapp, S., 2000. *The Observer*, 13 August.

Garner, L., 2004. *The Guardian*, 6 August.

Harvie, J., 2005. *Staging the UK*. Manchester: Manchester University Press.

Holdsworth, N., 2008. 'The landscape of contemporary Scottish drama: Place, politics and identity', in N. Holdsworth and M. Luckhurst (eds). *A Concise Companion to British and Irish Drama*. Oxford: Blackwell, pp. 125–45.

———, 2010. *Theatre & Nation*. Basingstoke: Palgrave.

McLucas, C., 2000. 'Ten feet and three quarters of an inch of theatre', in N. Kaye (ed.). *Site-Specific Art*. London: Routledge, pp. 125–38.

Muller, A. and Wallace, C. (eds), 2011. *Cosmopotia: Transnational Identities in David Greig's Theatre*. Prague: Univerzita Karlova.

Pattie, D., 2008. 'Mapping the terrain: Modern Scottish drama', in R. D'Monté and G. Saunders (eds). *Cruel Britannia: British Political Drama in the 1990s*. Basingstoke: Palgrave, pp. 143–57.

Pearson, M., 2010. *Site-Specific Performance*. Basingstoke: Palgrave.

Pearson, M. and Shanks, M., 2001. *Theatre/Archeology: Disciplinary Dialogues*. London: Routledge.

Reid, T., 2011. 'Post-devolutionary drama', in I. Brown (ed.). *The Edinburgh Companion to Scottish Drama*. Edinburgh: Edinburgh University Press, pp. 188–99.

Scullion, A., 2007. 'Devolution and drama: Imagining the impossible', in B. Schoene (ed.). *The Edinburgh Companion to Contemporary Scottish Literature*. Edinburgh: Edinburgh University Press, pp. 68–77.

Sierz, A., Middeke, M. and Schnierer, P., (eds), 2011. *The Methuen Drama Guide to Contemporary British Playwrights*. London: Methuen.

Turner, C., 2004. 'Palimpsest or potential space? Finding a vocabulary for site-specific performance'. *New Theatre Quarterly*, 20: 4, pp. 373–88.

Wilkie, F., 2002. 'Mapping the terrain: A survey of site-specific performance in Britain'. *New Theatre Quarterly*, 18: 2, pp. 140–60.

Wilkie, F., 2008. 'The production of site: Site-specific theatre', in N. Holdsworth and M. Luckhurst (eds). *A Concise Companion to British and Irish Drama*. Oxford: Blackwell, pp. 87–106.

Chapter 11

Acts of Poiesis: salamanda tandem

Mick Wallis and Isabel Jones

Introduction

Founded by Artistic Director Isabel Jones and others in 1989 and a registered charity since 2001, salamanda tandem makes cross-arts work with a wide spectrum of people. While only a small part of this is theatre in the strict sense, issues of theatre and theatricality are pertinent to the full spectrum of activity. To open this up, Mick interviewed Isabel over three days in July 2011, addressing three principal strands [1]:

Arts Work with People

This person-centred work with people with sometimes severe access-needs to making art addresses everyone's need to conduct *poiesis*. Another principle is gift – the artwork is often for someone. These together bring the work into the theatrical frame. This also figures antithetically: explicitly putting on a show in inappropriate circumstances alienates both the work and its makers. In the section Arts Work with People, we discuss arts work with people in institutional settings, where the issue is often institutionalisation of staff and service-users alike. Isabel presents the core principles of her work in Jones (2010).

In the section Living Room, we discuss *Living Room*, occasional participatory events that grew out of this institutional work. Artists manufacture live feedback into a space, where small groups of variously disabled people interact with each other, the aesthetic environment and salamanda tandem personnel as animateurs.

While much of the work with people is not made for explicit staging, in the section Arts Work with People we foreground an instance where it very successfully was – in the making and touring of inclusive performances for integrated audiences.

Training in Arts Work with People

While central to salamanda tandem's work, we have not foregrounded this. It is instead addressed in passing, where key principles such as embodied empathy, creating space, affordances, informed choice and self-reflexivity arise.

Professional Work for the Stage

At root here are issues around cross-genre work, within the wider frame of collaboration. In the section Professional Stage Work, we discuss this, place-specificity, community engagement, ritual, aesthetics, the role of the director/choreographer and other issues across a three-work sequence. We also touch on the interrelations between this work and arts work with people and on therapy.

We also explored an encompassing frame:

Company Organisation and Economics

Essential issues for all theatre companies and for a historical and political understanding of theatre, company organisation and economics help situate salamanda tandem as a particular practice. It is an organisation but not a theatre company. A company is formed for each explicit production, and, as described above, the idea of a company is anyhow not pertinent to much of the work. Like most arts businesses, salamanda tandem depends on funding – historically principally from the Arts Council and local authority Arts and Social Services departments. In the subsection Personal Budget (under the section Arts Work with People), we briefly discuss how salamanda tandem might best respond to recent changes in policy and funding frameworks.

Origins, Influences and Ethos

Foundational influences on Isabel's work map into three areas – other practitioners, her education and her family. But these were 'all tied in together'. Earliest was her blind father, Lewis:

> *He would send my sister and me out as a little game, maybe so he could sleep because he was suffering from severe depression. We had to find two identical stones, and he would assess them – through touch. He'd find a crack, a crevice, smoothness or roughness not visible to the eye. I suppose he wanted me to join him in his world – and I did. I've seen other children repeat 'Airplane' until the parent turns around and says, 'Yes, airplane'. But I had to work out at an early age that I had to take the thing and put it in his hands to get any attention. I started to get formed by that.*

At 11, Isabel won a ballet scholarship to the Royal Academy of Dance, London. But a feeling of futility grew: Lewis would never see her dance. Already trained in singing, viola and classical guitar – and brought up on sculpture – Isabel determined that rather than choosing between art forms, she should bring them together. Her undergraduate degree at Bretton

Hall (1979–82) allowed her to grow her own aesthetic and ethical direction, constructing an individual course across music, dance and theatre. Dance was the most challenging, due to her classical training. Instructed by Barbara Phillips to move naturally from an internal impetus, Isabel found herself trapped in her repertoire of learned movements. So she called on her father's experience as a blind child: *'I found that if I began with rocking and kept my eyes closed, the movement could quite naturally expand'.*

Bretton introduced Isabel to John Cage, from whom she gained a perspective on making space. Part of this was his personal generosity, taking time to engage fully with her when she approached him after a London concert: he valued and made space for others. This paralleled his aesthetic strategy of framing: in *4'33"* [*four minutes, thirty-three seconds*], the silence provides the frame that inducts the audience into hearing incidental sounds: *'He was interested in what was already there – not imposing something'.* In care, what is already there might be movements often regarded as tics that need correcting. But whether a tic or deliberate, the movement is often being used and valued by the person:

> *We never really know. Take the children on the autistic spectrum I work with. Flapping paper in the corner of their eye would be viewed as obsessive behaviour preventing them from learning or accessing the world – a block between them and others. But actually, it could be a starting point.*

And so Isabel typically provides a safe frame within which she can enter into creative dialogue with such movement – accepting the whole person. This perspective is informed by Isabel's learning about Dorothy Heathcote: *'Don't be frightened to dig and uncover what is there, to really join it'.*

A similar ethic informs the work of Wolfgang Stange, who Isabel's mother got to work with the Jones family and friends in 1983. During a postgraduate Drama in Education course at Goldsmiths' University of London in 1996, Isabel prepared for person-centred work with groups by independently furthering her contact with him. Isabel observed that everybody in Stange's work has their signature contribution, of which everyone in the group must be aware. Stange would solicit a movement – or stillness – from each member of the group, which the rest then echoed. Then he danced each, from memory – and *'you could see people grow'* – before clustering them into groups. Isabel admired Stange's directing of Amici for stage performance less. He would select the best dancers, and get angry as he struggled to make something work for an audience: *'I struggled to connect the two worlds – hospital and performance – rather than separate the two, as I think he did'.*

Isabel encountered a cognate separation in Steve Paxton – co-founder of contact improvisation. Eager to find ways to include Lewis when she and her then partner Peter Byworth set up salamanda tandem, they attended Paxton and Anne Kilcoyne's one-week course on the therapeutic application of contact improvisation at Dartington. But the egalitarian principles of contact were not much in evidence: while the dancers had a professional class every morning, the visually impaired participants were left at a rehabilitation centre. And Paxton would select the people most interesting to him to dance with in front of the others. Nevertheless, the course helped deepen Isabel's understanding of the relationships between dance and sightedness:

> You're dancing with a blind person and get stuck like you do in any contact improv. Then you sense that they are still in flow, tuning in to feeling the pressure between your hip and their waist. So you close your eyes and suddenly embodied touch becomes the driver of all the movement.

Key to that understanding is Isabel's relationship to Lewis. Paxton had invited Alito Alessi, founder of Danceability (Oregon) to Dartington: 'We danced together, but it went deeper. He is the only other dancer I have met who is also the child of a disabled person. We shared a common philosophy' (vide Jones 2010: 82–87).

While the other chief formative influences on Isabel in the Bretton years were from contemporary visual art and sculpture, some performance companies stood out – and a similar shape is evident. Isabel was inspired by the cross-arts work of Moving Being, but not its institution: 'It just wasn't inclusive of people in my sense – the performers were somehow separate and above'. L'Escalier (Lausanne) was a contrast: 'I really experienced the wide spectrum of people, and site-specific work, and a structure in place, rather than specific movements'.

Isabel also found the aesthetic institution of contemporary dance during excluding – declaring itself to be where the proper work was: 'Burying myself away when things were emerging for me was the best way to deal with it'. But she fought other aspects of the dominant head-on:

> Eye Contact went to as many audio-described performances as possible. I experienced one dance performance blindfold and was amazed. The voice just described the directions of the movements. The effort of imagining it exhausted me, and the wordy description cut across the music. Eventually, I turned the headphones off and listened to the music and clattering ballet shoes. My father had learnt from experience never to turn it on. We imagined making audio description into an art-form so enticing that all the audience, blind or not, would want to experience it. That got assimilated into all our early workshops and rehearsals. We worked smell, touch and taste into our shows. The sound and visuals became part of an integrated whole, with no necessity for special access facilities.

Arts Work with People

Non-Professionals on Stage

In 1990, weekly contact improvisation classes began for people of all degrees of sightedness. Depressed by what he identified as a dependency culture, Peter soon left. Isabel identifies two determinations: first, participants did not feel sufficiently empowered to generate something for themselves; second, many professionals passed through, but *'never taking a blind person with them'*. The culture changed as the group started making work for the stage, after Lewis and Isabel formed Eye Contact Dance Company in 1992. This was enabled by Isabel's development of person-centred approaches affording creative access through inclusive performance. 'Movement through Touch' displaced contact improvisation as their primary source for movement. The sense of taking control over one's destiny through art that one is creating things and is responsible for them – and especially in a community of makers – helped develop the sense of being a company.

Back in 1983, Isabel and her sister devised a hub-and-spoke string structure for non-sighted performers to navigate the stage: *'We'd realised as children that the whole world worked around the blind person fitting in with the sighted frame of reference. We wanted to create something the other way round'*.

Eye Contact's first piece, *Sound Round Robin* (NottDance, Bonington Gallery, 1991), adapted a contact improvisation call-and-response protocol by giving each person their sound signature, making sight redundant. For *Smell of the Blue* (1992), a dance floor with tactile edges and points directed performers. And funded collaboration with Drake Research introduced Soundbeam, triggering sounds and images when its ultrasonic beam was crossed. Duncan sampled and manipulated voices and mapped these onto a keyboard played by profoundly disabled Mark Rolland with his feet.

The maze-like installation for salamanda tandem's *Inaccessibility* (1990) by minimalist sculptor Jo Fairfax – introduced to Isabel by NottDance founders Don McClure and Stella Couloutbanis – critiqued the Bonington's lack of disabled access. But inclusiveness in the spaces of making and reception does not guarantee integrated work for integrated audiences: *'The music didn't connect my father to the dance, visuals or theme. I realised that the work needed to become more synaesthetic. There was a journey ahead of me'*.

Sub Vision (1994–98) developed multisensory performance. The cast peeled oranges, filling the auditorium with the aroma. Welsh cakes were cooked and passed warm to the audience.

Eye Contact rapidly developed a multi-part audience demographic. NottDance brought a contemporary arts audience. And their local disability audience comprised the *Inaccessibility* group and Isabel's personal network of family, friends and associates. *'Everything was interconnected'*. Touring to Dash Festival in Shrewsbury, Isabel first encountered the then prevalent cabaret-style disability aesthetic. Next to this, *Smell of the Blue* (1993) appeared 'arty' – but without difficulty. It equally suited contemporary arts audiences at the Deptford Albany, London's Purcell Rooms, and that at the Royal National College for the Blind in Hereford. This gig was instructive: *'We played to a totally blind audience, which blew our minds so much that we felt that we'd really got to open up into the other senses'*.

On Composition, Aesthetics and Perfection

The dramaturgical structure of *Inaccessibility* framed free improvisations by a group of young learning-disabled people Isabel had known since the early 1980s. And for *Smell of the Blue*, each dancer developed a solo based on their chosen colour – providing core movement material for the complete work: *'They could lead their parts in something like a jigsaw. We stored the pieces as tactile and visual notes, including 3-D clay. These could be shuffled'*.

This is organic collective composition. But as director, Isabel nevertheless takes responsibility for its final form and quality. We mentioned Isabel's resistance to Wolfgang's drive for aesthetic perfection. To what extent is Isabel herself a perfectionist?

> *With non-trained performers, their first emergence of movement is often the best, and they struggle to go back. My directorial notes were mostly about getting them to return to that deep feeling, to recover what had been lost in the business of repetition. This is partly why I have ditched remembered performance.*

But Siebers (2011), for instance, traces the ways in which the western construct of aesthetic value positioned the disabled as its essential other. Is there not 'abstract' beauty in salamanda tandem's publicity images?

> *Sometimes I look at the stuff I have produced, and it's too ordered, too beautiful. But in the early days my father was in the Disability Arts Forum and said he didn't believe in art about disability. That's how they were defining it then. He didn't want to know about the degradation. Why couldn't it be beautiful? It's almost as if salamanda tandem became an antidote. We created a company dealing with all that stuff that surrounds the disabled person so that they could create something of beauty, and* Smell of the Blue *was a thing of beauty.*

Gift and Communitas: Nottingham Prison

In 1994, Don asked Isabel to develop creative movement work with the *Inaccessibility* group and men on life sentences at Nottingham Prison. Jazz pianist Tony Baker improvised to the activity in the room:

> *They were exploring life-death cycles. And this child remained lying on the floor. This is a classic moment. Most of the time, staff would go, 'Come on, get up' – frightened that they're going to disappear into depression. I created a gathering around the person, to embody this feeling of death. Tony played the Funeral March. And this lad was lifted and carried. He ended up putting his hands across, playing dead.*

The boy was not excluding himself from the session by remaining still. He simply found it appropriate to that moment. Isabel made that judgement. And it turned out that his performance was much deeper than play-acting. A close relative had died and he'd not gone to the funeral; it had not been complete. While family and carers had all too typically not given the boy space and time to mourn, here he was given and took the opportunity to create his own private ritual within the safe and generative frame of *communitas*:

> *He was carried across the space and laid down and I whispered in his ear, 'What happens now?' He said something about a frog. So I made that big and suddenly he's croaking and he's up, doing it. That week, Tony's best friend had died in a car crash. So he was playing for real himself, just like that lad.*

The session was not for an audience, but for the people there, for the moment. But Isabel agrees that it is still theatre, because it is to do with giving and receiving. The participants are audience to their own creation in a deep and intimate way. The lad symbolically played out his feelings, and that was embraced by those around him.

In *The Gift* [1923] Mauss theorised the collective reciprocation of gifts as a foundational principle of human society (Mauss 2002). We do not need to construct foundational myths of theatre to recognise theatre as a cognate mechanism for exchange and thereby – as Raymond Williams (1987: 70) coined it – an act of *convening*. Turner's notion of *communitas* helps us capture the simultaneity of the desire to join for common purpose (Turner's 'normative' or sometimes 'ideological communitas') and the *generation* of togetherness ('spontaneous communitas') available through theatre (see Turner 1969: 132). Isabel's creation of the micro-stage described here organically manipulates these potentials.

Being Heard and Working Through: Nathan's Journey

From 2004, salamanda tandem delivered a series of inputs to a project for learning-disabled people in Telford run by Disability Arts Officer Kevin Hodgetts. Frustrated by the atmosphere when salamanda tandem went home, Kevin invited Isabel to train the local support workers engaged in his work with children. It was challenging work: *They took the point of view that these people literally needed a shove to get them moving, rather than be enabled to make a decision'.*

Kevin went on to devise a project, 'Work and Play', to initiate something of similar quality to salamanda tandem's work locally, on a continuous basis. Contracted as evaluator, Isabel re-framed her work as action research – circulating moment by moment between evaluation and the development of informed-choice strategies:

> *It was a case of getting people into the ethos of reflective thinking. They did things without thought, and you saw people shutting down instantly, the classic stuff. So I asked participants to explore – through painting, drawing and suchlike – where we were at, and built up enough individual interaction to teach the support staff and artists how to bring them on.*

But after two years, by July 2010, Isabel still could not help staff reach one young man properly, disadvantaged by his compliance – sufficiently cooperative and quiet to be ignored – and the constant presence of his minder, draining his energy. Isabel brought focus and the benefit of long experience to the situation.

For a community garden project, participants were led in generating a collective design by cutting images from magazines:

> *Nathan cut out a picture of a fire, which was ignored because it would have been a problem. I asked him about it. He said underneath the fire is a tomb containing the ashes of his grandfather. But he hadn't had any chance to mark his death and was absolutely bereft. The garden project as originally conceived wouldn't provide a frame for the fire and tomb; so Kevin and I steered it towards individuals making a piece of work to be installed there.*

Each participant made a bird sculpture, including Nathan.

> *But there was no sense of connection to his grandfather. He was just joining the group activity. Finally, there was an exhibition. The birds were stuck into the ground across the lawn. And his grandmother and mother came.*

At this point, 'theatre' provides a useful model to analyse various relationships. The work was for sale. So Isabel engineered a situation where Nathan's relations would buy his. This might finally constitute an act of mourning with Nathan as genuine performer – staging his loss and grief by fashioning his own rite of passage, through the gift at the heart of the theatrical contract. This is the deep and proper theatre of the situation. But a contradictory piece of theatre was going on:

> *This community dance person decides they've got to flap their arms! So Nathan and the others are turning to him and other leaders because they can't remember what they are supposed to be doing. Nathan is 26 and quite cool – he's got headphones and he's a rapper. But because he's learning-disabled, he can be told to flap his arms.*

In this shallow spectacle, 'community dance' is a form of policing, contrasting starkly to person-centred work. Nathan was especially distressed – probably by his mourning being again interrupted. Isabel conjured up her own piece of theatre, to cut the community dancer out:

> *I spoke to his relations. His grandmother immediately wanted to buy this bird for her garden, and talked about a bird seen on the fence on the day her husband died. No one's ever bought his work before. I set up a photo opportunity. And there was Nathan with his grandmother looking up at the bird.*

An exchange of gifts had been won. But recall that Nathan was not much invested in the bird. However, Isabel had meanwhile been nurturing Nathan's verbal creativity. On a group visit to an Anish Kapoor exhibition, Isabel recorded people talking stream-of-consciousness: *'Nathan walked with me, heard how I did it and just talked. He could go on about things like the colour red – it was fantastic, he could expand'.* And during the garden project, as Isabel and Nathan walked in the garden,

> He looked up at a bird, and I asked, 'If you were that bird, how would you be thinking?' He went straight into the body of the bird and talked about being frozen and dusting off his wings, yet still feeling the power to fly, to connect to home. The bird was a vehicle for his self-expression. I typed quickly as he talked, and read it back to him. And he went, 'Yeah, that's me, that's my poem.'

Nathan's journey with Isabel took him to making a short movie, *Can't Stop Me Shining* (see Campbell 2011a, b). We see Nathan's bird sculpture, which Isabel interprets as a symbol for his grandfather's tombstone. The day before the bird pantomime, Nathan told Isabel he wanted to collaborate with her artistically. Hugely focused work over a few hours followed, in which Nathan improvised vocally, while Isabel recorded and provided an active listening frame. When he stumbled, she encouraged him to resume, explaining that he would choose what others would hear. That same guarantee allowed him the space to work through some of his deepest anxieties and fears. That done, he chose to put into the world the beautifully affirmative lines that became the basis for *Shining*. While it was many months before the film was completed, Nathan determined its shape that day by deciding the edit. The closing crescendo affirms – aesthetically – 'I am a whole person'.

Personal Budget

With reports and programmes such as *Valuing People* (Department of Health 2001), the UK Blair government caught up with the person-centred approach, albeit in a more instrumental and far less productively intimate way than in arts work with people. The key principle was to ascertain and then address the specific needs of each individual, rather than treat people as genres through blanket coverage. This has recently developed into the provision of an assessed personal budget, which the disabled person can spend as a consumer on the approved services they select – including, for example, day centres but not as yet arts work with people on the salamanda tandem model. Work over several years of the type done with Nathan – and with her parents, both disabled – has led Isabel to conceive of the role of 'artist advocate', mediating between care professional and arts professional, in this context. Part of the project would be to generate 'communities of interest' around the person, both socialising and professionalising the context of their choices. This would counter the danger of atomisation implicit in the consumer model – and enhance informed choice.

Living Room

Immersion and Empowerment

Living Room enables participants to create together equally, using body and voice to regenerate a given space – making it their own. Live processing, sampling, digital interfaces and visual technologies enable performance interventions involving dance, visual arts, film and music.

Mick invited *Living Room* to Leeds University's Bretton Campus in 2006. He recalls:

> *You've set a single wooden chair in the large, dark space. You've invited groups of five to ten variously disabled children, from different institutions. Two or three groups participate together for around 40 minutes. Early in one session, a lad approaches the chair, a light comes on above and his spoken reaction is fed back into the space. They start playing together, testing what will happen. They're projected onto the wall, from a live-feed camera. One of them is given a camera and films their peers. Soon, a learning-disabled lad takes a young man in a wheelchair through an exercise he's experienced: he and other kids gently waft his arms up and down. A blue light bathes their bodies. It's delightfully intimate, safe, sharing. They seem absolutely focused, creative, flowing. Fifteen minutes later, it's like a rave at 3am – huge energy but totally intimate and safe.*

Duncan and Stuart live-mixed sound and image; Kevin Hodgetts passed cameras and microphone amongst participants; Julie Hood and Lisa Craddock animated movement; and Isabel improvised vocals. Their interactive work created the environment in which creative interaction flowed easily and joyfully between participants. All players were engaged in one territory of making. Two people were especially empowered that day. One was the learning-disabled lad:

> *Four years later, Ricky was still going on about it: 'That man's carer dumped and left him. He was frightened and didn't know what was going on, and I helped him, didn't I? I gave him the microphone, said 'Where are you?' and he said 'I'm in the sea'. So I said 'There's blue all around us', and I talked, I did it, didn't I, Isabel, I talked?' So he's got the idea of performance – and he still talks about the world that was created; but he's also got this idea of him doing something practical, that made a difference.*

The other was learning-disabled dancer Victoria, who facilitated by weaving her way round the space, fully immersed. That she was able to facilitate so well derives from salamanda tandem's deep practice. Victoria had spent years working with Isabel, Julie and Lisa, intensified at a short preparatory residency at Bretton:

She began to emerge as a creator, forming structures with her body to enable people to interact with her. When structures are the wave, people can create from a simple immediate stimulus. Then suddenly, all these choreographers and composers start emerging.

Isabel holds that the choreographer is the person who asks what dance could be. With salamanda tandem, Victoria did not simply learn to dance, but what dance could be for her, and thence for others.

From the Snoozlum and Back Again

Living Room emerged from resistant practice. Consulting on arts provision for disabled people in Staffordshire, Isabel and Duncan encountered the Snoozlum in 1993 – a 'sensory room' containing projectors, lights, cushions, sound equipment and other equipment. It was in extensive use, but to isolate and placate troublesome individuals – 'timing out' – rather than to stimulate. '*We witnessed what we call the psychedelic padded cell – everything was switched on and the door locked*'.

One determination on this corrupted use was the then dominant policy of 'normalisation'. The 'age appropriate' protocol ruled that service-users should be engaged in things normal for their age. While good in principle, it hampered good practice when not communicated well. Thus, care professionals declined to display drawings made by people in a salamanda tandem workshop because they looked like 'children's scribbles' – and chose Disney posters instead.

A further aspect of the policy is the ethos of work:

> *In one 'adult training centre' we visited, a production line was painting pigs pink. And cast aside, there was this beautiful sculpted head. It was explained to Duncan that one of the people on the line sculpted it in breaks.*

The pigs were destined for sale in shops. But those painting them were not paid. They were suffering alienated labour, without even the compensation of being constructed as consumers. And if they behaved 'inappropriately' on the production line, they were sent to the Snoozlum.

A turning-point came at an adult training centre in Burton-on-Trent, whose service-users had been released from mental hospital after 30–40 years. Isabel and Duncan found the care professionals hostile to their work, and chose to lock themselves in another room with the group, leaving the staff out:

> *Ironically, we chose the Snoozlum. The first thing we did was turn all the equipment off. And they began to tell us about the abuse. It became a refuge from the rest.*

Everybody understood that once you were in it, it was not about productivity – we were doing something different. It was painting, movement, sound, all integrated. Stuff would go straight up around the room until the whole place was completely swamped with colour and movement. Then people would share what they thought about what they had done.

Isabel and Duncan were, without conscious planning, reinventing the Snoozlum space – into one dedicated to person-centred practice. The decisive turn was their introduction of appropriate technology, derived from salamanda tandem's broader work at the time: for example, live sampling and an echo machine in live interactions enabled participants to hear themselves back; speakers turned over made the floor vibrate, so deaf-blind people could feel their own sound; blinking could be sufficient to conduct musicians.

Deeply informing this research was Isabel's experience as a young practitioner, working with children lacking active relation with the world. Stimulated by Ashley Montague's (1986) theory of 'acting on' – whereby for instance the infant sets up a chain of causality by sucking at the breast – she asked,

Could we create an environment where profoundly disabled people could set up such chains? Ultimately, Living Room *is a place in all the dimensions, which makes it possible for people to create a world of their own making.*

Living Room is a concentrated instance of the dialectic identified by Lefebvre (1974), whereby space determines social behaviour and social behaviour determines space. Building on Lefebvre, Soja (1996) calls for praxis (dialectic of practice and theory) addressing the interrelation between the historical, social and spatial. *Living Room* figures, for Mick, at this level as a model for the transformation of spatial design so as to make a historical shift in the social construct of dis/ability. The thought owes much to Constant Nieuwenhuys, while resisting the utopianism of his vision (see Wigley 1998). In this connection, the concluding phrase in the last quotation recalls queer theorist Michael Warner's notion of 'world-making' (2002: 67–118) – the project of an ongoing (re)construction of relational selves, as opposed to residing in identities. In the frame of theatre per se, *Living Room* might be seen to meet the current desire for immersive performance, while resisting its appropriation by capital (see Tomlin 2013: 171–206).

Living Room, Theatre and Decorum

The mutual giving on improvised micro-stages makes *Living Room* amenable to description as theatre. But it has twice crossed into theatre in an unwelcome way. In a performance at Derby Dance Centre by Indigo – young learning-disabled dancers with Julie as Artistic Director – conversations between dancers triggered wall-projections, and others created movements in response. The cross-over between immersive mutual stagings and bicameral ostension caused release and joy for some, but severe discomfort for others. When Faith and Madeleine 'let rip about their families', Faith's parents were deeply embarrassed – 'by the sheer scale of them'. It might not be too patronising, meanwhile, to suggest that that discomfort is rather like a growing pain: *'I think learning disabled people are too often dampened down. This is exactly what these young women needed, to expand'.*

At Nottingham Trent PowerHouse, the seating was not retractable, and Arts Council assessors sat there. This, and their unfamiliarity with *Living Room*, evidently encouraged them to think in terms of theatre for consumption. But Ricky, totally empowered by the Leeds experience, could not surrender the microphone. In more intimate conditions, with good time, he could have been helped let go – or have others join his enthusiasm. But interaction had turned into show – and Ricky was breaking decorum. Deeply unimpressed, the officers recommended that salamanda tandem lose its funding. Reflecting back on the whole journey recounted here, Isabel reflected,

> *Ricky and several others say that* Living Room *was the biggest and best thing they have ever done. There we were, turning the lights off of in the psychedelic padded cells; yet we've created something enormously psychedelic. But it's within people's power. They can see themselves in it. Every mark is theirs. And don't you think that, if you hit a drum very hard yourself, it's okay, but if someone next to you hits the drum very hard, it hurts?*

Professional Stage Work

Collaborations and Contradictions

At the time Isabel encountered Cage at Bretton, she also learned about Meredith Monk. Struck by Monk's ability to summon images through wordless vocal sound, she felt another connection: like Isabel, Monk was both choreographer-dancer and singer-composer. In 1993, Isabel embarked on a project shaped both by a desire to experiment with her dual identity as singer-dancer, and her introduction to Jo Fairfax (see page 201):

> *Musicians like to think of me as a dancer, and vice versa. Wherever there is a gap, I fill it or create space for someone else. I always felt that I was trying to advocate vanishing. And is it possible to sing well technically, and dance at the same time? I decided to work with a pure dancer and a pure singer, occupying both territories as well as a middle ground – pushing the boundaries of both forms, while bringing them together.*

Isabel's project, to *'bring together movement, voice, light and environment, blurring the boundaries'*, drew in medieval and Eastern European song specialist Vivien Ellis, Butoh dancer Naomi Mutoh, and minimalist sculptor Jo. The project became action research into artistic collaboration, over a series of productions.

There were challenges. While Isabel *'couldn't operate without the idea of the environment, the object'*, Vivien resisted distraction from pure singing and Naomi felt encumbered by costumes. And criticism of her occupation of the 'middle ground', and duets with Naomi, in *A House Is My Reflection* (Purcell Rooms, 1994) challenged Isabel's artistic identity: *'If I couldn't stand there in the dance field as a dancer, then I wasn't a choreographer'*.

For *Lighthouse* (Wollaton Hall, Nottingham 1996), Isabel increased the team to five, while withdrawing herself from pure dancing. She and Vivien quickly began experimenting with hocketting:

> It works up quickly, until you can't tell whose voice it is. We spent hours learning how to be one in the sound. We would also provide support for each other – one the drone with the other going off.

The work became the principal vocal score, punctuated by an Elizabethan madrigal – *'like an artefact'* – to connect with the venue.

Isabel's work with people provided an affordance for both Vivien and Naomi. Vivien had first approached Isabel because she wanted to engage in that work. Meanwhile, studying Butoh in Paris with Naomi's teacher, Isabel found its physical regimes difficult and felt experientially distant – it was grounded in a very particular historical experience. But

> Naomi said to me, 'Isabel, your work is Butoh'. She was thinking about my work with people. She saw that embodied in my work was my own disturbance. I realised that in that first piece, I had mistakenly tried to use a form derived from a culture different to my own. I needed now to bring my own dance, which had emerged from hours and hours echoing disabled people [2].

Lighthouse was very testing, as Isabel gradually asserted herself as director, while remaining committed to collaborative process: *'I was starting with collaborative methods, as in Eye Contact. Then after a night's sleep a whole structure would come to me, organically'*.

But as third-generation Butoh, Naomi was frustrated not having a wholly authoritative director define a structure from the start, and interpreted Isabel's collaborative directorial process – the two spending hours nurturing movement Isabel created – as expropriation. From this dynamic tension came a fracture. While Naomi later wrote in conciliation, the confrontation remained traumatic for Isabel.

Vivien too had difficulties with Isabel's inclusive methods. When a tray of lighted candles Jo fashioned for Vivien to carry while singing collapsed and burned her feet, she declared that she was finished with Isabel's preparedness 'to work with all this stuff – and it's not even complete'.

But Vivien also encouraged Isabel:

> She said, 'You're a fantastic director; so just do it.' And one day a dancer asked why I didn't audition. I automatically thought no, I work with the people there – but then thought again. I think what made Triptych *different* was that I decided to audition, as the sort of author.

Place-Specific Ritual Performance

A key stimulus came from the *Lighthouse* venue, an Elizabethan mansion that had become a civic museum. Its glass jars containing specimens in formaldehyde had Isabel fascinated as a child. Flying over remote Canada near the time of *Lighthouse*, she imagined an explorer removing items and putting them into the museum. She wanted to capture that sense of something being plucked from its natural environment and put on show – relating to her difficulties around blind people performing in front of sighted audiences. The concrete beginning was serendipitous. Isabel and Jo were experimenting in the Bonington:

> A white plinth remained from the previous show. I turned the box upside down, got in and began to move. Jo filmed. We went on to make about seven solos. Unsure whether or not I was the sculptor and he the choreographer, we decided we were going to be non-territorial.

Jo's ability to create scenes was crucial. He would make a sculpture and co-direct Isabel's interaction with it. This iteratively affected his sculpture, from his first piece giving Isabel little affordance to simple structures providing a richly choreographic frame. Experimenting with light, Jo had a box fabricated from Perspex and lit Isabel's movement within its confine. This had its own effect on Isabel:

> He liked the way I was struggling for real. He wasn't interested in flow, but more pedestrian movement – simple and pared down – and encouraged me to stay in that world longer. But, as I got to know the box, I knew the struggle was lessening. To stay in that zone, I needed to find new things every time.

The research process ended, Nottinghamshire County Council granted £30,000 to develop Nottinghamshire audiences with a piece for Southwell Minster. An advertisement for dancers attracted the remarkable Julie Hood:

> This time I didn't want people opting out of collaborating – absolute integration on every level. Julie and I worked side by side throughout the whole process. I thought

this was my most directorial and selfish piece of work. She, having worked with Michael Clark, said she'd never been in such a collaborative situation.

The core company was shaped as before but expanded. The addition of Southwell Minster choir, working with Vivien, led to a productive rethink of the proxemic design. While the choir-master was very responsive, leading choristers into new theatricalised ceremonies, their 'churchy' physical register frustrated Jo. Choristers would sway, as if carrying bible or cross, and singers brush their nose before singing. The core company had developed their own ritual register; and both the churchiness and pedestrian banalities grated with it. The solution was a spatial distinction between the core company, and the choir and Vivien as outer layer – doubling as denizens and animators of the building. The dramaturgy made a productive liaison between the two elements, rather than melting-pot synthesis. This evidently aided the sense of ownership by the Minster community.

In *Triptych*, within a relaxed formal, ecclesiastical envelope is held an intense and primal ritual performance. Members of the core company had developed personal ritualisations:

> *The first part was life and death. Vivien saw it as the different stages of an archetypal female life. And in a photograph of Julie on the box, she has this look of ancient wisdom. There was a very strong narrative for me, largely about loss, not having a child. I learnt from Butoh to go back in time to a moment and move forwards.*

Bell (1997: 92–102) writes of 'ritualisation' rather than 'ritual' to foreground the *activity* – 'a practical way of dealing with some specific circumstances'. There are clearly a number of ways in, and levels at, which ritualisation operated within *Triptych*. At the same time, these together constitute a ritual channel in which each instance – through the operation of ritualisation – is supported.

Touring *Triptych* to Lincoln Cathedral brought an invitation to create an Easter Saturday ritual, when candles are lit after a period of darkness. Structured in stages, *Stabat Mater* (2003) was set in the choir, with the congregation on either side. In one part, each female dancer lay within a tomb-like structure – a bed under a Perspex arch. Sculptor Rosalind Stoddard made the Perspex malleable, so that light would play through it. This was a ritual made for the cathedral's celebrants. Even so, ritual performances as much as theatrical ones have their own backstage – where the sense of common ownership and purpose can be shared in other than ritual ways:

> *We were warming up in the vestry, the choir and clergy getting ready to parade with their crosses in their adornery. Just before we entered, this bloke comes along with his cross, looks over and gives us a wink. There was an absolute sense of camaraderie. We were all in this – creating this ritual together.*

Triptych and more resolutely *Stabat Mater* occupied a space between site-specific theatre and community performance.

> *My approach was no technology apart from light, totally acoustic sound, and the environment. And part of the environment is the people. Vivien and I were allies in involving other people, and that links with her interest in my work with people. Julie started to go that way too, and is now a care professional. I wanted to integrate the two worlds, because I felt it had been a balancing act.*

On professions, Therapy and Art

While Isabel's work with people begins resolutely with the person, she felt the need to make her own art. Trained as an artist at Bretton, she then found herself in a therapy context – and at Goldsmiths developed an understanding of arts work with people.

> *But I had to ask, what is it then to be an artist, working with people? From the start of salamanda tandem, I wanted to assert the artistry, to ask myself, could I be accepted by a mainstream audience?*

This goes deeper than professionalism:

> *From my childhood, I had a terrible sense of self. I wasn't sure where I ended and the other person began. I would feel my father's grief – him lying there, at the seaside. Empathy has got to be a good thing, but I put myself entirely in my father's shoes and suffered from it.*

So independent artistic work, for Isabel, has been somewhere to find and be herself. The collaborative work has been an extension of this:

> *I was tortured by collaboration at an early stage. But with Jo making something non-reverential, or Vivian something beautiful, it would start to become universal – no longer about my personal angst. It's a sort of therapy for me.*

Yet in the early years of her arts work with people, Isabel was adamant that she was not doing therapy:

> *Therapy as I knew it then was to do with a distance between the one with the knowledge and the one being treated. But the frame has changed hugely. The principle of person-centeredness now reaches right across the field. So I am more blurred about it now.*

We might argue that all art is therapeutic, in that it works to adjust us to our world, processes experience. Thus, while no therapist is present in person-centred arts work with people, the self-expression, self-exploration and creativity of the person is therapeutic, because it is art. To this perception, Isabel adds a dimension that brings us back to the theatrical:

> *If you're telling your counsellor, you're paying them to listen to you. But in an art context, we find a way for our work to be appreciated by others and that appreciation comes back – and that's how we feel better.*

In the transactional space of arts work with people, as much as the theatre, there is a reciprocation between the act of giving and the act of appreciation.

Coda

The social definition of disability displaced the previous emphasis on impairment to challenge how the non-disabled world disables others. This politicisation has helped the development of self-affirmative discourses and representations around disability as an identity. Petra Kuppers (2011: 95–97) proposes a 'rhizomatic' definition, to reintroduce personal impairment as a challenge in itself. The move also brings back into focus the sort of trauma people like Lewis suffered in being wrenched from his synaesthetic childhood to the sensory depredations of blind school (Jones and Wallis 2011). Kuppers' coinage figures individuals negotiating these and other actualities simultaneously, horizontally.

Duggan and Wallis (2011) suggest a number of ways in which theatre is a privileged means to address trauma, and in particular to the process of working through. We see this above in particular in the case of Nathan's journey and the episode at Nottingham prison. These arise in the context of what Mick sees as Isabel's life-long process of working through the trauma she has shared through deep empathy: '[Lewis's] disadvantages were compounded by social prejudices. I felt the frustrations and injustices as a personal and intimate anxiety'. At the same time Mick has, over 20 years, witnessed Isabel's development of inclusive and person-centred arts practices, which, however much they are driven by that imperative, provide others with space and time for *poiesis* and gift.

The origins of the name salamanda tandem are instructive. Asked by Isabel what experience of movement he wanted, Lewis answered, 'To cycle very fast downhill'. Isabel made it happen: 'Me and dad went downhill very fast and it was extremely dangerous'. And at Mount St. Helens in 1988, Isabel and Peter saw a pond amidst the volcanic devastation. A small sign read, 'Please take care. Salamanders breeding here'. They recognised a metaphor: the salamander can re-grow lost body parts from a single cell; salamanda tandem goes through cycles, reducing to re-grow – but differently each time. Embedded in its name are some of the essentials of salamanda tandem: ingenuity, survival, resistance, regeneration, equality, and momentum, found through drilling down to a few essential properties that support growth and change – qualities essential to all our survival.

References

Bell, C., 1997. *Ritual: Perspectives and Dimensions.* Oxford: Oxford University Press.

Campbell, N., 2011a. 'Can't stop me shining'. *Mailout*, August/September.

———, 2011b. 'Can't stop me shining'. http://www.youtube.com/watch?v=kUcmTEM68Xg (accessed 31 July 2012).

Department of Health, 2001. *Valuing People. A New Strategy for Learning Disability for the 21st Century – a White Paper.* London: HMSO.

Duggan, P. and Wallis, M., 2011. 'Trauma and performance: Maps, narratives and folds'. *Performance Research,* 16: 1, pp. 4–17.

Jones, I., 2010. *Dance and Disabled People.* Leicester: Foundation for Community Dance.

Jones, I. and Wallis, M., 2011. Isabel Jones interviewed in Nottingham, 14–15 July, and in Clayton West, 29 July.

Kuppers, P., 2011. *Disability Culture and Community Performance: Find a Strange and Twisted Shape.* Basingstoke: Palgrave Macmillan.

Lefebvre, H., 1991 [1974]. *The Production of Space* (trans. David Nicholson-Smith). Oxford: Blackwell.

Mauss, M., 2002 [1923]. *The Gift: The Form and Reason for Exchange in Archaic Societies with a Foreword by Mary Douglas.* London: Routledge.

Montague, A., 1986. *Touching: The Human Significance of the Skin,* 3rd ed. New York: Harper & Rowe.

Siebers, T., 2011. *Disability Aesthetics.* Ann Arbor: University of Michigan Press.

Soja, E. W., 1996. *Thirdspace: Journeys to Los Angeles and Other Real-and-Imagined Places.* Oxford: Blackwell.

Tomlin, L., 2013. *Acts and Apparitions: Discourses of the Real in Performance Practice and Theory 1990–2010.* Manchester: Manchester University Press.

Turner, V., 1969. *The Ritual Process: Structure and Anti-Structure.* London: Routledge & Kegan Paul.

Warner, M., 2002. *Publics and Counterpublics.* Brooklyn, New York: Zone Books.

Wigley, M., 1998. *Constant's New Babylon. The Hyper-Architecture of Desire.* Rotterdam: 010 Publishers.

Williams, R., 1987. *Drama from Ibsen to Brecht,* revised edition. London: Hogarth.

Notes

1 The transcripts have been edited to retain Isabel's voice, while incorporating much of the material into the prose narrative.

2 The Butoh quality Naomi recognised in Isabel was from 'space dance', which explores the inseparability of dancer and environment. Later, Isabel worked in Tokyo with Japanese space dancers and children on the autistic spectrum – 'more tuned in to that work than any group I've ever worked with'.

Coda

Franc Chamberlain

When Tessa Jowell remarked that a nation was defined by its 'culture' (cf. Introduction), she might have given some thought to the looting of the Iraqi National Museum in Baghdad in April 2003. Whatever was too heavy for the looters to carry away was attacked with iron bars (Steele 2003). Statues from ancient Nineveh and Babylon were decapitated in symbolic acts which that echoed the removal, not simply of the oppressive regime of Saddam Hussein, but of any effective government in Iraq. These acts were also played out on the actual bodies of Iraqis and others caught up in the collapse. To be British was to be complicit in this destruction as the Blairite propaganda machine, aided and abetted by the Conservative Party, hoodwinked an estimated 67% of the UK population into believing the invasion was both necessary and legal. To be British was to show the world that we had moved beyond the Cool Britannia posturing of Blair's early days, from shopping and fucking to shocking and awing. If Jowell was right and *only* culture can define who we are, then there can be little doubt that the British participated in cultural genocide.

Ken Loach's *The Wind That Shakes the Barley* (2006) reminded us, if we had forgotten, that the British state has plenty of form when it comes to cultural genocide willing to use the otherwise unemployed as brutal oppressors of our 'own people'. Loach, an ardent opponent of the invasion of Iraq, was attacked, without any sense of irony, as having produced an 'anti-British film … designed to drag the reputation of our nation through the mud' by Harry MacAdam in *The Sun*. Michael Gove in *The Times* claimed that the film helped to 'legitimise the actions of gangsters' and, of course *The Daily Mail* and *The Daily Telegraph* also weighed in. George Monbiot, writing in *The Guardian* under the headline 'If we knew more about Ireland, we might never have invaded Iraq' (2006) challenges whether these other journalists had even seen the film and quotes Simon Heffer acknowledging that he hadn't seen the film because he didn't need to any more than he needed to read *Mein Kampf* 'to know what a louse Hitler was'. To refuse even to consider the parallels between the behaviour of the Black and Tans and the behaviour of British soldiers in Iraq, or the attitudes evidenced in a statement from US serviceman Jody Casey that 'when we first got down there, you could basically kill whoever you wanted' (Monbiot 2006), is to indulge in a prejudice that is almost anti-British in itself.

I am writing this afterword on the eve of the tenth anniversary of the invasion which occurred on 20 March 2003. I remember that I started a Boal class that day with: 'Today, I feel really ashamed to be British'. I wasn't previously unaware of our collective history of genocides and oppressions, of wars and conquests, but I hadn't felt that sense of shame before. The class was a good one though, as we explored all the positions pro-war and anti-war and even if we didn't arrive at any kind of consensus we were able to understand the arguments and feelings in the room.

Ten years after the invasion, most of which I have spent living outside the United Kingdom, I wonder why there is no mention of Iraq in this book. Isn't this an important part of what it has meant to be British over the past decade? Hasn't it had a significant effect on whether some people who were born here feel able to accept themselves as 'British'? Where is the theatre work that addresses this? I wonder how cultural historians in 25 years time will view the response of our small-scale theatre companies to the destruction of Iraq. But, of course, they may not consider it at all and be wondering instead why our theatre and theatre scholars were so slow to address the global ecological situation.

Looking forward it is difficult, if not impossible, to predict which of the productions of the past decade will be remembered and which companies will still exist in 2038 or 2048. The past 35 years of British theatre have been incredibly rich and vibrant and reading through the pages of this collection I am reminded of productions and companies I saw and have, occasionally, forgotten about. And I also noticed the absence of companies and productions which I thought would still be remembered and considered important in 2013. This is not a criticism of the choices that have been made in this book but rather a testament to the immense creative productivity of across a wide range of theatrical forms. There isn't any company or work discussed that I would have omitted, but there are those that I would have added and which I think speak directly to questions of what we might consider 'Britishness' to be, or what we might consider it to have been.

One evening in 1988, I travelled from Norwich to the New Wolsey Theatre in Ipswich to see Temba's production of *Romeo and Juliet* directed by Alby James. Set in nineteenth-century Cuba, the Capulet's were generally paler-skinned than the Montagues. Using 'paler-skinned' I'm not trying to avoid stating that the Capulets were 'white' and the Montagues 'black', but pointing to the interracial aspect of both the Cuba of the time and of the cast, an aspect which destabilised neat racial binaries. 'White' and 'black' were contested ideological constructs existing within a struggle for economic and social power. The parents of Romeo and Juliet sought to shore up these constructs: the upwardly mobile former slaves and the old slave-owning family. The complexities generated by this Cuban context, much closer to the historical moment of slavery than 1980s Britain yet more integrated, combined with strong performances and high production values, touched me in a way no other production of *Romeo and Juliet* has before or since. At the same time, the balcony scene seemed to exist in an affective space that was, momentarily, beyond any consideration of race and economic power [1]. This was a production that implicitly refused any kind of racial classification and, by doing so, challenged an easy marginalisation of the work. At least that's how I remember it.

Temba's *Romeo and Juliet* is production that continues to do its work in my memory and imagination in 2013 and if anyone had asked me in 1988 to predict shows that would be remembered and celebrated 25 years later, then this would have been one. Yet not only is this production barely remembered, the work of Temba, a company active between 1972 and 1993, has received relatively little critical attention.

In an interview with Sandy Carpenter published in *TDR* (1990), Alby James pointed towards those in Britain who thought that: 'Temba ought to be doing its own thing – always separate' and 'they don't wish to see us integrated into the mainstream of English theatre' (1990: 32). This resistance to Temba's acceptance into the mainstream was also reflected in the difficulty in finding commercial sponsors. James claimed that the production of *Romeo and Juliet* was 'much too controversial' for the sponsors because of its 'interracial' cast (1990: 33). Reading these comments 25 years after watching the production it seems hard to believe that's how it was. In my view, Temba's production stands comparison with the best of the RSC productions of the time and rather than finding it controversial, I thought that it was 'mainstream' in the most positive sense: a production of a canonical text with classically trained actors which was accessible and addressed important matters of contemporary concern. But maybe that's the product of faulty memory, maybe I knew it was 'controversial' in a broader sense and that's what contributed to my excitement at the time.

A year before I saw *Romeo and Juliet*, I was in Exeter Arts Centre to see a show by John Lee and my attention was drawn to a small, simple notice pinned to a board with the words 'Making Faces'. It was an announcement of a four-week mask laboratory hosted by Pan Project in London with master-teachers in Nyau, Noh, Topeng and Dixi. I signed up for the course and made contact with a company that had been founded in 1986 by John Martin, Jacqui Chan and Tim Jones. Pan Project (or Pan Intercultural Arts as they are now known) are still going strong after 27 years yet their work has also received little critical attention.

When Martin [2], Chan and Jones formed Pan Project they were interested in the possibilities of an intercultural theatre asking: 'What might an intercultural theatre be like?' To this end they set up a series of four summer schools or laboratories to investigate these questions together with master teachers such as Peter Badejo, I Nyoman Wenten and Akira Matsui. These summer schools led to Pan's first production *Under the Moon* (1988), which opened at the ICA and then undertook a short national tour. Peter Badejo joined the company in the same year and, in 1989, they organised the Commonwealth Theatre Laboratory in Bhopal. Over the next five years Chan, Martin, Badejo and then Mallika Sarabhai created a number of shows that toured both within the United Kingdom and to India, South Africa, Portugal, Germany and West Africa. *Itan Kahani/Story of Stories* (1992) was a storytelling performance that had two storytellers (Badejo and Sarabhai) and three musicians. The traditional stories dealt with issues of gender power and oppression and the two performers, using their own traditional performance languages to play off each other and to undercut and challenge those stories which seemed to reinforce gender stereotypes and roles.

Itan Kahani received funding from the British Council to tour India and West Africa as an example of 'what can come out of a multi-cultural Britain' work which didn't erase the differences between cultures but had 'plenty of room for explorations and togetherness' (Martin 2013: personal communication). Whilst all of the productions from *Itan Kahani* onwards, such as *I have Seen Her Behind the Bamboo Screen* (1995) and *Sita's Daughters* (1996) dealt with intercultural relationships and identities in more than a purely formal sense, a key shift in the company's work occurred following a performance of *V for ...* (1996). A member of Camden Equalities Unit approached the company and asked if they would be willing to use their theatre techniques to find ways of easing the violence between elements of Bengali, White and Somali communities in the Summertown area near King's Cross. It was an area of high unemployment where there were few or no positive role models and where previous attempts to improve the situation, such as funding football teams and youth clubs had only made the problem worse (Martin *pers.comm.* 2013). The *Arts Against Violence* project, which began in 1997 and was Mojisola Adebayo's first engagement with the company, was a result of this query and is still ongoing in March 2013.

Pan continued to produce new pieces of intercultural theatre such as *Itan Kahani 2* and *Mirror Lore* (both 2000) but the emphasis of the company's work had firmly shifted towards arts for social change and participatory performance both inside and outside the United Kingdom. In the United Kingdom they continue to work with victims of torture (from 2003), trafficked women (from 2010) and young people involved in gang culture (from 2009) whilst engaging in post-conflict trauma work in Pakistan, Afghanistan and Southern Sudan.

Twenty-seven years of exploring questions of interculturalism and multiculturalism through aesthetic and participatory forms deserves a much more intricate discussion than is possible here. Will people be discussing Pan's work in 2038? Is this a direction that more British theatre companies will take in the future? I'm not sure that it matters, what matters is that this work needs doing now and it's being done. We can pass on whatever skills and knowledge we have to those who come after to help them make their own choices as to what the theatre and the world needs then.

Perhaps no-one will even identify as 'British' in a decade's time, perhaps we will think more about 'Englishness' and 'Welshness' or maybe even 'Europeanness'.

In the meantime there are so many stories to tell ...

Huddersfield, 19 March 2013

References

Carpenter, S. and James, A., 1990. 'Black and British theatre forges the mainstream: An interview with Alby James'. *The Drama Review: TDR*, 34: 1, pp. 28–35.

Martin, J., 2013. Telephone conversation. 12 March.

Monbiot, G., 2006. 'If we knew more about Ireland, we might never have invaded Iraq'. *The Guardian*, Tuesday 6 June. http://www.guardian.co.uk/commentisfree/2006/jun/06/comment.world (accessed 19 March 2013).

Steele, J., 2003. 'Museum's treasures left to the mercy of looters'. *The Guardian*, 14 April. http://www.guardian.co.uk/world/2003/apr/14/internationaleducationnews.arts (accessed 19 March 2013).

Notes

1   Juliet was performed by Georgia Slowe and Romeo by David Harewood.
2   The information on Pan Project comes from my personal engagement with their work, the company's website http://www.pan-arts.net and telephone conversation with John Martin on 12 March 2013.

Notes on Contributors

Chapter 1

Graham Saunders is Reader in Theatre Studies at the University of Reading. His books include *Love Me or Kill Me: Sarah Kane and the Theatre of Extremes, About Kane: The Playwright and the Work, Patrick Marber's Closer* and co-editor of *Cool Britannia: Political Theatre in the 1990s* and *Sarah Kane in Context*.

Roland Rees was Artistic Director of the theatre company Foco Novo from 1972 until its disbandment in 1988. The company specialised in producing revivals of classic plays ranging from Christopher Marlowe to Brecht as well as new writing; these included writers such as Bernard Pomerance and Howard Brenton as well as the work of black British writers including Alfred Fagon and Tunde Ikoli.

Trevor R. Griffiths is Visiting Professor in Humanities at the University of Hertfordshire and former Professor of Theatre Studies at London Metropolitan University, and has published widely on Renaissance and twentieth-century theatre. He is Editor of the Nick Hern Books Drama Classics series, and Theatre Notebook (the journal of the Society for Theatre Research).

Chapter 2

David Grant has enjoyed a varied career in theatre throughout Ireland as director, teacher and critic. He has been Managing Editor of *Theatre Ireland* magazine, Programme Director of the Dublin Theatre Festival and Artistic Director of the Lyric Theatre, Belfast. Publications include *Playing the Wild Card: Community Drama and Small-Scale Theatre in Northern Ireland* and *The Stagecraft of Brian Friel*. He has been a lecturer in Drama at Queen's University since 2001.

Tim Loane has worked extensively as a writer, director and actor in film, television, theatre and radio on local, national and international stages. He co-founded Tinderbox Theatre Company in 1988 and was Joint Artistic Director until 1996. For the stage he has written the political satires *Caught Red Handed* and *To Be Sure* and for BBC radio, the inner-city thriller *The Tunnel* and the post-ceasefire ensemble comedy *I Can See Clearly*. His screenwriting includes the comedy films *Out of The Deep Pan* (BBC) and *Reversals* (ITV), and he was creator and lead writer of BAFTA-nominated *Teachers* for Channel 4. He has also written the conspiracy thriller *Proof 2* (RTE), the three-part family drama serial *Little Devil* (ITV) and the 2009 update of 1980s television classic *Minder* (Channel 5). In addition to numerous theatre productions, he directed the short film *Dance Lexie Dance* that was nominated for an Academy Award in 1997.

Chapter 3

Gareth Somers is an independent researcher who has worked as a director and performer internationally since the early 1990s. He has worked in a number of universities and conservatoires.

Steve Fisher co-founded Volcano Theatre (1987–92) and he has worked in film, TV radio and theatre. He has premiered works by a number of Welsh playwrights: Roger Williams, Ian Rowlands (in the United Kingdom and in New York), Mark Jenkins, Thomas and Gary Owen. In 2000 he became Associate Director with the Sherman Theatre, Cardiff, directing productions and running the Education Department. He has directed for the Royal Welsh College of Music and Drama and is currently Senior Lecturer in Drama at the University of Glamorgan.

Chapter 4

Ekua Ekumah is a trained actor and lecturer. She holds an MFA in Theatre Arts from the School of Performing Arts, University of Ghana, Legon after earning a BA (Hons) in Theatre Arts from Rose Bruford College of Speech and Drama. She lectures in the Department of Theatre Arts, University of Ghana and is recipient of an AHRC-funded PhD research bursary in the Theatre and Performance Department, Goldsmiths College, University of London.

Femi Elufowoju Jr founded and was Artistic Director of Tiata Fahodzi from 1997 to 2010. The company specialised in touring commissioned new writings by artists of African Diaspora backgrounds living in Britain including the highly acclaimed Ola Rotimi's *The God's Are Not to Blame* and Roy Williams's *Joe Guy*. His 2010 production of Oladipo Agboluaje's *Iya Ile* was nominated for an Olivier award for 'an outstanding production in an affiliate theatre'. After 13 years of leadership Elufowoju left Tiata Fahodzi to pursue a freelance career as an actor, theatre director and radio producer.

Chapter 5

Kene Igweonu is Senior Lecturer and Programme Director for BA (Hons) Drama at Canterbury Christ Church University. His interests cover African and African Diaspora theatre and performance, as well as cultural and performance theory. His current research and practice focus particularly on somatic practices in performance training, issues of identity in performance and cross-art practices.

Patricia Cumper is an award-winning playwright, writer and director. She is a graduate of Girton College, Cambridge University where she obtained a degree in Archaeology and Anthropology in 1973. After five successful years at the head of Talawa Theatre Company, she was succeeded as Artistic Director in 2012 by Michael Buffong.

Chapter 6

Tony Gardner is a theatre academic at the University of Leeds's School of Performance and Cultural Industries with a special interest in contemporary practice that explores social and political engagement through performance work. He has previously published on the influence of Antonin Artaud, as well as critical perspectives on time and duration in performance.

Rod Dixon joined Red Ladder Theatre Company as Artistic Director in 2006, after a number of years as Associate Director at Plymouth's Barbican Theatre and director of Cornwall's The Hub Theatre School. He has also performed with various companies, including Kneehigh Theatre. Major productions directed for Red Ladder include *Riot, Rebellion & Bloody Insurrection, Big Society!* and *Promised Land*.

Chapter 7

Victor Ukaegbu is Associate Professor in the Department of Media, English, Cultural Studies and Performance, University of Northampton. He has published in the areas of African, black British and African Diaspora theatres, in applied theatre and ethnodrama as well as in intercultural and postcolonial performances. He is co-founder of African Theatre Association (AfTA), co-Artistic Director of Jawi Theatre Collective, and Associate Editor, *African Performance Review*. He is on the editorial board of *Journal of Applied Arts and Health* and is a contributing researcher and member of the North Africa/Middle East Board of World Scenography.

Jatinder Verma is Artistic Director of Tara Arts, the pioneering cross-cultural theatre company he co-founded in 1977. Among his many contributions to the development of cross-cultural theatre, his 'Binglish' approach to contemporary British theatre has stimulated the rise of other theatre companies and generations of artists. Tara Arts has produced and toured over 150 productions nationally and internationally, including producing at the National Theatre. Jatinder has contributed essays to many publications, including in *Theatre Matters* (1998) and *Theatre in a Cool Climate* (2000).

Chapter 8

Eirini Kartsaki writes and performs. She has presented her work nationally and internationally (including at V&A, Arnolfini, Whitechapel Gallery, Camden People's Theatre, East End Collaborations, The Place, Biennale d'Art Contemporain de Lyon) and has published in journals *Activate, PerformArt* and *Choreographic Practices*. Eirini is Senior Lecturer in Drama in Anglia Ruskin University, Cambridge.

Lone Twin Theatre work with other artists to tell stories about the jigsaw of people's lives. The group come from all over the world, so are an eclectic combination. They are drawn to catastrophes, some violent and dramatic, others slighter and more everyday. But their approach to narrative is always playful – the darker the night, the louder we sing. Olé! Lone Twin Theatre are: Guy Dartnell, Antoine Fraval, Paul Gazzola, Molly Haslund, Nina Tecklenburg, Cynthia Whelan. Associate performers: Bob Karper, Nadia Cusimano, Vic Llewellyn. Dramaturge: David Williams. Artistic Directors: Gregg Whelan, Gary Winters.

Chapter 9

Patrick Duggan lectures in Theatre and Performance Studies at the University of Exeter. His research is interdisciplinary in focus and explores the sociopolitical efficacy of performance. Patrick has contributed to a range of academic and non-academic publications on subjects from trauma theory, to Live Art, ethics, politics and popular theatre. He is author of *Trauma-Tragedy: Symptoms of Contemporary Performance* (Manchester UP 2012) and co-editor of *On Trauma*, a special issue of the journal *Performance Research* (2011). As well as being an academic, Patrick is also a theatre director and curator.

Jemma McDonnell is the co-founder and Artistic Director of The Paper Birds Theatre Company. Jemma has undertaken a BA in Theatre Acting at Bretton Hall, Leeds University and an MA in Theatre Collectives at the University of Chichester. As well as devising and performing in all of the company shows since its inception in 2003, Jemma is also a guest director and lecturer at a number of universities around the United Kingdom.

Chapter 10

Trish Reid is Deputy Head of the School of Performance and Screen Studies at Kingston University. She has published on Anthony Neilson, the National Theatre of Scotland and post-devolutionary Scottish playwriting. She is the author of *Theatre & Scotland* (Palgrave 2012) and is currently working on a longer monograph for Palgrave on contemporary Scottish theatre and performance.

Ben Harrison is co-Artistic Director of the multi-award winning Scottish theatre company Grid Iron. He works almost exclusively in the field of location and site-responsive theatre. Ben's award winning productions for Grid Iron include *The Bloody Chamber* (1997), *Deccy Does a Bronco* (2000) and *Roam* (NTS 2006), the first piece to be performed in an international airport. He also works extensively as a freelance director and has taught site-responsive theatre as far afield as Lebanon, New Zealand, Portugal and England.

Chapter 11

Isabel Jones is a dancer, singer, composer, choreographer and director with 18 years' experience of making arts work with people. She is the artistic director and founder of the charity salamanda tandem, formed in 1989. Her work brings together cross-arts and cross-disciplinary teams, both disabled and non-disabled, to research, redefine and cross boundaries between people and art forms. Isabel has directed and choreographed nine full-length works with salamanda tandem, and other shorter performances with other artists.

Mick Wallis is Professor of Performance and Culture at the University of Leeds, where he is also Pro-Dean for Research and Innovation in the Faculty of Performance, Visual Arts and Communications. He works at various interdisciplinary interfaces with performance studies, from social and cultural history to robotics and complexity. Mick was a salamanda tandem board member 2001–08.

Index

The below is not an exhaustive index but represents a set of keywords identified by individual contributors and referenced across the whole volume. As such, page numbers are given as normally expected in an index, alongside chapter references (in bold) which point to contributions which have that keyword as a key concern in some way.